STATE GOVERNMENT IN TRANSITION

Reforms of the Leader Administration, 1955-1959

Government Studies

FELS INSTITUTE SERIES
University of Pennsylvania Press

This volume is one of a series devoted to
problems of current and long-range significance
which are of particular interest
to students of local and state government.

VOLUMES IN THE SERIES ARE:

Stephen B. Sweeney and Thomas J. Davy (Eds.), *Education for Administrative Careers in Government Service*

Stephen B. Sweeney and George S. Blair (Eds.), *Metropolitan Analysis: Important Elements of Study and Action*

W. H. Brown, Jr. and C. E. Gilbert, *Planning Municipal Investment: A Case Study of Philadelphia*

Reed M. Smith, *State Government in Transition: Reforms of the Leader Administration, 1955-1959*

Harold Herman, *New York State and the Metropolitan Problem*

Oliver P. Williams and Charles R. Adrian, *Four Cities: A Study in Comparative Policy Making*

FELS INSTITUTE OF LOCAL AND STATE GOVERNMENT
UNIVERSITY OF PENNSYLVANIA
PHILADELPHIA

STATE GOVERNMENT IN TRANSITION

REFORMS OF THE LEADER ADMINISTRATION, 1955-1959

By Reed M. Smith

Fels Institute of Local and State Government
University of Pennsylvania

PHILADELPHIA
UNIVERSITY OF PENNSYLVANIA PRESS

To My Wife

Library of Congress Catalog Card Number: 63-7864

7399
Printed in the United States of America

PREFACE

Most writers on state government usually emphasize gubernatorial leadership as both a measure and an objective of administrative reorganization and reform. In the past, few governors were actually equipped to govern because they lacked the structure, tools, or authority for executive leadership and control. "The American governorship was conceived in mistrust and born in a strait jacket, the creature of revolutionary assemblies."[1]

Although the notion of executive integration is now a familiar one, its application may be open to controversy in any particular jurisdiction. Less abstract and therefore more relevant for present purposes is the question whether any particular governor has at his command the means for effectuating his program. Every governor searches for available tools, relying in some cases upon novel or untested improvisation. The success of such efforts cannot be stated categorically, for success, like one's knowledge, is always a relative matter.

Students of American government are inclined to regard most of our states as somewhat behind both the federal government and our more progressive cities in the business of administrative reform. This assumption of relative retardation may soon be, if it is not already, open to serious

---

[1] William H. Young in Robert L. Morlan, ed., *Capitol, Courthouse and City Hall*, 2d ed. (Boston, Houghton Mifflin Co., 1960), p. 125.

challenge. At least many of our state governments are now in a period of transition.

More particularly, close observers of Pennsylvania government at the time of the Leader administration, 1955–59, are inclined to speak of an administrative revolution in the Keystone State. Energetic efforts were made at Harrisburg in those years to help close the gap between knowledge and practices at the state level. At the time of the Pinchot reforms in the early 1920's and 1930's, Pennsylvania could be regarded as in the forefront of the state administrative reorganization movement. The number of independent departments and agencies was then vastly reduced, and the governor's powers were consequently enlarged. That reform was embodied in the Administrative Code of 1923, as amended in 1929 and subsequently. However, Pennsylvania government failed to keep pace with changed conditions during the next generation, and, by 1955, the central staff services were generally acknowledged as inadequate by close observers from both political parties.[2] Yet political realities in a state with a strong tradition of political patronage, added to certain nonpartisan factors, resulted in no effective action towards state reorganization and reform until the time of the Leader administration. By that time conditions were ripe for the most sweeping reform the state had experienced since the Pinchot era, with the possible exception of the brief "Little New Deal" interlude, which reached its climax in 1937.[3]

[2] *The State Government Survey Committee Report* to Governor Fine, Harrisburg, February 11, 1953.

[3] Richard Keller, "Pennsylvania's Little New Deal." Unpublished Ph.D. dissertation in history, Columbia University, 1960.

The present study can be taken as a case study in state administrative reform, based upon the experience of the Leader administration in Pennsylvania, 1955–59. It is hoped that the materials presented here may provide at least partial answers for three questions, each somewhat more specific than the one before:

1. When or in what circumstances are the conditions ripe for basic administrative reform at the state level?
2. What particular type of reorganization is appropriate to achieve executive integration in a state such as Pennsylvania?
3. Did Governor Leader's Bureau of Program Evaluation within the Office of Administration make a significant contribution to gubernatorial leadership and control?

Because the data on program evaluation represents, in my opinion, the most novel and original aspect of this case study, nearly half of the material presented deals with the third question. Subsidiary hypotheses or questions, such as the following, are raised and treated in that section:

1. Is program evaluation a basic administrative process, which should be separately identified and structured?
2. Where should this function be performed, or more specifically, how should it be related to other central staff services?
3. Was the experience of Governor Leader's Bureau of Program Evaluation a successful one? That is, did this unit perform the function for which it was created?
4. Does this experience throw any light on the general question of the role of the political scientist in government?
5. Finally, how does Pennsylvania's experience with this new unit compare with similar developments in other

states, and how does it relate to the general literature on public administration?

In a study of this length, not all of these questions can be given definitive answers. For one thing, the Leader administration is too recent and probably too brief to permit the fully objective or mature perspective which a political or administrative historian desires. It is hoped, however, that the data presented here will provide at least partial answers and provide the basis for future observation and study.

METHODOLOGY AND ACKNOWLEDGMENTS

The Leader Papers, located in the Pennsylvania Historical Collection of the Pennsylvania State University Library, provided many of the raw materials for this study. Additional materials were obtained directly from the Governor's Office and the Office of Administration in Harrisburg, whose cooperation is hereby acknowledged. Particular help was supplied by Governor Leader himself and by his brother, Attorney Henry B. Leader, as well as by several members of Leader's cabinet. Considerable information was also secured from Governor Leader's secretary, Attorney David Randall. I am also indebted to the members of Leader's preinaugural Advisory Committee, especially Dr. Stephen B. Sweeney, chairman, and Dr. Harold F. Alderfer, recently deputy superintendent of public instruction. Important assistance was also provided by Leader's successive secretaries of administration, Dr. James C. Charlesworth and Dr. John H. Ferguson. The author also consulted Dr. William C. Seyler and Dr. Robert A. Christie, the first and fourth directors of program evaluation, whose terms in that office preceded and followed that of Dr. Ferguson and Dr. Alderfer. Additional information was secured from Dr. Edward F. Janosik, University of Pennsylvania, Dr. Gayle Lawrence, Temple University, members of the staff of the Fels Institute of Local and State Government, University of Pennsylvania, in addition to several members of the legislature, the press, the bureaucracy, the political parties, and the public. Altogether more than one hundred interviews were conducted with persons associated with the Leader administration in some way. These interviews provided significant guidance for other materials found in government documents, library sources, and official papers.

Special acknowledgment is made of the painstaking work and advice of Dr. Wallace S. Sayre, who supervised the research upon which this book is based, and of his colleague, Dr. Lawrence H. Chamberlain, both of Columbia University. The basic research for this study was made possible by the generous grant of a senior research fellowship by the Fels Institute of Local and State Government during the year 1959–60.

The Fels Institute
Philadelphia, 1962

REED M. SMITH

CONTENTS

CHAPTER I

THE NATURE OF THE GOVERNORSHIP
OF PENNSYLVANIA

The problems of American state government have been diagnosed and dissected in at least three different directions:

1. Problems in our state political systems.
2. Constitutional, that is, chiefly organizational, problems.
3. Problems of executive leadership and personnel.

Pennsylvania has suffered from shortcomings in all three areas, and the history of the governorship of Pennsylvania illustrates how these three types of problems are related.[1] We begin our survey of the governorship in this chapter placing special emphasis upon the political problems. Chapters II and III deal with the constitutional and organ-

[1] In vastly oversimplified terms the relationship can be stated as follows: (1) Pennsylvania's political system was such that there was relatively little effective demand for administrative reform. (2) Pennsylvania's governor is further handicapped by the constitutional limitation of only one consecutive term, which in turn hampers both his policy leadership and his opportunities for organizational reform. (3) Both political change in the direction of a better balanced two party system and organizational reform were required to enable the Pennsylvania governor to grow "from figurehead to leader," to borrow Lipson's phrase.

izational problems, and succeeding chapters discuss the problem of staffing for executive leadership and control.

Pennsylvania's experience generally confirms the doctrine that two parties in active competition are essential to governmental improvement. As Professor V. O. Key has pointed out:

> On the American scene a high priority would generally be given to the requirement that parties compete for power. . . . A belief in the corrective efficacy of competition permeates American political thought as well as other aspects of American life.[2]

Yet, just as a close look at our American economy reveals large areas which are not in active competition, so also in half or more of the American states the parties have not been well balanced or very competitive for fifty years or more:

> Within a large proportion of the states only by the most generous characterization may it be said that political parties compete for power. . . . [In fact] over a half century the vigor of competition between parties within the states has, on the whole, declined.[3]

Pennsylvania has had a most striking record of one-party control at the state level. In 1948, Pennsylvania historian, Wayland F. Dunaway, wrote, "Next to Maine and Vermont, Pennsylvania has been the most consistently Republican state in the union." [4] For all but four of the sixty

---

[2] V. O. Key, Jr., *American State Politics: An Introduction* (New York, 1956), p. 11.

[3] *Ibid.*, pp. 13, 14.

[4] W. F. Dunaway, *A History of Pennsylvania* (2nd ed., New York, 1948), p. 523.

years from 1895–1955, the governorship was held by members of that party. The exception was Democratic Governor George H. Earle III, who rode into office at the time of the New Deal landslide, 1935–39. Prior to that, in the nineteenth century, Democratic Governor Robert Pattison had captured the State House twice at the time of factional splits within the Republican party (1883–87, 1891–95). Thus of the twenty men elected governor in the ninety-four years from 1860 to 1954, all had carried the Republican banner except Earle and Pattison.

Since Pennsylvania has been until recently a modified one-party state,[5] it is possible to observe the effect of that political system upon the governorship in particular. We can then observe what political changes were needed before organizational changes or reforms could be made. These organizational reforms are then further examined with respect to the problem of executive leadership and control.

THE PERIOD OF ONE-PARTY RULE

The Republican party's grip upon the government at Harrisburg had been so long standing that the major contests for the governor's chair frequently took place in the primary. In the general election the Republican gubernatorial candidates stacked up majorities ranging from one quarter of a million to nearly three quarters of a million votes, in a total vote ranging from one to three million.

[5] Austin Ranney and W. Kendall, "The American Party Systems," 48 *American Political Science Review* (June, 1954), p. 483.

In the generation from World War I until after World War II, these Republican majorities were as follows:[6]

	Republican	Democrat
1914:	135,325—Martin G. Brumbaugh	over Vance C. McCormick
1918:	247,222—William C. Sproul	over Eugene C. Bonniwell
1922:	250,071—Gifford Pinchot	over John A. McSparran
1926:	737,543—John S. Fisher	over Eugene C. Bonniwell
1930:	58,560—Gifford Pinchot	over John M. Hemphill
1934:	–66,329—William Schnader	*under* George H. Earle
1938:	279,148—Arthur H. James	over Charles A. Jones
1942:	217,634—Edward Martin	over F. Clair Ross
1946:	557,515—James H. Duff	over John S. Rice

The largest majority, 73.3 per cent of the total vote, was achieved in 1926 by Governor Fisher, after a bitter struggle in the primary. Two decades later, Governor Duff achieved a majority of over half a million, or 58.5 per cent of the total vote. As recently as 1948, the Democrats reached their nadir as an opposition party, losing in that year the remaining state-wide elective offices to the Republicans.[7]

[6] 93 *Pa. Manual*, p. 1053. Republican fortunes in the next three gubernatorial elections shifted as follows:

1950: John S. Fine, Rep., 85,764 over Richardson Dilworth, Dem.

1954: Lloyd H. Wood, Rep., –279,196 *under* George M. Leader, Dem.

1958: A. T. McGonigle, Rep., –76,083 *under* David L. Lawrence, Dem.

[7] Only five state executive officers are elected at large in Pennsylvania: governor, lieutenant governor, auditor general, state treasurer, and secretary of internal affairs. Pennsylvania Constitution, Art. IV. For an analysis of gubernatorial elections, see H. F. Alderfer and F. H. Luhrs, *Gubernatorial Elections in Pennsylvania, 1922–1942* (State College, 1946).

The Pennsylvania legislature had also been in Republican hands over half a century prior to 1955, with the exception of three elections during the Franklin D. Roosevelt era. Republican majorities in the General Assembly generally reached a magnitude of four or five to one from 1906 until the New Deal period. Even then the Republicans were ousted from their control of the state senate only one biennium (1937–39) and from the house only three times (1935, 1937, and 1941). Following the Democratic interlude at the time of Governor Earle, the Republicans restored comfortable majorities in the Pennsylvania legislature from 1943 until 1955.[8] Governor Leader had a Democratic majority in the house (112 to 98) only during his first two years, and the senate remained in Republican hands up to 1961, at which time there was a tie, which gave the Democrats a majority only by the deciding vote of the presiding officer, the Democratic lieutenant governor. Thus as recently as 1954, Pennsylvania had been characterized by *Time* magazine as "the anchor and pride of Republicanism." [9]

CHARACTERISTICS OF THE MACHINE

For more than fifty years after the Civil War, the Republican party in Pennsylvania operated a rather tight organization. Pennsylvania was a prime example of "machine politics" during this period, and the nature of the governorship can only be understood in terms of the "machine" which put the governors into power. Three great Republican "bosses" dictated the politics of this era: Simon D.

[8] See *Pennsylvania Manual,* Vol. 93, p. 1019; Vol. 94, p. 1023.
[9] Vol. 64, No. 20 (November 15, 1954), p. 27.

Cameron (1865–87), Matthew S. Quay (1887–1904) and
Boies Penrose (1904–1921). Each of them established a
base in the Keystone State and then continued to manipu-
late the political strings in Pennsylvania as United States
senators in Washington, D.C.

These political "bosses" set the pattern not only for
Pennsylvania, but in many matters for the nation as well.
They "made and unmade" mayors, governors, legislators,
senators, congressmen, lesser officials, and sometimes even
had an important voice in the choice of a president. The
party machine operated an essentially self-serving operation, in which political jobs, contracts and other official
favors (including the type of legislation and law enforcement desired by party contributors) were exchanged for
votes and contributions to the party coffers. In its fuller
dimensions the machine handled the selection and thus
the control of the whole gamut of officials and public serv-
ants, down to the street cleaners, police, janitors, and gar-
bage collectors. Many of the judges were appointed by the
machine; others were "rubber-stamped" into office by ma-
chine-controlled elections. County sheriffs, prosecutors,
commissioners, councilmen, local clerks, and assessors, in
both large and small communities were recruited, maintained, or removed, if not directed, by the party organization. In return, much of the party's organizational work
was carried out by these lower officials. Without the support of the lower bureaucracy and the "small man," the
political bosses could not have remained in power.[10]

[10] For various accounts, see J. T. Salter, *Boss Rule, Portraits in
City Politics* (New York, 1935); David H. Kurtzman, *Methods
of Controlling Votes in Philadelphia* (Philadelphia, 1935); *The
Autobiography of Lincoln Steffens* (New York, 1931).

Pennsylvania Republican leaders also developed close ties with the business community. This included not only manufacturing interests, for which Pennsylvania has long been noted, but also railroads, utilities, oil, shipping, and other interests. These interests, in turn, frequently dictated the candidate for governor. Among the corporations playing an important role in the internal affairs of the Republican party, the Pennsylvania Railroad was well known. In the days of the Penrose machine, the president of the Pennsylvania Railroad was paid a salary of $50,000 a year and controlled 150,000 employees, whereas the governor was paid $10,000 per year and controlled but a fraction as many employees.[11] One "lubricant" of the system of "railroad politics" was the issuing of free passes to office-holders and legislators. Another influential voice was the late Joseph R. Grundy, organizer and president of the Pennsylvania Manufacturers' Association, from 1910 to 1943. Writing in 1949, one observer noted:

Since the death of Penrose [in 1921] no man has received the Republican gubernatorial nomination unless he has had the approval of [Mr.] Grundy. And only one of those nominees was beaten in the general election.[12]

[11] According to Thomas P. O'Neill, formerly political editor, *The Philadelphia Record*, "Gen. Wm. Wallace Atterbury, P.R.R. president, 1925–35, . . . exercised veto power over Republican slate-making for all important municipal and state offices. . . . The real ruler was—[not Vare or Penrose—but] Broad Street Station." From Robt. S. Allen, ed., *Our Fair City* (New York, 1947), p. 68. See also, Robt. D. Bowden, *Boies Penrose, Symbol of an Era* (New York, 1937), p. 70, and E. J. Stackpole, *Behind the Scenes with a Newspaper Man* (Philadelphia, 1927), p. 25.

[12] Herman A. Lowe, "Pennsylvania, Bossed Cornucopia," in Robt. S. Allen, ed., *Our Sovereign State* (New York, 1949), p. 114. See also, Jesse R. Wike, *The Pennsylvania Manufacturers' Association: a*

In the late 1930's this picture changed slightly, when Joseph N. Pew, president of the Sun Oil Company in Philadelphia, joined forces with Mr. Grundy to return the Republicans to power in Harrisburg in 1939.[13]

Under these circumstances of close economic and political alliance, Pennsylvania politics was characterized by the use of enormous sums of money to influence elections. Even primary campaigns were sometimes very expensive. In 1926, for example, over $2,000,000 was spent for all candidates in the Republican primary, about $750,000 of it on behalf of William S. Vare's campaign for the United States Senate.[14] As a result of these excessive campaign expenditures, Vare was ultimately denied his seat in the senate on December 6, 1929.[15]

Although vast campaign funds were required to reach Pennsylvania's large and far-flung population, which reached about ten and a half million by 1950, there is evidence that the use of money in Pennsylvania politics went far beyond the cost of normal publicity and election administration. As Professor Dunaway put the matter:

The Republican organization was still further entrenched in its position by reason of the large and easily influenced

---

Study of a Political Interest Group in the Governmental Process, Ph.D. dissertation, University of Pennsylvania, 1955, published by the University Press, 1961. Mr. Grundy died early in 1961.

[13] James Reichley, *The Art of Government, Reform and Organization Politics in Philadelphia.* A Report to the Fund for the Republic (New York, 1959), p. 8.

[14] Sylvester K. Stevens, *Pennsylvania, The Keystone State* (New York, 1956), Historical Vol., p. 626. See also, Wm. S. Vare, *My Forty Years in Politics* (Philadelphia, 1933).

[15] Joseph R. Grundy was appointed to this senate vacancy by Governor Fisher, 93 *Pa. Manual,* p. 1034.

foreign vote in Pennsylvania, which was captured for the most part by the Republican party bosses, amply supplied with campaign funds by the corporations. . . . This condition of affairs encouraged machine politics, inefficient government, and political corruption, since there was no formidable opposition party to jeopardize Republican control and thereby to keep that party on its good behavior.[16]

Yet money was not the only persuader. In the heyday of machine rule, the party also resorted to some physical coercion and intimidation at election time, sometimes with the aid of the courts, the jails, and the police. In the tough anthracite mining towns, bullies were hired to intimidate known opposition voters.[17] Economic threats were also used. In many small "company towns" the workers were notified by the owners that if they did not vote for the Republican candidates the plant would be closed. As recently as 1937–39, a Philadelphia grand jury investigated the close connection between the Police Department, organized crime and vice, and various political forces, including Mayor Wilson and the city machine.[18]

When bought votes, bribes, and intimidation failed, there was always the possible recourse to ballot-box manipulations. Such fraudulent voting, counting, and record-

[16] Dunaway, *op. cit.*, p. 522.

[17] *The Speeches of Hon. John Wanamaker on Quayism and Boss Domination in Pennsylvania Politics* (Phila., Business Men's Republican League, undated, c. 1898), p. 7. Also, Committee of Seventy, "The Public Conscience of Philadelphia," undated brochure (Philadelphia, c. 1952), p. 2.

[18] *Fifteenth and Final Presentment of the October, 1937, Grand Jury of Philadelphia County.* See also, T. Henry Walnut, "S. Davis Wilson, Mayor of Philadelphia," in J. T. Salter, ed., *The American Politician* (Chapel Hill, 1938), pp. 282–303.

ing is so well known that it need not be described in this section. According to reports in the Philadelphia newspapers, vote frauds had not yet been fully eradicated up to 1960–61.

THE GOVERNOR AND THE IMPORTANCE OF PATRONAGE IN PENNSYLVANIA

The Governor's Office has long been the focal point of the party organization in Pennsylvania. Aside from his being the titular head and the standard-bearer of the state party, there is a more practical reason for the governor's being the chief name on the ticket. Whoever occupies the Governor's Office administers practically the entire state administration. This is particularly the case in a state, such as Pennsylvania, which has so few independently elected executive officials. None of the four elected officials, aside from the governor, heads a major executive or administrative department. Thus the governorship is the major political prize, without serious rival in Pennsylvania, with the possible exception of the position of United States senator.

The political significance of the governorship is greatly enhanced by the fact that Pennsylvania's government operates largely on a "patronage" rather than on a merit or "civil service" basis. Patronage can be defined as the practice of making appointments to public office as a reward for service to the party.[19] The term also includes government contracts and other official benefits awarded on a

[19] Austin Ranney and Willmore Kendall, *Democracy and the American Party System* (New York, 1956), p. 376.

similar basis. However, the present discussion deals chiefly with the political appointments available to the governor, rather than the broader meaning of the term.

The available evidence indicates that the governor of Pennsylvania has general authority over more patronage positions than any other governor in the Union, and perhaps even more positions than are available to the president of the United States. By Leader's time, the governor had appointive power over some 50,000 persons. At least that many state government appointments were made outside the civil service or merit system.[20] Although the governor does not personally select all of these persons, their appointments are cleared, if not arranged, through the patronage secretary located in the Governor's Office. In consultation with the party the governor personally selects some twenty-two department heads, members of boards and commissions, deputy secretaries in each department, and in some cases even bureau chiefs and other officials.[21] The number that the governor personally decided upon differs with the circumstances and with the governor in office from time to time.

Such a concentration of appointive power has an important effect upon the governorship of Pennsylvania. One

[20] Pennsylvania has had a Civil Service Commission since 1941, but on the eve of the Leader administration only eleven agencies, or 13,640 of some 65,000 total state employees, were under the merit system. See *Sixth Biennial Report*, Pennsylvania Civil Service Commission (1952–54), pp. 2, 3. For further description of the patronage operation, see Chapter III.

[21] Based upon interviews with Governor Leader and his secretary, Mr. David Randall, March 3, 1961, and August 10, 1960, respectively.

result is that the governor is closely tied to the party organization, since the official governmental position of so many of the party leaders is in his hands. Another result of this interdependence is that it has historically been difficult, if not impossible, for the governor to dissociate himself very much from the type of machine politics which has just been described. In other words, the structure of the state government, as well as that of the party, has traditionally served to make the governor the most official beneficiary of the party machine.

Thus, the governor in Pennsylvania, even more than in other states, came to be primarily a political executive. This extensive patronage made his political responsibilities so enormous that he had rather little opportunity to provide energetic program and policy leadership. Not only is the governor constantly in touch with the party organization on matters of appointment; many of the party leaders are also dependent upon the governor for their own jobs on the state payroll. Thus the Pennsylvania governorship has traditionally been a highly political operation. These circumstances were not favorable to the development of a genuine chief executive. In fact, many of the governors recruited by the party machine turned out to be rather undistinguished persons. The party bosses desired a pliant governor, who would also be congenial to the various corporate interests upon whom the party relied for support. Not only did these governors lack leadership abilities; they also lacked knowledge of the managerial skills and the grasp of public issues which are necessary for an able public administrator.

Pennsylvania governors, then, during the one-party era were brokers more than leaders. They traded official favors for political support. They were intermediaries between the party and the government. Since there was only one party of importance they had no necessity to accommodate the rival demands of two groups with vastly different orientation. The party secured governors who could bend, if necessary, the needs of the public service to fit the patronage requirements of the party.

THE "TYPICAL" PENNSYLVANIA GOVERNOR— SOME COMPARISONS

Although there were important differences in the character and qualifications of the governors recruited by the party machine, the record is generally one of little previous experience in state legislative or executive office.[22] There was no one certain route to the Pennsylvania governorship, but the overwhelming majority prepared for this high office by way of the legal profession. Four of the eighteen governors prior to Leader were recruited from the judicial branch; others had served as district atorneys, and one had been attorney general. In general, previous experience in state government was no more, and in many cases, less prominent than experience in politics or business. A few governors had experience in city government or in the federal service, however. Although their educational background was above the average for governors nation-wide, Pennsylvania governors had little higher education in fields other than the law. Few Pennsylvania governors wrote anything about their experience as chief ex-

[22] For a comparative chart of the governors since the Constitution of 1874, and their background, see Appendix A.

ecutive.[23] With regard to both intellectual background and scholarly attainments, Governor Pennypacker was an exception.

On the more difficult question of the inner workings of the governor's party, and particularly the relation of the governor to the regular party machine, only scattered evidence is available. However, on the basis of public statements and external evidence, it is clear that not all of Pennsylvania's governors were equally pliant or complacent "puppets" of the Republican machine. A rapid survey indicates that at least as many administrations defected as fully conformed to the "boss" or to the regular party organization.[24]

[23] Only four Pennsylvania governors left memoirs: Samuel Pennypacker, governor, 1903–1907, wrote *Autobiography of a Pennsylvanian* (Philadelphia, 1918). Gifford Pinchot's *Breaking New Ground* (New York, 1947), dealt with his experience with the U.S. Forest Service, rather than with his two terms as Governor, which began in 1923 and 1931. William A. Stone, the predecessor of Pennypacker, wrote his memoirs, *The Tale of a Plain Man* (Pittsburgh, James Macmillan Printing Co., 1917), 194 pp. Quite recently, Governor Edward Martin published a brief autobiography in limited edition: *Always Be On Time* (Harrisburg, The Telegraph Press, 1949), which contains 19 pages on "The Governorship Years, 1943–47." Back in 1759 Benjamin Franklin published in London *An Historical Review of Pennsylvania From its Origin . . .* , tracing the record of early colonial Governors, some 20 years prior to his own term as Governor of the Province of Pennsylvania.

[24] The defections and revolts against the regular Republican organization (including the Democrats) involved the following eight governors (or ten administrations): Hoyt, Pattison, Hastings, Sproul, Pinchot, Earle, Duff, and Fine. Some of these developed their own organization. The ten governors who, on balance, were apparently more conformist were: Hartranft, Beaver (until near the end of his term), Stone, Pennypacker (to some degree), Stuart, Tener, Brumbaugh, Fisher, James, and Martin. See Appendix A.

The governor's ability to challenge the regular party leaders and to establish his own organization is greatly hampered by the constitutional prohibition upon successive terms. A few governors, such as Curtin, Hoyt, Pinchot, Duff, and Fine, sought to supplant the regular organization, but in most of these cases, the organization survived better than the governor did. In cases such as Pinchot, the governor's relatively greater independence from the party was possible because of a factional situation, which developed after the death of Boies Penrose, the last of Pennsylvania's great party bosses, in 1921. Moreover, Pinchot's appeal to certain citizen groups was increased by his steps towards political and administrative reform. Prior to his time most of the defections from the regular party organization were short-lived, and reforms were of a minor character. The machine accommodated the demand for reform by periodically selecting as a "front" a very able candidate, who could rehabilitate the party's name.

The "Pinchot wars" then, in Pennsylvania, in the 1920's and 1930's, were the result of the rise of a new progressive faction within the Republican party, after the time of the "big bosses," as the period from 1865–1921 was known.[25] Pennsylvania's progressive era was in part just a reflection of the Progressive Movement, which had begun in Wisconsin a decade or two earlier. Then came the further political dislocations resulting from the Great Depression and the New Deal, during which time Governor Earle, 1935–39, broke the pattern of solid Republican rule. After the

[25] See Robert Bowden, *Boies Penrose, Symbol of an Era* (New York, 1937), and Edward F. Cooke and G. Edward Janosik, *Guide to Pennsylvania Politics* (New York, 1957).

New Deal period, western Pennsylvania became a stronghold for the revived Democratic party, and the politics of the Keystone State began to move closer to a two-party system. Though Pennsylvania Republicans made a remarkable come-back in Harrisburg during and immediately after World War II, the rapid social changes and dislocations which took place in the generation since the Great Depression were bound to be reflected in changes in the state's political institutions. Pittsburgh went Democratic in 1932, and Philadelphia in 1951, and it was just a matter of time until this political shift in the state's two major cities would be reflected at Harrisburg as well. The handwriting was already on the wall at the time of Governor Fine's narrow election in 1950, as confirmed by the fact that the state went Democratic in 1954. In this political upset, Governor Leader carried with him Democratic candidates for three of the five elective state offices, and the majority of the house for the first time since 1937.

Elected at thirty-six, George Leader was a very young and appealing candidate, who stood in rather sharp contrast to the "typical Pennsylvania governor" as described earlier in this section. He slipped into the running rather unexpectedly early in 1954, when the previous Democratic standard-bearer, Philadelphia's Richardson Dilworth, decided not to run for governor again. Born on a farm, January 17, 1918, George was the third of seven children. His father, Guy Alvin Leader, was of Pennsylvania Dutch ancestry, and his mother, Beulah Boyer Leader, was of German–Swiss parentage. The family had been Pennsylvania farmers six or seven generations, since colonial times. It was not unusual for Pennsylvania to choose her governor from an old German–American family. The Pennsylvania

Dutch (as they are improperly known) have given the state about as many governors as any other group. Altogether, ten or a dozen had such parentage, the remainder having been fairly evenly divided between the English and the Scotch–Irish.[26]

Many of George Leader's qualities, such as his directness, sincerity, and humanitarian concern, were the product of his background. It was most unusual for a farmer to become governor of Pennsylvania, at least in the present century. Just before his election, Governor Leader was engaged vocationally in a poultry breeding and hatchery business, although he had actually completed his college training in the field of education. Most Pennsylvania governors had been lawyers, in fact, twelve of Leader's eighteen immediate predecessors, including all those since Governor Earle, had been recruited from that profession, as were twenty-two of the thirty-eight governors since 1790. Most of Leader's predecessors were also older, the average age being about fifty-two, as opposed to thirty-six. Leader's youth was both a political asset and a liability, praised by his supporters and admirers, and scorned by his political enemies.

Leader's education was also in contrast to that of the "typical Pennsylvania governor." Although all ten of the governors from 1915 to 1959 were college graduates, none apart from Leader had done much graduate study outside of the field of law. From 1935–38, Leader attended Gettysburg College, Pennsylvania, where he studied primarily philosophy, economics, and political science. In 1938, he transferred to the University of Pennsylvania, where he

26 Ralph Wood, ed., *The Pennsylvania Germans* (Princeton, 1942), p. 18. Also, Dunaway, *op. cit.,* p. 368.

completed a social studies major, graduating with a Bachelor of Science in education in 1939. After a short period back on the farm, which interrupted his earlier plans to go into teaching, Leader returned to the University of Pennsylvania to do post-graduate work at the Wharton School in the field of administration. Although this program was interrupted by military service the second semester, Leader completed seven courses in the Wharton Graduate Division and its constituent Institute of Local and State Government. Leader's professor of public administration, Dr. James C. Charlesworth, was later appointed first secretary of administration in the Governor's Office, 1955–56, and Dr. Stephen B. Sweeney, director of the Fels Institute of Local and State Government, served as a close advisor to Governor Leader throughout his term.

Not only was Leader's academic background exceptional among the recent governors; he also regarded himself as an intellectual. Governor Leader was interested in ideas. He surrounded himself with academic experts in many fields, and he had great respect for intellectual attainment. Thus Governor Leader's grasp of many of the great issues of government in the modern world was an asset not possessed in the same degree by several of his recent predecessors. His intellectual interests and qualities are perhaps best recorded in his many speeches, not only during the campaign, but throughout his term. He put a great deal of personal time and effort into speech-writing, and several of them have been published.[27]

---

[27] See 15 *The Township Commissioner* (Winter, 1956), p. 2; 64 *Pan American Federation* (A.F.L., May, 1957), p. 8; 300 *Annals of the American Academy of Political and Social Sciences* (July, 1955), p. 1; and in Stephen B. Sweeney, ed., *Education for Careers in Gov-*

Political experience is difficult to measure, since it may include many different things. Since the Leader family had long been active in York County politics, George's education in political matters began at an early age. His father had been fairly well known as a state senator and a leader in the county Democratic organization, both of which positions were later held by the future governor. George Leader's political experience can be summarized as follows:

1. Secretary of the York County Democratic Committee, 1942–46.
2. County chairman, 1946–50.
3. State senator, 1950–54.
4. Justice of the peace, York County, 1951.
5. Nominee for state treasurer, 1952.
6. Governor of Pennsylvania, 1955–59.

Although Leader had fewer years in public office than most of his predecessors, he had been active in county politics for ten or twelve years, and a state legislator, an experience which few of his immediate predecessors had enjoyed.[28]

Leader was also a veteran of the Navy, having spent ten months in the Pacific on the U.S.S. *Randolph* during the later part of World War II. He later noted that his three

---

ernment Service (Philadelphia, University of Pennsylvania Press, 1958), pp. 218–231. Also, his *Final Message to the General Assembly* (separately printed, Harrisburg, January 6, 1959, 116 pp. with Supplement), and other speeches and messages as printed in the Pennsylvania *Legislative Journal*, 1955, 1957 sessions.

[28] Only two of the eighteen governors since 1874 had been elected to the state legislature: Fisher (1901) and Sproul (twenty-two years, beginning in 1896). Governor Arthur James had previously presided over the Senate as lieutenant governor, however.

years as a supply officer gave him some experience with administrative problems, in another branch of governmental service.

George Michael Leader, II, brought a fresh breath of life to the State House at Harrisburg. Prior to his time the Governor's Office had been a rather quiet place. Some of his recent predecessors spent a good part of their time signing their names to various papers. Under Leader, the Governor's Office became the scene of a different kind of activity. The staff was expanded, and paper work streamlined, so that the governor could give more attention to other things. More ideas were aired, more programs initiated at the governor's desk, and more questions of departmental or state-wide concern were brought to the chief executive.

Governor Leader himself was largely responsible for this change, although there was also the salutary effect of having an entirely new team, a new leadership group at the top. Much of the new spirit, however, was a product of the governor's own personality. His youth was supplemented by an eagerness to do great things.[29] George Leader was enthusiastic about his job, and his sense of urgency was contagious. There was much to be done in a short time. Described by one close associate as "a tremendous personal salesman," Leader inspired the devoted loyalty of all those

[29] The only younger governor under the Pennsylvania Constitution of 1874 was Robert Pattison, who was first elected at thirty-two in 1882. George Earle (1935–39) was forty-five, and William Bigler (1852–55) was thirty seven. See Appendix A.

around him. In his speeches and meetings with citizen groups, Governor Leader invariably made an excellent impression. An extrovert by nature, Leader had a great personal appeal and he was able to "warm up" an audience of strangers in a short time. As governor, Leader could not be personally austere and formal, nor would he allow himself to be merely a figurehead, or a ceremonial factotum. Leader impressed people as human and understanding, although not exactly warm. He was a man of conviction and action.

People who saw Governor Leader in action speak first of his idealism and his sincerity—two qualities which few could doubt. Some observers say that Leader was too idealistic. He was a pragmatic idealist—a doer and not just a theorizer. He liked to discuss ideas, but he also wanted results. George Leader was inclined to absorb ideas from observation and conversation rather than from reading, but he did his homework, as well. He dug into all aspects of state government and knew both the organization and the programs. He pressed hard and vigorously for changes, trying to get action immediately, rather than waiting for political timing or acceptance.

Leader's sincerity was not simply a matter of fidelity to his promises and of personal relationships. It was a matter of his devotion to certain ideals. As one associate noted, Leader had a passion for certain things, towards which he pressed at every opportunity.[30] Governor Leader seemed to like people, though he would not tolerate the slightest

[30] One observer summarized a number of Leader's concerns in this humorous caricature: "He wanted legislation to send overaged, handicapped, unemployed Negroes to college to learn higher education." Interview in Harrisburg, May 9, 1961.

moral defect or acceptance of graft on the part of a state employe. Thus Leader not only made friends readily; he made enemies quickly, too. Leader's attitude manifested strong religious convictions about right and wrong. He stood firmly and immovably on issues such as betting on horse races, which he regarded as moral issues. This type of moral idealism made Leader more rigid and uncompromising than many politicians.

Leader's characteristic firmness was early observed by both friends and enemies. Friends would be inclined to admire his tenacity of purpose, while his critics thought of the governor as just plain stubborn. On the other hand, the long deadlock with the Republican Senate on the tax issue tended to give Leader an exaggerated reputation for stubbornness. Leader understood politics as "the art of the possible," and he made many compromises, as for example, in his legislative program.[31] Yet his compromises were seldom smooth. Partly as a result of his eagerness to make certain new departures and to achieve certain objectives, Leader failed to cultivate the art of a deft compromise in which he could retain the initiative. Rather, the governor readily identified the forces emerging for a "showdown," and he warmed quickly to the fray. Even some persons who were devoted to Leader acknowledged that he was one of the most determined persons they ever knew.

Leader was not afraid of disagreeing with people, and if the disagreement was sharp enough tempers were known to rise. These spirited encounters were not unusual for a young man with great determination. Tall, alert, and highly articulate, Leader often tended to dominate the sit-

[31] One example was Leader's acceptance of the age limitation on the F.E.P.C. bill.

uation. His language was as forceful as his manner, and close associates asknowledged that on occasion Leader changed their opinions. Though Leader was a good listener on other occasions, he was also an incisive person. He knew his subject and was well prepared to hold his own. He didn't tackle something until he was knowledgeable and well armed. He visited, for example, every one of the state hospitals, prisons, and institutions in order to know what he was talking about.

Even Leader's political enemies had to acknowledge that his burning interest and personal concern for education, for the mentally ill, and the handicapped, for example, was so genuine that he brought to the Governor's Office a new quality.[32] Many remarked that he would make an excellent secretary of health, education, and welfare.[33] Near the end of his first year in office, Leader spoke to the State Education Association annual meeting in these words:

> A Governor is governor to *all* the people in the State. He has a poignant concern for the hungry, the physically or mentally ill, the poorly housed and schooled. . . .[34]

[32] At the end of his term Leader characterized his program for the handicapped as, "the most gratifying achievement of my administration." (From 1954 to 1958 the number of handicapped children in special public school classes jumped from 47,910 to 110,163, and the number of such classes increased from 1165 to 2391.) *Press Release* #866, September 22, 1958.

[33] Persons opposed to governmental expansion were, however, less enthusiastic about Leader's approach.

[34] Governor's Office *Press Release* #454, December 29, 1955, p. 2. See also Leader's commencement address to the University of Pennsylvania, *Press Release* #934, February 9, 1957, p. 1. Reprinted in Stephen B. Sweeney, ed., *Education for Administrative Careers in Government Service* (Philadelphia, 1958), pp. 218–231.

Unlike many persons in high office, Governor Leader was very direct. Though he was sometimes asked in press conferences for information he could not disclose, Leader was not inclined to be evasive in normal circumstances. He was more apt to err on the side of being too outspoken, if not a trifle blunt at times. Once he issued the statement that if the legislature did not authorize the State Police to use radar for catching speeders, it would be responsible for the loss of hundreds of lives.[35] Even more serious was the time Leader indicated in a press conference, in response to a direct question, that he did not feel his lieutenant governor, Mr. Roy Furman, possessed all of the qualifications needed for a future governor.[36]

However, it is important to place Leader's approach to office into the historical setting. The Democrats had been out of office for sixteen years, and they had not really expected Leader to win. When Leader came to office, almost new and untried (if not a political unknown), there were many who thought their turn had come to "move in and take over." Those self-appointed regents were quickly disillusioned. They found in the Governor's Office not a pliant farm boy, nor a power vacuum, but a passionate liberal, who was determined to be nobody's tool. George Leader was his own boss, and he did not propose to yield to pressure on matters of principle.

After he began to realize the full powers of his office, Leader was even less inclined to court the favor of the county chairmen, a plausible cause for his failure to carry the full support of some of them in the 1958 campaign

[35] *Press Release* #A220, June 12, 1957.

[36] Mr. Furman can be regarded as a representative of the regular Democratic organization.

for United States senator. On the other hand, Governor Leader thought of himself as a party man to a certain extent. He did not agree with those "reformers" who would have him make "whipping boys" out of some of the county chairmen. Instead of disrupting the party, Leader wanted to help build, sustain, and improve it. He believed the reformers and the politicians should work on the same team, and he worked hard with both groups to bring this about.[37] However, both groups apparently misunderstood the governor's conviction and blamed him for following either too much or too little the rules of the political game.

In spite of this political problem, Leader made an enormous contribution to the governorship of Pennsylvania. His contribution can be identified in three major areas: administrative reorganization, improved personnel, and legislative program. His administration is also of special interest in terms of the structures and techniques used to enhance executive leadership and control. Chapter II discusses Leader's reorganization program, placing particular emphasis upon changes made in the Governor's Office as a result of the introduction of the Office of Administration. Succeeding chapters will describe other changes made by Governor Leader, with special reference to the experience of his Bureau of Program Evaluation. This was a new and somewhat experimental staff unit created to do program and policy research within the Governor's Office.

[37] Leader believes that both the "good government" reformers and the party leaders have a vital role to play, and that neither group is as venal as the other group would make them seem. Interview at Dover, Pennsylvania, August 14, 1960.

CHAPTER II

REORGANIZATION
OF THE GOVERNOR'S OFFICE

Leader's administrative reforms built upon the foundation established by the Administrative Code of 1923 (now known as the Code of 1929). This code, introduced under Governor Pinchot, was a major step in the establishment of a manageable administrative system. It consolidated some 139 agencies into seventeen (later twenty) departments, ten independent boards and commissions, three state authorities, and three other agencies.[1] Despite this leap towards consolidation, the new departmental organization preserved a considerable decentralization, which

[1] The State Police, the Turnpike Commission, and the Highway Planning Commission. Tanger, Alderfer, and McGeary, *Pennsylvania Government, State and Local* (rev. ed., State College, 1950), p. 121. Additional boards, commissions and agencies had been added by 1950, as noted above. A. E. Buck simplified the Pinchot reorganization slightly, when he wrote that the 1923 Code consolidated 105 agencies into "fourteen departments and three commissions. Only twenty-two of these agencies . . . were actually abolished; the others were transferred to various departments." A. E. Buck, *The Reorganization of State Governments in the United States* (New York, 1938), p. 205. In 1927, a Department of Revenue was added, and in 1929 the Code was expanded, with the addition of a fiscal code.

was regarded as one of the chief virtues of the new code. Professor Clyde L. King, of the University of Pennsylvania, who assisted Governor Pinchot in this reorganization, described the chief goal to be "reasonable centralization of fiscal responsibility with a proper decentralization in administration." [2]

One of the means of maintaining a degree of decentralization, or at least of collegial responsibility, under the new system was to create an Executive Board, with basic responsibility for matters of internal organization and management, for all the departments and agencies responsible to the governor. This board, the budget system, and central purchasing represented the three major features of the system established by the Administrative Code.[3]

THE EXECUTIVE BOARD AND THE CABINET

The Executive Board is a feature of Pennsylvania government which is quite unusual. Tanger, Alderfer, and McGeary describe it as, "in effect, a little cabinet . . . [or] a combination personnel and efficiency board." [4] It is

[2] Quoted by Buck, *ibid.,* p. 208. Thus, the major accomplishment of 1923 was the installation of an executive budget system.

[3] Leonard P. Fox, "Pennsylvania Reorganizes; Pinchot Code Now Effective," 12 *National Municipal Review* 9 (September, 1923), pp. 527ff.

[4] *Op. cit.,* p. 124. Section 709 of the *Administrative Code of 1929* gives the powers of the board, which include such things as the qualifications and wages of state employees (under the governor), the state administrative organization, including the creation of new bureaus or divisions within various agencies, the establishment of branch offices, rules governing work hours, extra compensation, expense accounts, fidelity bonds, purchase and use of state automobiles and the disposal of noncurrent records and files.

not precisely an *ex officio* board, since its membership is determined by the governor, who also serves as chairman. The board consists of the governor and six department heads, as designated by the governor from time to time. Four of the seven members constitute a quorum.

Although the Executive Board provides some departmental representation at the point where top operating decisions are made, it had not been used by recent governors as a consultative body. By the early 1950's, the board served primarily a *pro forma* function, "rubber-stamping" such matters as classification and salary changes in a round-robin fashion. The cabinet was not a consultative body either. Since many of the recent governors did not concern themselves greatly with internal departmental operations, such desuetude could be expected.[5]

Governor Leader revived the Executive Board and used it much more than had been done for many years. For example, all of his reorganization plans were "thrashed out" and ultimately approved by the Executive Board. The board was also the body responsible for implementing the new classification and compensation plans, and for the extension of civil service coverage—which has since been known as the "Executive Board civil service." Leader also started out with monthly cabinet meetings. However, he soon found the cabinet to be too large and heterogeneous a body to serve as either a policy-making or an advisory body:

The cabinet was never used to discuss how to tackle a problem. It was never an advisory body. . . . Public questions were

[5] It was reported that Governor Fine never met with his cabinet. Based upon interviews in Harrisburg and Philadelphia.

not discussed in cabinet meetings. It was a medium to transmit matters of common interest to the various departments.[6]

As in the federal government, Pennsylvania's cabinet has no statutory basis. Thus, Governor Leader could and did alter its membership according to his wishes.[7] Leader also had available the State Planning Board, which was shifted from the Commerce Department to the Governor's Office by Reorganization Plan #1 under the Act of 1955.[8] The Planning Board was thus given approximately the same status as any other advisory board, of which Leader had a good many. However, the traditional concern of the Planning Board was with physical, natural resource, or state economic development, rather than questions closely related to state administrative operations.[9]

Thus, up until 1955, there was a kind of vacuum at the administrative apex in Harrisburg. Neither the cabinet, the Executive Board, nor the Planning Board were able to provide the governor with vital policy, administrative, or advisory services. This vacuum was filled by the crea-

[6] Interview with Dr. Charlesworth, Philadelphia, June 27, 1960.

[7] By precedent, the heads of the major departments are all included, but in Leader's case, this did not include the elected treasurer and auditor general, who were Republicans. Leader's cabinet also included the governor's secretary, the budget secretary and secretary of Administration, the chairman of the Liquor Control Board, and the vice-chairman of the Turnpike Commission, making a total of about twenty-four persons. 93 *Pa. Manual,* p. 276.

[8] The Planning Board consisted of fifteen part-time members appointed by the governor for four year, staggered terms. Three of these were *ex officio* members, the secretaries of commerce, highways, and forests and waters. The board has a small staff.

[9] The State Planning Board now (1962) has certain responsibilities for evaluating state programs in connection with capital budget planning.

tion of the Office of Administration within the Governor's Office in January, 1955. This new agency is regarded as one of the major contributions of the Leader administration, the long-term significance of which may be as great or greater than the political upset in Harrisburg in 1955.

THE OFFICE OF ADMINISTRATION

Since the Office of Administration was created by executive order, rather than by statute, it was originally taken less seriously even by sections of the bureaucracy than would otherwise be the case. After all, what one governor could order, another could rescind. However, Governor Lawrence, Leader's successor, has continued this entire operation largely intact. Thus, by 1960, observers generally regarded the office as a permanent feature of the state administration. There was never any question of the governor's constitutional and statutory authority to set up this new agency within his office, since he has full power not only to reorganize his own office, but also to supervise the common affairs of the several departments, in such a way as the Office of Administration does. The governor's legal power to establish the office was never challenged.[10]

Like most other important governmental changes, the

---

[10] Aside from the governor's constitutional mandate, the *Administrative Code of 1929,* Section 701, as amended, further elaborates the powers and duties of the governor, under twelve headings. These include such specific powers as "To prescribe . . . a uniform system of accounting, reporting . . . ," to prescribe forms for accounts and . . . records," "to submit . . . a budget," "to prescribe the filing system [for] each department, board, and commission, . . . [to manage or destroy] records . . . to assign space . . . or quarters . . ." All of these things are performed in some degree by the Office of Administration.

idea of such a central staff agency had a history in Pennsylvania—it did not just spring from the head of Zeus or from Adam's rib. By the 1950's, several of Pennsylvania's political scientists could see the basic need for central reorganization. In the 1950 revision of their textbook, Tanger, Alderfer, and McGeary touched upon the reorganization problem with two summary statements.

One of the dangers of centralization is the development of complex mechanisms for relatively simple processes. This incurs delay and red-tape. . . . The eradication of useless procedures is one of the most important improvements still to be made. . . .[11]

In the second place, they noted that many additional agencies had been added, which had "not in all cases been fitted into the reorganized administrative structure." [12] In a pamphlet published about the same time, Professors Alderfer and McGeary elaborated the problem as follows:

One of the main improvements that has to be made is to develop machinery in the Governor's office that will ease the Governor's load and accelerate the routine of day-by-day administration. The original reorganization was made in order to concentrate power in the hands of the chief executive so that action on a uniform basis would be forthcoming. Now

[11] *Op. cit.*, p. 132. This point was made slightly more specific in the concluding chapter, where the authors speak again of the ineffectiveness of the Executive Board: "In actual practice, many of the lesser decisions such as the appointment of employees in the lower echelons usually are made by the Governor himself. Because of the great variety of demands upon his time, the Governor's desk has become a bottle neck in state administration. It is also apparent that not enough real responsibility has been given to cabinet officers and heads of departments. . . ." *Ibid.*, pp. 361, 362.

[12] *Ibid.*, p. 132.

improvements have to be made in order to decentralize not his ultimate power but administrative procedure. It may be that, as has been suggested in other states, the Lieutenant Governor should be given increased responsibilities, or that the executive board should be re-activated, or that in the Governor's office there should be administrative assistants, under his direct supervision and guidance, who will lighten his burden. . . . For the Governor is the leader, the chief executive; his larger responsibilities do not permit him to be an administrator of detail. . . .

As a whole, however, the structure and organization of the state administration in Pennsylvania is solid and sound. No fundamental changes need be made, but constant care and repair of the complicated machinery is necessary.[13]

In January, 1953, Dr. James C. Charlesworth, the future secretary of administration, went further in his task force report to Governor Fine's State Government Survey Committee.[14] Dr. Charlesworth recommended the establishment of the following staff and/or auxiliary units directly under the governor:

1. The secretary with his staff.
2. A Management Department, headed by a secretary.
3. A Department of Law (with the State Police).
4. The State Planning Board.

Moreover, all of the regular line departments and agencies were to be grouped under five or six administrations, plus

[13] Alderfer and McGeary, *Pennsylvania Government: 1950: The Shape of Things Today and the Shape of Things to Come*, pp. 8, 9.
[14] This Committee is generally known as the Chesterman Committee.

two operating departments.[15] According to a brief "Foreword," this scheme was designed to reduce the governor's span of control, to coordinate departments with related programs, to free policy agents from line duties, to make lines of responsibility more clear and definite, and to provide line executives with adequate staff and management assistance.[16]

Dr. Charlesworth's proposal was fairly close to what ultimately emerged in 1955 as Governor Leader's Office of Administration. The proposed management department was to contain seven bureaus. Four of these, plus a personnel office, which was to be attached to that department with a separate board, were actually included in the Office of Administration. The proposed seven bureaus (those actually established in 1955 are italicized) were as follows:

Budget	Buildings	Public information
Accounting	*Program analysis*	(Plus, Office of *Personnel*,
Supply	*Procedures*	with board, as indicated.)

Just two years later, in January, 1955, Governor Leader called upon Dr. Charlesworth to preside as secretary of

15 The administrations were to be economics (with four departments), finance (three departments), public works (three departments), welfare (four departments), and possibly education (with two departments). Military affairs and the state department were to be separate. Twenty-two organizational charts were attached to this task force report.

16 Three years earlier (February to June, 1949), in his public administration seminar at the University of Pennsylvania, Dr. Charlesworth and his students had worked out a similar but less elaborate scheme. See Institute of Local and State Government, University of Pennsylvania, *Proposed Reorganization of the Executive Branch of the State of Pennsylvania*, 1949. (Mimeographed, 31 pp., with charts.)

administration over five of these seven or eight units that he had suggested.

The Chesterman Committee presented its final report to Governor Fine on February 11, 1953, less than a month after receiving Dr. Charlesworth's task force report. In this short time, it is doubtful that the full implications of the various task force reports could be fully examined. In any case the final report of the State Government Survey Committee, as it was officially known, pared down Charlesworth's proposals somewhat. Thus the recommendations of the full committee moved in the same direction, but at a slower pace. The committee recommended adding only two new units directly under the governor:

1. A new Management Administration (headed by an Executive for Administration—a kind of deputy to the Governor)

2. A new Department of Accounting (to formulate and operate . . . sound bookkeeping and accounting practices . . . for every operational unit of the state government).[17]

Special emphasis was also placed upon the need for "improvement of personnel administration by . . . a uniform classification system . . . salary revision . . . and the provision of job security for more professional and technical employees."

Neither Governor Fine nor the state legislature took any specific action on the basis of this report. This was partly due to the fact that in the latter part of his term,

[17] Commonwealth of Pennsylvania, *The State Government Survey Committee Report* (Harrisburg, February 11, 1953), 94 pp., at p. vii. Mr. Francis J. Chesterman, chairman, is retired president of the Bell Telephone Company, Philadelphia. More than two hundred citizens participated in the work of this committee, assisted by a staff under the direction of John N. O'Neil.

Governor Fine did not enjoy the full support of his own party in the General Assembly. Adoption of the recommendations was also handicapped by the fact that Mr. Chesterman and his associates declined to make themselves available to legislative committees, in order to discuss or support their proposals. However, many of the ideas in the report were utilized in 1954 by the Pennsylvania Economy League, and by Governor-elect Leader's preinaugural Advisory Committee, in two activities to which we now turn.

THE ECONOMY LEAGUE PLAN

Governor Fine was aware of the inadequacy of his executive office staff. The organization of the Governor's Office had been "established by the Executive Board in 1927, and consisted of the following organizational units, headed by a secretary to the governor:

Administrative Bureau
Personnel Bureau
Budget Bureau." [18]

On the one hand, the governor was burdened with so much detail, such as issuing commissions, making appoint-

[18] *A Suggested Plan for the Organization of the Governor's Office, Commonwealth of Pennsylvania,* Pennsylvania Economy League (1954). Some expansion also took place under Governor Earle.

On June 1, 1940, there were twenty-six employees in the Administrative Bureau under the secretary to the governor, sixteen in the Budget Bureau, under the statutory budget secretary, and ten persons in the Personnel Bureau, making a total of fifty-two in the Governor's Office altogether. For a description of the duties of each bureau, the salaries of all employees, and the object expenditures of the Governor's Office for the three biennia, 1937–40, see the Turner Report (*Report on the Organization and Administration of Pennsylvania's State Government,* Harrisburg, January, 1941, pp. 101–110).

ments, signing papers, and performing ceremonial functions, that he had insufficient time to devote to the larger policy questions. For another thing, he lacked the information, staff, and controls needed to keep sufficiently in touch with departmental operations.[19]

Consequently, Governor Fine asked the Pennsylvania Economy League, whose Harrisburg branch had specialized in state governmental matters for some years, to make a special study of the Governor's Office and to prepare a plan for its reorganization. This study was completed in the fall of 1954, and its substance was approved by Governor Fine. However, he realized that implementation at the eleventh hour of his term would be of little advantage. In his first meeting at the capitol with the governor-elect, Fine turned this plan over to him for his consideration. Leader was delighted to have this proposal, and went to work on it immediately. The fact that this report had originally been prepared at the request of Governor Fine gave this Plan a bipartisan, if not a nonpartisan character, which was very desirable. Governor Leader

. . . accepted the recommendations in this report almost in toto and proceeded to staff his office accordingly. The only

[19] Governor Fine's problem was by no means exceptional for many modern governors. See Homer E. Scace, "The Governor Needs Staff," 40 *National Municipal Review* (October, 1951), p. 462. Mr. Scace, of the New York State Chamber of Commerce, described the jobs to be performed by a governor's staff as follows: (1) public relations, (2) preparation of the governor's legislative and administrative program (including the use of objective research, expert legal advice and review), (3) preparation and presentation of the executive budget, together with control of expenditures, (4) concern with the quality and performance of state personnel, and (5) administrative coordination and control. See also, by the same author, *The Organization of the Executive Office of the Governor,* Institute of Public Administration (New York, 1950).

significant alteration to the recommended plan was the creation, by the Governor, of a Bureau of Program Evaluation under the Secretary of Administration. The functions of the Bureau of Program Evaluation are the review, evaluation and projection of objectives, programs and accomplishments of state agencies.[20]

Thus the heart of Governor Leader's administrative reform was recommended by a nonpartisan group of experts retained by the Pennsylvania Economy League. The Economy League utilized trained and professional observers of the state government, who, in turn, compiled the ideas of numerous persons and groups, such as those cited above. The Economy League Plan was more specialized than the Chesterman Report since it dealt only with the organization of the Governor's Office, rather than the state administration as a whole.[21] The Economy League noted that "the functions and responsibilities of the Governor can be grouped into two classes, *i.e.,* political and ceremonial, and administrative." The Governor's Office was to be reorganized to reflect this bifurcation. The administrative activities were to be placed under a secretary of administration, while the political and ceremonial activities were to be placed under the secretary to the governor. It was asserted in the plan that,

The centering of the direction of these activities under two top aides will minimize the number of people reporting directly to the Governor, thereby relieving him of excessive detail and conserving his time.

[20] Leslie D. Howe, "Pennsylvania Governor's Office Revamped," 44 *National Municipal Review* (July 1955), p. 366.
[21] The Plan comprised eleven pages, as opposed to ninety-four pages for the Survey Committee Report (with acknowledgments).

SECRETARY TO THE GOVERNOR

The first of these two aides, the secretary to the governor, should help him to perform the following political and ceremonial functions:

1. Maintain relationships with legislators and party members.
2. Deal with the press.
3. Consult with groups of all kinds.
4. Speak on administrative and public questions.
5. Represent the state in negotiations and meetings with other governmental jurisdictions.
6. Represent the state in ceremonies and public affairs of all kinds.[22]

Thus, the secretary is to serve as a personal aide and confidential secretary to the governor, helping him to deal with members of the public, the party, and the government. One of his major responsibilities is to screen persons to see the governor.[23]

----

[22] Pennsylvania Economy League, *A Suggested Plan . . . ,* p. 1. See chart on the next page.

[23] "From Fisher's term on, the affairs of the state government have increased so greatly that Governors have been obliged to lean more heavily than ever on their secretaries. Prior to Earle, confidential and assistant secretaries were frequently used, but they were given assorted titles in the staff. Earle found it necessary to set up an actual secretariat and had two assistant secretaries, in addition to several advisers and research technicians, placed elsewhere on payrolls in state government.

"The post of assistant secretary became a permanent one, and Governor James also had two assistants, who served, one as a press secretary and one as a correspondence secretary. Duff changed the title of one assistant secretary to executive assistant, and put his publicity man on the payroll of the Department of Commerce as a

The secretary to Governor Leader, Mr. David Randall, supervised the political and ceremonial activities of the Governor's Office[24] with the aid of these four major units, as recommended by the Economy League:

1. The legislative secretary (Mr. Henry B. Leader).
2. The public relations secretary (Mr. Thomas K. Hodges).
3. The personnel secretary (Mr. Robert H. Jones).
4. The chief clerk (Mr. Richard Heagy).[25]

Altogether, these four functions involved a staff of about forty-five persons, including clerical personnel.[26] Only Mr. Heagy, the chief clerk, had served in the Governor's Office for some years, actually since 1919.[27]

---

public relations specialist. The budget and personnel bureaus also have secretaries, who report to the Governor's secretary and are under him." Le Roy Greene, *Shelter for His Excellency, The Story of Pennsylvania's Executive Mansion and the One Hundred Governors of the Commonwealth* (Harrisburg, 1951), p. 339.

[24] Prior to this assignment Randall was "engaged vocationally in anthracite mining, preparation, sales and land management, and avocationally in politics." 93 *Pa. Manual*, p. 308. Randall resigned as secretary to Governor Leader on September 12, 1958, to enter the University of Pennsylvania Law School and was succeeded by Otis B. Morse, IV. Morse continued as secretary to Governor Lawrence and then became Democratic state chairman.

[25] The functions of these units within the Governor's Office are summarized in the Economy League Plan, pp. 2–4. The names of the persons involved appear in 92 *Pennsylvania Manual*, p. 1012. In Vol. 93, p. 377, Mr. Debs Myers had replaced Mr. Hodges, and the title had shifted to press secretary.

[26] According to interview with Mr. Randall, in Philadelphia, August 10, 1960.

[27] Mr. Heagy's knowledge of the routines, and his efficient management of the files and papers proved a great help both to the governor and his staff, and to the public. In fact, the care with which Mr. Heagy indexed and prepared the Leader Papers for storage at the Pennsylvania State University Library will be of great

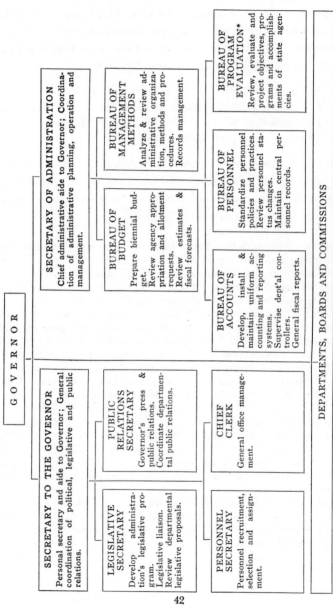

GOVERNOR

SECRETARY TO THE GOVERNOR
Personal secretary and aide to Governor; General coordination of political, legislative and public relations.

LEGISLATIVE SECRETARY
Develop administration's legislative program.
Legislative liaison.
Review departmental legislative proposals.

PUBLIC RELATIONS SECRETARY
Governor's press & public relations.
Coordinate departmental public relations.

PERSONNEL SECRETARY
Personnel recruitment, selection and assignment.

CHIEF CLERK
General office management.

SECRETARY OF ADMINISTRATION
Chief administrative aide to Governor; Coordination of administrative planning, operation and management.

BUREAU OF ACCOUNTS
Develop, install & maintain uniform accounting and reporting systems.
Supervise dept'al controllers.
General fiscal reports.

BUREAU OF BUDGET
Prepare biennial budget.
Review agency appropriation and allotment requests.
Review estimates & fiscal forecasts.

BUREAU OF PERSONNEL
Standardize personnel policies and practices.
Review personnel status changes.
Maintain central personnel records.

BUREAU OF MANAGEMENT METHODS
Analyze & review administrative organization, methods and procedures.
Records management.

BUREAU OF PROGRAM EVALUATION*
Review, evaluate and project objectives, programs and accomplishments of state agencies.

DEPARTMENTS, BOARDS AND COMMISSIONS

42

* The establishment of this unit was not included in the study recommendations, but was subsequently added by the Governor. (This chart was in the Pennsylvania Economy League Plan following page 1. Dated April 2, 1956.)

The work of the public relations secretary was greatly expanded under Leader. According to a member of the Harrisburg press corps, "One of the biggest things Leader did to educate the public, was to make available all the information he could to the press." As a result, Leader's immediate relations with the newspaper correspondents were very good. However, as one observer put it, by the time some of this press material filtered into the news and the editorial columns of some of the big city papers, it was often much less favorable, and rarely complimentary in tone.

The office of legislative secretary was new. It was established in 1955 much as the Economy League had recommended. There had been a certain amount of legislative liaison before, through the secretary to the governor. However, this new position served to institutionalize, regularize, and expand this whole operation. Special procedures were now established to secure the views of all departments interested in or affected by legislative proposals. These views were collected by the legislative secretary and discussed from the viewpoint of the governor's program. Democratic members of the legislature found this to be of great service since they now had an authoritative statement of the governor's views, together with departmental notations on every important matter up for consideration. The job had never been conducted in such a systematic way before. The position was at the center of some tension, however, at times when legislative–executive relations be-

---

assistance to historians of future generations. (Mr. Heagy retired at the end of Leader's term, after forty-six years in state service, since 1912.)

The functions of Mr. Jones, the personnel secretary, are described in Chapter III.

came strained. In addition to institutional jealousies and some personal strains, the legislative secretary stood in a rather exposed position. He was at the point where most of the grievances of the legislators on patronage matters were relayed to the governor. Thus the job of the legislative secretary was not restricted to matters involving new legislation.

SECRETARY OF ADMINISTRATION AND BUDGET SECRETARY

The Office of Administration, the other wing of the Governor's Office, was created in 1955 to free the governor from as much of the management detail as possible, in order to leave some "time available for policy matters and state leadership." [28] The governor's responsibility for administrative oversight and supervision was extensive in view of the sheer size of the state apparatus. In 1954, the state administration consisted of the following:

  20 Departments (seventeen with head appointed by governor, three elected)
  10 Independent Boards and Commissions
125 Departmental Administrative Boards, Commissions and Offices, each of which is placed in one of the above administrative units
   3 State Authorities
     Pennsylvania State Police
     Pennsylvania Turnpike Commission
     State Council of Civil Defense
     Highway Planning Commission[29]

The Office of Administration had been recommended to

[28] Pennsylvania Economy League Plan, 1954, p. 4.
[29] *Ibid.,* p. 5.

the governor to perform the following more specific functions:

1. Budget formulation and execution.
2. Management research.
3. Accounting control and systems.
4. Personnel administration.[30]

The Pennsylvania Economy League suggested that the governor should select as secretary of administration a man possessing

... extensive background of business or public administration experience. He should be able to maintain good working relationships with administrative agencies and be capable of effectively representing the Governor before the legislature in support of his budget program.

The Office of Administration was to be comprised of four bureaus, corresponding to the functions just listed. The budget secretary was the only one of the ultimately six bureau chiefs whose position had been specifically named in statute, though the language of the enabling Section 211 of the Administrative Code was broad enough to include also the rest of the Office of Administration.[31]

---

[30] *Idem.* To these four were added the functions of the Bureau of Program Evaluation in 1955 and the Bureau of Capital Expenditures, c. 1956, as further explained in Chapter IV. See also 93 *Pa. Manual,* pp. 307, 308.

[31] "The Governor shall appoint, to serve at his pleasure, a Secretary to the Governor, a Budget Secretary, and such consultants, experts, accountants, investigators, clerks . . . and other employes as may be required for the proper conduct of the work of his office and of the Executive Board, and shall fix their salaries, wages, fees or other compensation." Section 211, *The Administrative Code of 1929.*

Section 601 gives further detail on the functions of the budget secretary.

The budget secretary performed all the usual functions of receiving and reviewing departmental requests, making decisions as to size of program, preparing the budget document, and then executing the budget, as approved, with the aid of allocations and budgetary reviews. In the fall of 1956, the offices of budget secretary and secretary of administration were combined in the same person.[32] There was Economy League support for this arrangement of combining the positions of budget secretary and secretary of administration. Though the original Plan (1954) provided a separate description of the budget secretary, this followed immediately as a subhead to the topic, "Budget and Administration (Secretary of Administration)" (*sic*). When the Pennsylvania Economy League restudied this Office nearly four years later, their first recommendation was such a combination.[33] In fact, the 1958 report suggested expanding the Budget Bureau to provide central stenographic, messenger and duplicating services for all the bureaus (presumably within the Office of Administra-

[32] By that time, Leader's first budget had already been prepared and adopted, and many other initial problems had been solved. Thus, these two functions could now be better combined than in the first year, when the policies, procedures and program emphases of the new administration had not yet been adumbrated. Based upon interviews with former members of the Office, in Philadelphia, June 27 and June 29, 1960.

[33] "Prepare and introduce legislation to give statutory recognition to the Secretary of Administration, and to transfer to him the present statutory duties and responsibilities of the Budget Secretary." *Recommendations Concerning the Future Organization and Functions of the Office of Administration,* prepared for Secretary John H. Ferguson by the Pennsylvania Economy League, Inc., State Division, June 18, 1958, p. 1. Other observers have felt this combination to be unwise.

tion).[34] The major objective of the Budget Bureau was officially set forth in August, 1958, as follows:

To ensure that the formulation and execution of the Governor's budget are directed toward the achievement of the goals of the Administration.[35]

BUREAU OF MANAGEMENT METHODS

The Bureau of Management Methods was designed to conduct management research and to "serve as a trouble shooting unit for the Governor for locating bottlenecks and organizational weaknesses in administrative units, analyzing them, and making recommendations for improvement." [36] The 1958 report of the Governor's Office puts the objective more simply as the "development and application of modern management methods to the administration of the State government." Various observers have

[34] *Ibid.*, p. 2. Six other major recommendations were outlined for the Budget Bureau, one of which was to "Consolidate program research and evaluation with budget preparation and control, within the Budget Bureau. Program evaluation might be performed by a separate unit appropriately staffed to make continuous and special analyses of operating program proposals and performance, assist in program phases of budget preparation. . . ." *Ibid.*, pp. 5, 6.

[35] *Role of the Office of Administration,* Governor's Office, Commonwealth of Pennsylvania, August, 1958, 8 pp. mimeo., at p. 3. Fourteen specific duties were listed, which embrace the customary aspects of budget preparation and execution. However, these rather unusual duties were also included: #10. To encourage the professional development of budget personnel throughout the executive branch. #11. To keep agencies currently informed on developments in the field of budget management. #12. To serve as a clearing house and provide information for investments, bond issues, tax anticipation notes, etc.

[36] Economy League Plan (1954), p. 6.

pointed to this bureau as an illustration of the newly invigorated interest in administrative improvement under the Leader administration. Moreover, unlike Program Evaluation, Management Methods was accepted as one of the standard features of present-day administrative practice —already established and identified in other jurisdictions.

In the preceding administration,

> . . . only two agencies, Bureau of Employment Security and Department of Public Assistance, had anything resembling management methods units, and these two had small staffs that dealt mostly with procedures analysis alone. In the last year of Fine's administration a records management division was created in the Budget Bureau . . . [with] a small staff. . . .[37]

When the new Bureau of Management Methods was set up in January, 1955, with a limited budget, a number of persons were borrowed from the three existing units just noted, plus others who had some administrative and/or supervisory background. Shortly the new bureau was operating with a director, assistant director, secretary, and from two to six analysts.

The idea was always to have a small nucleus in the Office of Administration who would be "generalists" to guide management methods all over "the hill," so that a larger staff was not desired. Through three training classes some sixty men were instructed and then sent out to work in the agencies and were administratively responsible to their agency heads.

[37] "How Administrative Planning and Direction Are Used for Establishing the Administrative Management Function in State Government," panel discussion by Dr. Robert A. Christie, director of Management Methods and Program Evaluation, Commonwealth of Pennsylvania, at the Fels Institute, October 15, 1959, p. 2.

The original goal had been to have one management analyst for every thousand employees. Such a number was approached, with the aid of the sixty analysts trained by the bureau itself. However, some of the better trained methods analysts were lost to this program, because they were promoted to become bureau chiefs and to other line supervisory positions. The O and M training was thus not "lost," since many of these persons were still employed by the state, though a full complement of management methods units was never actually obtained.

To facilitate the infiltration of management methods ideas throughout the various agencies Governor Leader created a Management Methods Council. This group was designed to nurture common goals, techniques and methods:

A good example of the use of standardized procedures was the Bureau's preparation and promulgation of a manual of office planning and layouts, which is still being used.[38]

After some eighteen months of operation, a report of the Office of Administration listed eight or ten activities and accomplishments (of a total of some thirty-two) which fall into the area of management methods. It is unnecessary to give the details, but the scope and significance of such services can be indicated from the following summary:

#11. New organization charts . . . for nearly all agencies and approved by the Executive Board.
#12. Approximately 50 management analysts at work in the various agencies . . . conducting continuous and sys-

[38] Prepared text of Dr. Christie's remarks, p. 4.

tematic analyses of departmental organization and
procedures. . . .

#19. Office space allocation, through Office of Administra-
tion: . . . fuller utilization of available office space.
. . .

#20. Forms control was instituted by this Office. . . .

#21. A complete audit is in progress of the uses made by
the Commonwealth of automatic business machines.

#22. A plan . . . for improving institutional food serv-
ices. . . .

#28. A program of work measurement is in the process of
development . . .

#32. A record management program has been devel-
oped. . . .[39]

Other studies conducted early in the Leader regime by
the Bureau of Management Methods revealed serious
weaknesses in such matters as inventory control, records
management, and use of floor space. On the fifth floor of
the capitol, floor space adequate for some thirty office
rooms had been "wasted," since it was used for storing
"tons of rubbish, outdated records, old furniture, yellowed
stationery, outdated printed forms, and unused valuable
steel file cabinets." In one such room, "stationery and outdated printed forms estimated in excess of three tons were
discovered . . . long since forgotten." [40]

Evidence of the fact that management methods had
come to Harrisburg to stay can be found in the fact that
the bureau was given even more assignments in the early
part of the Lawrence administration. Its authorized com-

[39] Staff report of the Office of Administration, "Report of Activities," August 15, 1956, 6 pp. (Mimeographed.)

[40] Governor's Office *Press Release* (unnumbered), April 22, 1955,
issued by the Office of the Secretary of Administration.

plement was increased from thirty to forty-seven in 1961, forty-two of these to be professional and technical people.[41]

BUREAU OF ACCOUNTS

The new Bureau of Accounts was created as a third section of the Office of Administration in 1955. This bureau filled a special need because of the chaotic condition of the commonwealth's previous accounts. Some idea of the confused state of the accounts can be grasped by the following incident. Although Governor Leader delivered his first budget message to the General Assembly on April 19, 1955, he did not know as late as March 31 just what the state government's current obligations were.[42] The fact that the state's accounting methods were obsolete had long been known. They had been continued largely through inertia. As Governor Leader himself observed, accounting, like other things, has evolved and changed with the times, but the state government failed to keep pace with such changes.[43] In 1953, the Chesterman Committee had emphasized the necessity for accounting reform, and suggested the establishment of a new Department of Accounting, in order to achieve a uniform accounting system. An earlier step in this direction had been taken by the establishment of the Budget Bureau under Governor Pinchot in 1923, but by 1955 the accounts had again become too uncoordinated to disclose the information needed. The Administrative Code of 1929, as amended, provided the governor

[41] Interview with Mr. Donald Probert, assistant director, Bureau of Management, March 7, 1961.

[42] Statement made by Governor Leader to his *Press Conference,* March 31, 1955, p. 1 of mimeographed typescript.

[43] Governor's Office *Press Release* #85, March 4, 1955, p. 2.

with authority, "To prescribe and require the installation of a uniform system of bookkeeping, accounting, and reporting, for the several . . . departments. . . ." [44] The governor has other accounting functions, such as the duty to:

(2) Supervise the departmental comptrollers who, with the exception of a few agencies, are directly responsible to and are employes of the Governor as a result of legislation passed in 1953;

(3) Maintain pre-audit control of purchases and expenditures through the supervision of departmental comptrollers;

(4) Obtain pertinent data on departmental expenditures and supply it in proper form to the Budget Division for effective budget administration. [45]

Though the governor possessed ample authority in the accounting area, these powers had not been fully and adequately utilized prior to 1955. Thus, the commonwealth's financial problems were compounded because of inadequate fiscal tools and inaccurate fiscal information. The state suffered not only from an inadequate fiscal policy, but also from fiscal mismanagement and misinformation. [46]

[44] *Administrative Code of 1929,* Section 241. (See *Purdon's Pennsylvania Statutes Annotated,* Title 71, Section 241, d.)

[45] As summarized by the Pennsylvania Economy League Plan, p. 7.

[46] *The Philadelphia Inquirer,* September 12, 1954, p. 15, "Fine's Tax Estimate Called Phony by Barr." See also Governor Leader's speech to the Pennsylvania Political Science and Public Administration Association, at Mechanicsburg, April 12, 1957:

"Accounting methods were needlessly and outrageously complex when I took office. No one was able to figure out the exact financial status of the Commonwealth. We found—unbelievable as it may sound—a system of bookkeeping which did not disclose liabilities running into millions of dollars . . . We completely overhauled our accounting system and had a new one in operation by January 1, 1956." *Press Release* #71 (should be A–71), April 12, 1957.

A large variety of accounting records and types of recording were used in the various departments—so much so that central control was almost impossible. Some departments used manual entries, whereas other departments had installed some accounting machines of various types and designs. There were even instances found where data was kept in memorandum form on slips of paper in a bureau drawer. In another case, similar information was recorded in a voluminous filing system using sixty elaborate forms and folders, where one would suffice.[47]

Even more serious than the lack of uniformity was the fact that heretofore the commonwealth maintained only single-entry cash accounts. This meant that although the governor could secure figures as to the state's cash position any particular month or day, such figures were misleading, since they did not take into account sums that had been obligated or contracted, but not actually disbursed. The real problem was the lack of an accrual type of accounts, which would reflect the total financial position of the commonwealth, rather than just its momentary cash balance or degree of solvency. The significance of accounting procedures is evident from the fact that the commonwealth's expenditures amounted to $2,584,178,028 for the biennium ending May 31, 1953, and had already reached $2,405,232,-992 for the next biennium by January 31, 1955. Yet this large financial operation was accounted for by a single entry system of bookkeeping on a cash basis. The self-bal-

[47] Governor's Office *Press Release* #85, March 4, 1955, p. 2. It could be argued that such a set of facts could be made the subject of some rhetorical exaggeration for political purposes. Certainly smaller departments would not require exactly the same type of machine equipment as the larger departments. The real issue is to what extent the data is comparable.

ancing control features of a double entry system were lacking. The old procedures were described by the Governor's Office in these terms:

> Revenues due to the Commonwealth are not reflected on the books as assets unless collected in cash, and payables owed by the Commonwealth are not reflected on the books as liabilities until they are approved for payment by the Auditor General, although services contracted for may have been rendered and goods purchased may have been received. Under the present system it is not possible to draw up a clear and correct statement of the Commonwealth's total resources and obligations at any given time. The cash system of accounting not only permits but actually requires the preparation of statements which are at variance with the facts.[48]

Moreover, cost information by units of work was generally lacking. In fact, the entire disbursement system was so bad that it was decided to call in an outside firm of administrative experts to renovate the accounting system.[49]

Not only were the disbursement accounts in a chaotic condition; the accounts receivable were also quite unsatisfactory. The result was that the commonwealth lacked reliable information concerning revenue collections and taxpayer delinquencies, according to official statements. Although the governor did not assert that a number of tax collections had actually been evaded, he did maintain that

[48] *Press Release* #85, p. 2.

[49] The Public Administration Service of Chicago was engaged for one year beginning March, 1955, to develop a double-entry accrual type of disbursement accounting. The contract was for the sum of $50,000. The Manual prepared by PAS was distributed by the Governor on August 1, 1956, and was still in operation, with some amendments, in 1961. See *Manual of Accounting and Related Financial Procedures*. Commonwealth of Pennsylvania (1956).

the system he inherited provided no assurance that all the revenues actually due had been collected, and no certainty that the collections had been as prompt as would have been proper. In fact, the revenue situation was so critical, that this part of the accounting reform was tackled even earlier than the Public Administration Service project just described. Less than a month after he took office, Governor Leader signed an agreement with two accounting firms to modernize the accounts receivable bookkeeping system of the Department of Revenue.[50]

The next task of the Bureau of Accounts was to introduce more mechanization into the bookkeeping system. This was done by means of IBM punch cards. Machine accounting had already been begun in some departments under Governor Fine. What Leader did was to install the same type of accounting machine in every department, in every controller's office. After such mechanization revenue receipts were punched daily and mechanically added in various categories, in order to provide revenue information on a current basis.

Later, the Leader administration undertook to mechanize the payroll system, and installed a Univac electronic data processing center, which was used not only for the operating statistics of the various departments, but also for various phases of general and fiscal accounting. Although this electronic machinery was originally leased by the state at a monthly cost of $25,000, it was expected to

[50] This work was done by two Philadelphia firms, Laventhal, Krekstein and Co. and Price, Waterhouse and Co., at a total cost of about $85,000. *Press Release* #44, February 15, 1955. The weaknesses of the revenue system had been described in a study by the Joint State Government Commission in 1950.

pay for itself and save the commonwealth about $300,000 per year.[51]

Another objective of the accounting reform was to decentralize the system, in order to avoid duplication, as well as the clutter of detail which results from too much centralization of routine operations in the office of the chief executive. This was done, partly, by making the controller in each department responsible for the basic fiscal data, but subject to the technical control of the Governor's Office of Administration. Thus there were centralized controls operating within a system of decentralized accounting. Legislation passed in 1953 authorized the governor to assume responsibility for the departmental controllers, but such supervision was not actually exercised by the Governor's Office until the Leader administration. Under the new system, the controllers were responsible to the secretary of administration.

In summary, the specific objectives of the Leader administration's new accounting system were set forth in the following terms:

1. Coordination of the systems of accounts kept by individual departments and agencies with those of the Office of Administration.
2. Uniform and consistent accounting practices among all State agencies.
3. Consistency and coordination between accounting and budgeting procedures.
4. Current and accurate information relating to the financial condition and operations of the State.[52]

[51] *Press Release* #A 500, January 10, 1958. It was later (1960) purchased.

[52] *Manual of Accounting and Related Financial Procedures* (1956), "Foreword." This manual, prepared by the Public Administration

In announcing the new accounting system to be put into effect on January 1, 1956, Governor Leader said that the commonwealth now would have its first effective system for financial management in about twenty-five years.[53]

OTHER FISCAL REFORMS

Another aspect of fiscal mismanagement which came to light early in the Leader regime had to do with the custody of state funds. Heretofore each department had the practice of depositing funds in banks under many different accounts. The effect of depositing many small and partially inactive funds under so many different accounts and subaccounts was to forfeit a considerable amount of interest, which might be available under a consolidated bank deposit.[54]

The shortage of qualified personnel was another handicap which the commonwealth suffered, in nearly all aspects of fiscal management and operations. This matter became so serious that after the sales tax was increased by Leader's first legislature, it was found that an additional field staff of 432 trained accountants was needed for that

Service, represented itself as the first "complete presentation of the method of administering State fiscal affairs" in the history of the state.

[53] *Press Release* #393, November 4, 1955.

[54] Consolidating state funds in unsegregated accounts would permit an estimated reduction in active bank balances of approximately $10,000,000 daily. Investing such funds in short-term government securities might enable the state to earn $100,000 a year in interest. *Press Release* #178, May 7, 1955.

This change required legislation since the state treasurer and the auditor general were not under the governor's control, and efforts since 1936 to secure such legislation had failed. Such legislation was passed under Governor Leader, Act #102, *Laws of Pennsylvania,* 1955–56, p. 285.

operation alone. To secure qualified accountants and auditors, salaries were raised and these positions were placed under the merit system.[55]

Although the state had established a system of central purchasing through the Department of Property and Supplies as early as 1923,[56] the commonwealth was not enjoying the full benefits which could be gained by a modern and efficient system in 1955. One problem was that a great many goods and services, such as insurance, supplies, leases, and contracts,[57] were handled on a political patronage basis through the Governor's Office. In the insurance field, for example, it was found by a subcommittee of Governor Leader's Advisory Committee that previous practices were "inefficient, inadequate and extravagantly costly." Higher premiums were apparently not only the result of some favoritism in the placement of policies, but were also due to the fact that over 4,000 out of approximately 9,000 state automobiles carrying accident insurance were insured on an individual car basis. It was estimated that changing this coverage to a car fleet basis, approximately fifty per cent of the annual premium of some $250,000 might be saved. As it is further described below in Chapter V the liability coverage was ultimately increased and the cost of coverage was reduced at the same time, according to official sources.[58]

[55] The first state-wide examination for accountants was to be conducted by the state Civil Service Commission on March 9, 1957. Following an active campaign of recruitment, some 800 persons qualified to take this exam. *Press Release* #938, February 8, 1957.

See also the governor's address to the Pennsylvania Institute of Certified Public Accountants, Harrisburg, March 19, 1957. (*Press Release* #1002.)

[56] See Section 2401 of the *Administrative Code of 1929*.

[57] On leases and contracts, see *Press Release* #7, January 20, 1955.

[58] The "exceedingly uneconomical" insurance practices formerly in effect were described in *Press Release* #127, March 27, 1955.

Another form of fiscal folly turned up in the bonding practices for state employees. It was discovered by the same insurance subcommittee that a blanket position bond might be secured for some 3,000 state employes requiring coverage at a savings of fifty to seventy-five per cent of the $75,000 currently spent for these premiums.[59] In fact, centralized purchasing by the state was found to be in disrepair in a number of areas. For example, in the single field of drugs and medicines, it was found that improved procurement methods might net the state a savings of some $1,262,277 per year. Such a figure would mean a reduction in the listed price of various drugs and medicines ranging from twenty to fifty per cent, on various items. Governor Leader analyzed these procurement wastes as due primarily to three factors:

1. Favoring certain suppliers.
2. Poor and antiquated purchasing methods.
3. Carelessness or lack of interest on the part of those concerned.

The governor then announced and itemized a six-point program designed to realize the projected savings.[60]

[59] A ruling by the attorney general was required, however, to determine whether the individual "faithful performance" bonds might legally be replaced by such blanket bonding, guaranteeing honesty only. *Ibid.,* p. 2. See also, *infra,* p. 188ff.

[60] First, a new catalog of drugs and medicines was prepared, which eliminated forty per cent of the former listings, many of which were duplicate items.

2. Encouragment of competitive bidding.
3. Changing from the common or generic name to trade name.
4. Realizing bulk or quantity discounts.
5. Directing hospitals and institutions to buy drugs and medicines that can be stockpiled in large quantities, and
6. Advertising for bids on anticipated needs, but ordering such perishables when needed. *Press Release* #776, October 10, 1956.

The purchase and care of automobiles had also been badly managed by officials at Harrisburg. In one spot survey it was found that thirty of the seventy-one automobiles examined were "unserviceable." Many of the official automobiles had been left outside in winter to deteriorate, without the necessary paint, maintenance, or repair. Two inexpensive cars of fairly recent model were parked unused simply because they lacked batteries. Aside from the necessity of proper maintenance, additional savings could have been realized by organizing an efficient motor pool, such as is utilized by the federal government and elsewhere. In other cases, it was found that the state could have realized economies by allowing employes to utilize their own automobiles on a paid mileage basis.[61] Later, it was found that the automotive maintenance bill was much larger than required, because of the use of so many superannuated vehicles. Related to this was the fact that new cars could be purchased upon the basis of quantity bids in fleet lots, and then sold at auction after one year, for a market price equal to or greater than the wholesale price at which they were procured. The fleet purchase plan had already been put into effect in Maryland, New Jersey, and other states. Its subsequent adoption in Pennsylvania was estimated to result in a savings of $4,000,000 to $5,000,000 per biennium.[62]

[61] *Press Release* #138, April 1, 1955. As of December 29, 1954, about 2597 automobiles were under the jurisdiction of the Department of Property and Supplies. An additional 615 automobiles were assigned to the Highway Department. *Ibid.,* p. 3. About two years later, the governor reported the Commonwealth had a fleet of about 3600 automobiles, plus 9,000 other vehicles. *Press Release* #1002, March 19, 1957, p. 4.

[62] The fleet purchase plan was suggested to Governor Leader by Governor Meyner of New Jersey. A meeting of automobile dealers

In this, as in other administrative reforms, Governor Leader ran into some resistance from those who had heretofore relied so heavily upon the state's patronage. Fleet purchases and auction sales were, however, continued, although inflation and other factors resulted in greater geographical decentralization in purchases and sales, and ultimately in the decision to drive new cars two years, rather than just one year before resale. Thus the savings resulting from quantity purchases and auction sales were continued, but on a somewhat smaller scale than was originally the case.[63]

BUREAU OF CAPITAL EXPENDITURES

The Bureau of Capital Expenditures is the fourth and last of the bureaus of the Office of Administration to be discussed in this chapter. One proposed responsibility of the bureau was to work out with all the various state departments and agencies a capital budget, setting forth their projected capital expenditures for the next five or six years. Such a comprehensive financial plan is essential to an enlightened fiscal policy, and is in line with recommended practice in the field of public finance. Officials need a

---

was called to explain the plan on June 9, 1955 and the plan was promptly implemented. It was found necessary to stagger the time and place of the auction sales, however, in order not to upset the market. *Press Release* #224, June 10, 1955.

Better methods were also discovered for insurance and bonding automobiles on a quantity basis, with a resulting reduction of 95 per cent of the paper work, and an additional savings of $100,000 per year. *Press Release* #1002, *op. cit.,* p. 4.

[63] See, "State to Purchase New Automobiles Each Year." 28 *Pennsylvania Road Builder* (June, 1955), for the original plan. Modifications were described in various interviews at the Office of Administration, Harrisburg, April 8, 1960.

picture of foreseeable capital requirements in order to
make a rational decision as to the extent of borrowing
needed or as to the extent to which funds can be provided
upon a graduated, pay-as-you-go plan.

Such a bureau was not included in the original (1954)
plan of the Pennsylvania Economy League, nor had it
been included within the structure of the Office of Administration as first organized in 1955. Philadelphia had just
introduced its first capital budget under its new Home
Rule Charter of 1951. The Bureau of Capital Expenditures
was established at Harrisburg in 1956, but its first assignments involved office space allocation, the state authorities,
and related matters.[64] When the task of devising a capital
budget was finally undertaken, there were many difficulties
and false starts, as a result of which the commonwealth's
first capital budget did not actually appear until early in
the Lawrence administration, on August 31, 1959.

Since capital budgeting was an entirely new activity for
the commonwealth, new procedures had to be devised.
There were initial difficulties in deciding exactly what
should be classified as a capital expenditure, and upon
what basis the estimates should be made. It would be
obviously irrational to prepare a plan simply by asking
each department to indicate everything that they would
like to have. An impartial basis is needed for screening
future needs. To have such requires persons with maturity
and experience in public finance, and also with some
firsthand knowledge, as well as ability to appraise program

[64] The three major activities of the bureau were (1) allocation of
space, (2) planning for and expediting capital improvements, and
(3) acting as the governor's liaison with the three state authorities
and the Turnpike Commission. H. F. Alderfer, "Pennsylvania's Office of Administration." 9 *G.R.A. Reporter* (third quarter, 1957).

content. Then the additional problem arose of coordinating the capital budget with the regular biennial budget, the governor's tax and fiscal policies, revenue trends, and similar matters.

Various persons and units worked on the capital budget from time to time—program evaluation, management methods, capital expenditures, and the Budget Bureau. This was one of those responsibilities of the Office of Administration which for some time did not fit neatly within the bureau structure. Since nearly all of these units were understaffed, the problem was to find somebody free and capable of doing the job. The problem of manning this activity was complicated by some resignations and transfers to other departments. Each new person started somewhat "cold" on capital budgeting, which meant some waste of time and effort.

Thus, from the administrative point of view, capital budgeting at Harrisburg faced problems of conception or objective, problems of coordination, and problems of staffing. Finally, there was the political problem of timing. Governor Leader and then Governor Lawrence wanted the new capital budget to appear at the most expedient time, when the legislature might be most receptive. Though the lump sum figures and much of the detail was ready for publication in the spring of 1959, it was decided for political reasons to delay the release of the document until late in the summer of 1959. When it finally came out, relatively little political opposition appeared. Governor Lawrence finally introduced the capital budget in the following terms:

As you know, such a document as this is unprecedented in Pennsylvania. It seems to me, as I am sure it must to the Members of the General Assembly, that it is essential for the Commonwealth to develop a planned program of capital improvements. This budget, prepared by the Office of Administration in coordination with the staff of the State Planning Board and with departmental officials is, in my opinion, an important and valuable first step towards such comprehensive planning.[65]

Though the idea of a separate capital budget could be defended on the grounds of sound fiscal practice, it did not necessarily justify the necessity for a separate Bureau of Capital Expenditures. The decision to establish a separate bureau was partly due to other factors. For one thing, a separate bureau would signify the importance of this special kind of budgeting. More important was the fact that the ordinary operations of the Budget Bureau concerned chiefly those departments and agencies which were under the governor's full control. In contrast, much of the large capital spending was now being done by various independent or semi-independent state authorities, such as the General State Authority, the state Public School Building, and the Highway and Bridge Authorities. Though the governor was himself an *ex officio* member of these authorities, his personal membership was found to be insufficient for establishing satisfactory coordination and control. Various methods were suggested for increasing the governor's control over these new authorities. At one point, Governor Leader considered coordinating by making himself the active chairman of all the authorities. Then it was concluded that a capital budget, including the plans of the independent authorities, would be a logical method for securing the desired coordination and control.

[65] Message transmitted to the General Assembly, released to the press on August 31, 1959.

The experience with the new capital budget is too recent to judge to what degree the various objectives of this new fiscal tool have been obtained.[66]

To permit fuller treatment the new Bureau of Personnel will be discussed in Chapter III and the Bureau of Program Evaluation in Chapters IV and V. As already indicated these six bureaus completed the Office of Administration at the end of Leader's term of office:

Bureau of the Budget
Bureau of Management Methods
Bureau of Accounts
Bureau of Capital Budgeting
Bureau of Personnel
Bureau of Program Evaluation

Taken altogether these units provided the Pennsylvania governorship with one of the largest and most adequate staffs to be found in any state in the union.

[66] The question of the separate bureau for capital budget was resolved early in the Lawrence administration by the decision to consolidate this bureau with the regular Budget Bureau. See Appendix B.

CHAPTER III

OTHER GOVERNMENTAL CHANGES
UNDER LEADER

Although Governor Leader's administrative reforms were
centered chiefly in the Governor's Office itself, these
changes had important effects upon the line departments.
The entire state service was to some degree "tightened
up," in such matters as fiscal procedures, budgeting, accounting, and personnel. However, less could be achieved
in four years in reorganizing the line departments themselves. Governor Leader took a keen interest in a host of
particular departmental programs and policies, but he
could not in one short term accomplish basic structural
or institutional changes in very many line departments.
Aside from the enormous size of the state service, which
involved in Leader's time some 70,000 employees distributed among seventeen major departments and an even
larger number of boards and commissions, there was the
question of authority. As chief executive, Leader had full
authority to reorganize the executive office according to his
own needs, but as for departmental reorganization, he was
limited in many cases by statutory provisions.

However, Leader's interest in departmental matters was

whetted early in the game. To begin with, his four years in the state Senate provided a valuable orientation. He saw there not only the many state problems related to specific legislative proposals, but more specifically the organizational problems highlighted by the State Government Survey Committee—the Chesterman Report described in the preceding chapter. Other state governmental problems came to Leader's attention as he conducted his two statewide election campaigns—his unsuccessful bid for state treasurer in 1952 and his successful campaign for governor in 1954. In the latter campaign, for example, candidate Leader flayed the incumbent administration for laxity, weakness, if not corruption, in a number of departments, such as agriculture, commerce, highways, revenue, labor, and industry, and the Public Utilities Commission. The secretary of commerce, he said, did not even show up for work much of the time.[1] Thus Leader came to the State House not completely uninformed about the state departments under his jurisdiction.

GOVERNOR'S ADVISORY COMMITTEE

During his campaign, Leader had promised to set up committees of experts in various fields, such as taxation, industrial development, juvenile delinquency, consumers' rights, and fair employment practices.[2] Shortly after his election in November, 1954, this idea of calling upon citizen committees took root in the form of a preinaugural Governor's Advisory Committee. The initiative for this

[1] See *The Philadelphia Inquirer,* August 31, 1954, p. 6.
[2] See the lead editorial in *The Pittsburgh Press,* January 3, 1955.

particular effort was taken by Dr. Stephen B. Sweeney, director of the Fels Institute of Local and State Government at the University of Pennsylvania. Dr. Sweeney inquired through Mayor Clark of Philadelphia whether the governor-elect could utilize the services of the three institutes of government located at the Universities of Pennsylvania, Pennsylvania State, and Pittsburgh. Learning that Leader was receptive, Dr. Sweeney called the governor-elect and arranged for a luncheon meeting with the three institute directors at Harrisburg the next week on November 17, 1954.

When Leader met the three institute directors, Dr. Sweeney, Dr. Alderfer (Pennsylvania State) and Dr. Willis (Pittsburgh), he suggested they constitute themselves a Governor's Advisory Committee to serve, at least tentatively, until some time after the inauguration in January. In addition, Leader suggested that a larger committee of experts be selected to serve as consultants to the Advisory Committee on particular state departments. In one of his first press releases, dated December 31, 1954, Governor-elect Leader announced the appointment of the Governor's Advisory Committee, consisting of these three political scientists with Dr. Sweeney as chairman, plus some eighteen consultants selected by the committee. Ultimately, twenty-two experts in various fields were named as consultants, who, with the Advisory Committee of three, constituted a "brain trust" of twenty-five men. Almost all of these men, drawn particularly from the three institutions just mentioned, were deans, department heads, or senior professors at Pennsylvania's leading colleges or universities. As *The Pittsburgh Post-Gazette* put the matter:

Never before in Pennsylvania has an incoming governor had the assistance of a group of men capable of revving up such a high I.Q.[3]

[3] *The Pittsburgh Post–Gazette,* January 3, 1955. The twenty-two consultants are listed here according to the department or agency to which they were assigned:

Agriculture—Dr. John H. Ferguson, professor of political science and director, Social Science Research Center, The Pennsylvania State University.

Attorney General—Dr. Jefferson B. Fordham, dean of the Law School, University of Pennsylvania.

Banking—Dr. W. Carlton Harris, professor of finance, Wharton School, University of Pennsylvania, formerly special deputy secretary of Banking of Pennsylvania (1935–37), deputy city treasurer, Philadelphia (1938–41).

Commerce—Mr. Park H. Martin, executive director, Allegheny Conference on Community Development, Pittsburgh.

Corrections—Dr. Thorsten Sellin, chairman, Sociology Department, University of Pennsylvania. Formerly secretary-general, International Penal and Penitentiary Commission.

Forests and Waters, Fish Commission, Game Commission—Dr. William F. Schulz, professor of law, University of Pittsburgh, specialist on conservation law and administration.

Health—Dr. Thomas Parran, dean, Graduate School of Public Health, University of Pittsburgh, and Dr. Norman H. Topping, vice president for Medical Affairs, University of Pennsylvania.

Highways—Mr. Henry D. Harral, commissioner of streets, Philadelphia (then on leave from the staff of the Institute of Local and State Government, University of Pennsylvania).

Insurance—Dr. C. Arthur Kulp, chairman, Insurance Department, University of Pennsylvania. Formerly vice-dean, Wharton School, and Dr. Dan M. McGill, associate professor of insurance, University of Pennsylvania. Executive director, S. S. Huebner Foundation for Insurance Education.

Labor and Industry—Dr. R. Wallace Brewster, professor of political science, Pennsylvania State University. Formerly War Production Board staff during World War II.

Liquor Control Board—Dr. M. Nelson McGeary, professor of polit-

The Advisory Committee and this body of consultants agreed to serve the governor-elect on a voluntary basis as a temporary staff "to facilitate the orderly and constructive transition of the state administration." [4] The significance

---

ical science, The Pennsylvania State University (and author of a monograph on that subject).

Milk Control Commission—Dr. Gayle K. Lawrence, assistant professor of political science, Temple University.

Mines—Dr. G. R. Fitterer, dean of the Schools of Engineering and Mines, University of Pittsburgh.

Property and Supplies—Mr. Charles H. Frazier, executive engineer, Philadelphia Gas Works. Formerly Commission of Procurement, Philadelphia (1952–53). President, Philadelphia Chapter, Society for the Advancement of Management.

Public Assistance—Dr. Raymond T. Bowman, chairman, Economics Department, University of Pennsylvania. Formerly special assistant to secretary of public assistance, Pennsylvania, and also deputy secretary of public assistance. Organization consultant, War Production Board. Assistant administrator, Surplus Property Administration.

Public Utilities and State Authorities—Dr. Charles F. LeeDecker, assistant executive secretary, Institute of Local Government, Pennsylvania State University. Formerly, War Production Board staff.

Revenue—Mr. H. Michael Albers, management consultant, Institute of Local and State Government, University of Pennsylvania. Formerly treasurer and controller, Slater Systems, Inc.

State—Dr. Albert B. Martin, professor of political science, University of Pittsburgh. Author of task force report for the Chesterman Committee on the Department of State.

Welfare—Mr. Norman Lourie, executive director, Association for Jewish Children of Philadelphia. Consultant on child welfare, Institute of Local and State Government, University of Pennsylvania, and Dr. James P. Dixon, Jr., commissioner of health, Philadelphia. Professor, Department of Public Health and Preventive Medicine, University of Pennsylvania Medical School. Formerly manager of health and hospitals, Denver, Colorado.

[4] *Press Release* of Governor-elect Leader, Friday, December 31, 1954. This group should be designated as the preinaugural Advisory

of this new "brain trust" as a transitional device to help train and orient the new cabinet was stressed by the governor-elect and noted in the press at the time.[5] At the first meeting of the Advisory Committee and the consultants on December 31, 1954, Mr. Leader emphasized his desire to avoid the period of administrative chaos and confusion which so typically follows a major political upset at the state level. Leader said that normally,

. . . incumbent personnel, unsure of their status and uninformed about the policies of the new administration, have bided their time until they could tell which way the wind was blowing. The new department heads and their subordinates have required precious weeks and months to learn the functions, organization, and procedures of their departments— pretty much through trial and error methods—and to formulate their objectives and programs. During such interims, service to the people of the Commonwealth has suffered.[6]

Such a transition problem was particularly serious in a state such as Pennsylvania where the overwhelming majority of employees do not enjoy civil service tenure, and where the democrats had so long been out of power. In any case, Leader was eager to make a good start and to circumvent some of the transitional confusion which he had

---

Committee, as opposed to the enlarged and more permanent Advisory Committee, which continued to meet with the governor and the secretary of administration for a couple of years after the inauguration.

[5] See "Leader Plans for Change-Over." *The Philadelphia Inquirer* (Sunday, Jan. 2, 1955), p. 34.

[6] Quoted from some notes prepared for Leader's remarks at the December 31 meeting of the Governor's Advisory Committee.

described.[7] He felt that the first hundred days would be of key importance to his new administration, as it was in the case of Franklin D. Roosevelt:

In that period we fix our sights, get our key people, and set the tone and tempo of the government. It is vitally important that the decisions made in these first hundred days be based on knowledge and competence. . . . Mistakes made in this initial period are the most costly and their effects are often irrevocable. Often out of proportion to their significance, such mistakes condition the attitudes of people toward the new government and affect the morale and enthusiasm of employees in every department. We are determined that this administration from its very first day in office will have sound objectives and a high standard of performance.[8]

The Governor's Advisory Committee was not only a novel experiment in Pennsylvania political transitions. It also undertook an ambitious survey of some twenty-two major state departments and agencies under the governor's jurisdiction. The committee carried out its initial assign-

[7] The problem of transition was also stressed by President Truman in his memoirs. It can be recalled that a similar "brain trust" was employed by President Roosevelt, particularly in his early days. In 1952–53, Eisenhower also appointed an advisory committee consisting of Nelson Rockefeller, Milton Eisenhower, and Arthur Flemming. However, none of these transitional experiences undertook the kind of comprehensive department by department survey and evaluation which was carried out at the beginning of the Leader administration. Governor Pinchot had the services of a committee to investigate finances prior to his inauguration, and he provided similar pre-inaugural continuity for the interim term of Governor Fisher. This was a case of continuity between different factions of the same party. The comparison with Pinchot is, however, an important index of the fact that these two governors were particularly interested in the administrative aspect of their job.

[8] From prepared remarks for the December 31 meeting of the Advisory Committee.

ment in the following way. First, each consultant visited the retiring secretary of the department to which he was assigned with a member of the Advisory Committee,

> . . . to explain the Governor-elect's plan of having them serve as transitional consultants for the new department heads, to learn the ideas of the incumbent heads, and to obtain their approval . . . to make direct contact with departmental deputies and bureau heads.[9]

Retiring Governor Fine gave helpful cooperation for this operation. He instructed his department heads to cooperate with the consultants in every way. It was then planned that each consultant might confer in Harrisburg at least two days each week until the inauguration on January 18, and continue thereafter for such a period as agreed upon with the new department head.

Every member of the group apparently accepted the seriousness and urgency of his assignment, which was received when most persons were preoccupied with vacation and holiday activities. Not only was this work begun at an awkward time, but more striking is the fact that these pre-inaugural surveys were, with one or two exceptions, completed in just over two weeks, or about twenty days from the time of their appointment. Careful and explicit instructions, prepared by Dr. Sweeney's staff, were issued to the consultants, who collected relevant materials, arranged interviews, and wrote up their reports and recommendations by the time the new administration took over. Consultants were advised that their work was to be essentially anonymous and confidential. No public recognition was to be expected or sought. Rather, the group looked upon

[9] *Press Release* of Governor-elect Leader, December 31, 1954.

its assignment as a trust, in the public service, about which very little publicity was sought or received. The group was bipartisan in nature, and was asked to make "no comment or criticism, public or private, concerning either outgoing or incoming officials and employees." [10]

There were actually only two meetings of the full group of some twenty-five men. At the first one, on Friday, December 31, 1954, the governor-elect met his "brain trust" for the first time, and explained the purpose of the activity, as already described. At the second meeting, on the evening of January 19, 1955, the day after the inauguration, each consultant gave a brief five or ten minute oral report, backed up by the fuller written reports, which were, in general, submitted by that time.

Meanwhile, other physical arrangements had been made, such as a room in the capitol, which served as headquarters for the Governor's Advisory Committee. It had also been arranged that each consultant was to meet (on January 17 or 18) with a member of the Advisory Committee assigned to his area in order to review and discuss his findings and recommendations. On Thursday morning, January 20, the day after the meeting with Governor Leader, each consultant was sent to confer with the new department head. At these conferences, each consultant was armed not only with his own report, but also with John D. Young's booklet, *Taking Over a New Executive Post,* which had been prepared for the United Nations in 1952.[11]

[10] Memorandum to Special Consultants, Governor-elect Leader's Advisory Committee, entitled, "Purposes, Procedures and Obligations of Consultants," December 1954, p. 3.

[11] International Institute of Administrative Science (Brussels, 1952).

In this way, the Governor's Advisory Committee undertook to analyze and evaluate the organization, procedures and programs of the various departments under the governor's supervision. Such a rapid undertaking would have been impossible had it not been for the fact that nearly all of the consultants were already very well informed, and in many cases also familiar with the work of the departments to which they were assigned. One or two of the consultants had recently undertaken similar surveys for the Chesterman Committee in 1952–53. Several others had written books and articles about the activity they were now sent to observe.[12]

The consultants to the Governor's Advisory Committee had been asked to include in their reports such matters as the following:

1. Chart and description of present functions and organization of department.
2. Evaluation of the adequacy of departmental programs for accomplishing the objectives of the department's functions.
3. Evaluation of the organizational structure for accomplishing the objectives of the department.
4. Evaluation of the procedures used in administering the department's programs.
5. Identification of key positions and recommendations of desirable qualifications for these positions.
6. Evaluation, where appropriate, of working relationships

---

[12] About six of the twenty-two consultants were professors of political science. With the addition of two economists, two in law, and five or six in closely related social sciences, such as sociology, insurance, and finance, it can be said that at least sixteen of the twenty-two consultants were social scientists.

with other state departments and agencies, with federal agencies, and with local governments.

7. Evaluation of the adequacy of staff and management services available to the department head and his subordinates within the department.
8. Desirable program and administrative emphases to be adopted by the department.
9. Other points that the consultant thinks are important for the new department head.[13]

Presumably these topics were suggestive; a given consultant might not prepare reports on all of these subjects. The reports and recommendations were to be for the guidance of the new department heads, as well as for the planning and recommendations of the Advisory Committee, and ultimately for the information of the governor. Circumstances of time and distance prevented the Governor's Advisory Committee from actually working over all of these "task force reports," as the Hoover Commission and, in the state, the Chesterman Committee had done in order to prepare a combined report which would be consistent in all its parts. In the course of this activity, Dr. Sweeney's staff prepared a six-page outline for analysis of each department, which was supplemental to the above memorandum, and which might serve as a point of departure or a general procedure for program evaluation. This outline embraced five aspects of each department, within each of which additional matters were pinpointed:

1. Organization, expenditures and personnel.
2. Service objectives and programs.
3. External relationships and controls.

[13] Memorandum to Special Consultants, December, 1954, p. 2.

4. Executive direction and control.
5. Summary of studies or surveys of the department.[14]

The consultants' reports, some of which were mimeographed, and all of which were typed, collected in notebook form and preserved, proved to be of considerable value to the incoming cabinet heads. These reports varied in length from twelve or fifteen to as much as thirty or more pages in length. In addition to their findings and recommendations, many of the consultants prepared, collected and submitted charts, tables, publications, and other specialized materials as appendices, which constituted a rather bulky file on some of the departments.

To secure these reports and materials as promptly as possible, the chairman of the Advisory Committee had asked each consultant to submit a work schedule for the period up to January 18 and to submit interim reports in the form of memoranda on various aspects of his department as soon as each was completed. Such memoranda were supposed to emphasize the administrative aspects of each department, rather than the more substantive or technical policy matters.[15] It was also suggested that the recommendations should, in general, be matters designed for executive rather than for legislative action. However, there were points where such glaring deficiencies in the

[14] "Guides for Analysis and Evaluation of Departments by Consultants," Governor's Advisory Committee, January, 1955.

[15] Section II of the "Guides of Analysis . . ." did call for identification of the service objectives and programs of the department. However, the emphasis was upon an analysis of the capacity of the agency to grasp and meet its objectives, rather than upon the wisdom or advisability of these objectives, *per se*. (P. 3 of the memorandum cited.)

law were found that basic revisions in the scope or mandate of particular departments were recommended.[16]

Ultimately, the consultants' reports reflected a rather wide variation in quality and in fidelity to the guides and criteria suggested. In general, those prepared by political scientists and other social scientists were more valuable as administrative studies than some of those dealing with such topics as health, mines, insurance, state authorities, and revenue. Many of these were more concerned with the technical and substantive aspects of the departments involved. Altogether, these reports constituted a most valuable commentary on the specific conditions and problems prevailing within the various state departments at the time of Leader's inauguration. Various officials have since indicated that they were still working in the direction indicated by this group four or more years ago.

At the conclusion of this preinaugural activity, the three-man Governor's Advisory Committee was expanded to include representatives of the Pennsylvania Economy League, the new Office of Administration, and other persons. The secretary of administration frequently prepared the agenda and served as coordinator and subsequent chairman. The committee held luncheon meetings with the governor about every two weeks for the next two years. After that, meetings became less frequent. With the expanded Advisory Committee, various subcommittees were formed, such as that on insurance, and another on the Department of Public Instruction. A considerable volume of instructions, files, and reports was prepared for or by each of these, which ultimately served as supplemental

[16] See, for example, page two of the report on the Department of Welfare, with respect to the institutions for mental health.

sources, resources, and studies for the Bureau of Program Evaluation, though the work of some of the subcommittees, such as that on insurance, was of such importance that it was funneled directly to the governor by the secretary of administration without much reference or relation to other specific work then being done by the Bureau of Program Evaluation.[17]

Many of the agencies surveyed and programs evaluated by the Governor's Advisory Committee and its various subcommittees provided the basis for important administrative reorganization and reform throughout the course of the Leader administration. For example, one of the problems of fiscal control which was noted by many of the early consultants was the somewhat ambiguous position of the departmental controllers. As noted above (page 56), these officials were made the subject of one of Leader's first executive directives. Another question raised by the Governor's Advisory Committee was concerned with the authority of the trustees of the various state welfare institutions. As a result of studies made, regulations were modified to place these bodies in an advisory position, rather than in a position of line authority over the institutions in question. Such a change enhanced the control of the secretary of welfare and ultimately the authority of the governor over the state's own institutions. The Governor's Advisory Committee also pointed to the necessity

[17] See "Spheres of Interest of the Governor's Advisory Committee, February 16, 1955," which was duplicated in March, 1955, three pages. Page three of this memorandum further reduces the areas of concern of the earlier instructions to three major items:
1. Administrative organization.
2. Policy objectives.
3. Program review.

for better research, planning, budgeting, and personnel practices in many departments, as well as better training, reporting, and public relations. All of these matters became subsequent concerns of the governor, and in many cases, specific assignments for his Office of Administration.

A number of those associated with the early Advisory Committee continued to serve the Leader Administration either full- or part-time in other capacities.[18] Some of the consultants became state executives later in Leader's term.

USE OF PATRONAGE

When Governor Leader took office in January, 1955, he had about 50,000 patronage jobs to dole out, more than any other governor, and more than the President of the United States.[19] In 1956, the number of noncivil service

[18] This was true of Michael Albers, Dr. Alderfer, Dr. Ferguson, Dean Fordham, Dr. Kulp, Dr. Gayle Lawrence, Dr. LeeDecker, Norman Lourie, Dr. Sweeney, and Dr. Willis. Some of these who did not actually become part of the administration served such groups as the 1957 Commission on Governmental Reorganization and the 1959 Commission on Constitutional Revision.

[19] For a 1950 figure see Tanger, Alderfer, and McGeary, *op. cit.*, p. 101. See also, Ralph D. Tive, "Pennsylvania Begins to Rejuvenate its Civil Service," 74 *Good Government* (September–October, 1957), p. 48. (Publication of the National Civil Service League. Mr. Tive is executive director of the Pennsylvania Civil Service Comm.) According to the Bureau of Personnel, Office of Administration, there were an average of 64,322 employes under the governor's jurisdiction during the year 1954. Subtracting an average of 13,640 under the merit system, we reach a figure of 50,682 patronage positions under the governor's jurisdiction. The 13,640 figure appears on page three of the *Sixth Biennial Report,* 1952–1954, Pennsylvania Civil Service Commission. Only eleven state agencies were under civil service at that time.

or nonmerit system employes in Pennsylvania compared
with seven other similar states as follows:[20]

Pennsylvania	52,959	New Jersey	10,463
New York	7,433	Massachusetts	2,718
California	7,232	Maryland	2,678
Michigan	2,546	Connecticut	3,379

Even this comparison minimizes the contrast between
Pennsylvania and the other states, because Pennsylvania's
governor has under his jurisdiction essentially all of the
employes in the executive branch, excepting for about
860 under the auditor general, the treasurer, and the secretary of internal affairs. In other states, such as New
York, California, and New Jersey, the governor does not
have full appointive power over that large a percentage of
the non-civil service covered employes.

The use of the governor as a kingpin for partisan control, if not for spoils purposes, has both a constitutional
and a statutory basis in Pennsylvania. This power of the
governor has also been generally buttressed by court decision. The Constitution provides (Article IV, Section 8):

He shall nominate and by and with the advice and consent
of two-thirds of all the members of the Senate, appoint a Secretary of the Commonwealth and an Attorney General during
pleasure, a Superintendent of Public Instruction for four years,
*and such other officers of the Commonwealth as he is or may
be authorized* by the Constitution or by law to appoint; he
shall have power to fill all vacancies that may happen . . .
during recess of the Senate [until] . . . the end of their next
session. [Emphasis added.]

[20] *Pa. Statistical Abstract,* 1960, p. 160.

By statute, the governor has power to appoint "all members of . . . administrative and advisory boards and commissions, except a few otherwise provided by law." [21] In other cases, the governor's control over lesser officials and employes is derivative from the Governor's power over the head of particular agencies, who serves at the former's pleasure.[22] Legally the governor is responsible for practically all appointments in the executive branch, excepting those in the three independent agencies just described (auditor, treasurer, and internal affairs). As a general principle, the appointing power also has the power of removal.[23] The governor's authority even includes those employes under civil service protection, subject, however, to the limitations of those laws.[24] The forty administrative

[21] Tanger, Alderfer, and McGeary, *op. cit.*, p. 123. In most cases, the term is for four years and the incumbent is removable at the pleasure of the appointing authority. In the case of some of the boards, the membership is in whole or in part *ex officio,* that is, made up by law of those who hold particular state offices. Such are, for example, the Boards of Property, Pardons, and Finance and Revenue. *Idem.*

[22] Many other states employ this practice of appointing department heads with the understanding that the governor will have at least a veto over the selection of their departmental personnel. This is a kind of subcontracting arrangement. See, for example, *General Management of Michigan State Government,* Staff Report to the Michigan Joint Legislative Committee on Reorganization of State Government, Report No. 30, November, 1951, Lansing, Michigan, pp. II–19.

[23] Official Opinion of the Attorney General, #4 (Harrisburg, September 12, 1957).

[24] When the Civil Service Act of 1941 was passed Governor James insisted upon a provision giving the governor personally the power to remove even those under the merit system—a power which has rarely been exercised.

units under the governor contained the following employes prior to and near the end of Leader's term:[25]

	July, 1954	*July, 1958*	*Change*
Salaried:	45,774	53,232	7,458 (increase)
Hourly:	18,531	15,521	−3,010 (decrease)
Total:	64,305	68,753	4,448 (increase)
Covered by Civil Service:	−13,640	−22,747	9,107 (increase)
Patronage employes:	50,665	46,006	

Subtracting in the above table, those employes covered by the civil service merit system, which was expanded by about 10,000 during Leader's term, it is seen that the number of patronage employes subject to the governor decreased about 4,000 from 1954 to 1958.

Governor Leader did not personally appoint all of these employes, many of whom were actually continued from former administrations. According to Governor Leader's own estimate, about 29,000 patronage positions were processed during his first two years in office.[26] However, the governor participates personally in the selection and appointment of only a fraction of that number. In practice, he rarely examined the credentials of those whose salary was less than $5,000 per year.[27] The governor did concern

[25] *Pa. Statistical Abstract, 1960,* p. 160. Also figures secured from Bureau of Personnel, Office of Administration, Harrisburg, February, 1961.

[26] Looking back, Leader now regards this rate of turnover as too rapid for the good of the service. Interview, March 3, 1961.

[27] Interview with David Randall, March 5, 1961. There were, of course, merit positions over $5,000 not handled the same way.

himself with all department heads and their deputies, of whom there were three or four in some departments, all members of boards and commissions, plus certain bureau chiefs, and others whose appointment was brought to his attention for some reason—altogether perhaps 400 or 500 persons.[28] As Leader pointed out, the governor has full authority over nearly all patronage employes, whether or not he personally participates in their appointment or removal. In other words, by threat of removal the governor can make his influence felt rather far down into the ranks of the bureaucracy, although in many segments of the state service the governor's authority to remove is rarely if ever exercised.

There are several rather large clusters of patronage employes who must be regarded as really not available to the governor in practice. First, there are about 1,900 state policemen, whom the governor appoints on the basis of competitive examinations conducted by the state Civil Service Commission, though these positions are not legally under civil service protection. Secondly, there are about 10,000 permanent hourly highway maintenance positions, which are generally regarded as available to the county politicians in the areas where they are located. There is a special procedure here whereby the secretary of highways gives assurance of political clearance to the governor's patronage secretary. Of some 4,500 salaried positions in the Highway Department over 2,000 were under civil service protection by the end of Leader's term, but somewhat

---

[28] Governor Leader's estimate, March 3, 1961. The governor appoints some ninety-nine board members in the Department of Public Instruction alone. Many of these professional licensure boards, *e.g.,* are part-time, *per diem* positions, not included in the 50,000.

more than half of the remaining 2,500 were also treated as local "district" jobs, reserved for the county chairman.

Another sizable cluster of patronage jobs which for years have been handled without interference from the Governor's Office can be found in the various welfare institutions. There were, in 1958, about 17,000 institutional positions altogether, only about 3,200 of which were under civil service protection. The majority of the remaining 13,800 are scattered throughout the state and are in most cases regarded as available to county political leaders. Assuming there may be 10,000 of these institutional jobs locally dispensed, that makes a total of 23,100 out of some 50,000 patronage positions which are, in effect, not generally available to the governor.[29]

The county chairmen were also given the major voice in selecting some 300 local (state) prison positions, some of the field positions in the Department of Labor and Industry and about 140 local mine inspectors, plus at least 1,000 persons employed in the Pittsburgh and Philadelphia state office buildings, under the Department of Property and Supplies. The Department of Public Instruction is responsible for some fourteen state teachers colleges at which approximately 4,100 positions are also treated as local patronage. Of the Department of Revenue's 3,613 employes (in 1958), over 2,500 were then in the central office, leaving a balance of 800 or 900 field positions which are treated as primarily local patronage. Another 2,000 such local jobs can be found in the various state sanatoria. Add-

[29] Information obtained from Bureau of Personnel, Governor's Office, Harrisburg, April 25, 1961. Furthermore, during his term of office, Leader's Secretary of Welfare, Harry Shapiro, eliminated political clearance for those positions in the institutions.

ing the 7,090 or more jobs mentioned in this paragraph to the previous total of 23,100, we are able to account for over 30,000 patronage positions which are not really available to the governor.[30] All of these positions are subject to the governor's legal authority, however, and in case of serious disagreement with local party leaders, various clusters of jobs can be withdrawn by the Governor's Office from local determination or selection.

During Leader's term, the patronage appointments could be divided into two groups, those nominated by the county chairman and those recruited in other ways. By far the largest number of patronage appointments were made in the former manner through the personnel secretary in the Governor's Office. Leader's personnel (or patronage) secretary was Robert H. Jones, a Scranton recreation director and former football coach, popularly known as "Pop" Jones.[31]

Although the majority of patronage employees were

[30] There are additional noncivil service positions under various state boards and commissions which are somewhat insulated from the governor by the semi-independent nature of some of these bodies, such as the Fish, Game, and Public Utilities Commissions. P.U.C. commissioners, *e.g.*, are appointed for ten-year overlapping terms, and there is a large measure of stability in the permanent staff, which has developed a kind of unofficial career system partly because of the technical nature of the operation. Source: Bureau of Personnel, Governor's Office, interview April 25, 1961.

[31] Jones "is a political lieutenant of Lackawanna County Commissioner Michael F. Lawler, one of the real powers of the party in Pennsylvania." "Leader Names Chief for Jobs." Philadelphia, *The Evening Bulletin* (December 15, 1954). Michael Lawler's brother, Joseph J. Lawler, was Leader's first secretary of highways. According to a comment received from Governor Leader, January 9, 1961, "Pop Jones had nothing to do with the selection of top personnel except to process the papers." Also, "Mike Lawler had no greater influence as a result of Jones."

secured in Leader's term through the regular party organization, which made their applications to the governor's personnel secretary, there were certain agencies for which the governor or his department heads undertook recruitment on their own or through other supplementary channels. One striking example was Leader's recruitment of nurses and doctors for the state mental hospitals on a nation-wide basis. Direct, or nonpolitical recruitment was also used for such positions as highway engineers, foresters, and bank examiners. Governor Leader was determined to secure more able technical and professional people in these critical areas, and found he could not secure the personnel needed through normal political channels. In order to meet the traditional requirement of political clearance for some of these persons not secured through the county chairman, the device was adopted of having the governor's secretary, David Randall, listed as the political sponsor.[32] Although this method of outside recruitment caused some disaffection for the governor within the party organization, it provided Leader with a greater reservoir to draw upon.

Governor Leader made an important improvement in the patronage operation itself. He required all of those cleared for office by "Pop" Jones to have their qualifications rechecked by the Bureau of Personnel within the new Office of Administration. Thus the merit principle was injected to some degree into the patronage system. The addition of this nonpolitical check both strengthened the hand of the personnel secretary, in his own screening operation, and put pressure on the county chairmen to nominate better qualified persons.

In his speeches and press releases Leader drummed re-

[32] Governor Leader estimated several hundred were given political clearance in this manner. Philadelphia interview, March 6, 1961.

peatedly on the urgency of securing higher quality employes by the extension of the merit system. According
to Ralph Tive, executive director of the state Civil Service
Commission:

Although he [Governor Leader] gave the patronage system
time to prove its worth, he soon found that it was the primary
reason why professional and technical people refused positions
with the Commonwealth, in spite of an exceptional new public
welfare program, which had received high praise.[33]

And in his Final Message, Leader spoke to the same point:

In all of the Commonwealth's programs, one fact stands out:
No program can be effectively carried out unless we have first
rate people in jobs which call for special training or special
skills. . . . We cannot get, or keep these people through the
time-worn methods of patronage as usual, for we are forced
to compete with . . . industry. . . .[34]

Formerly, the merit system covered only about 14,000 employes, those under federal grants, or under the Liquor
Control Board. Leader by Executive Board action extended
this to include about 10,000 more persons. The legislature
refused to provide a statutory basis for this extension both
before and after the Executive Board action.

Almost as important as the governor's power of appointment under normal circumstances is his power to fill vacancies, not only in those offices which he controls, but on

[33] *Good Government* (September–October, 1957), p. 48. On January 9, 1961, Leader commented: "I did not delay to test the patronage system. I delayed to give the legislature a chance to act. I delayed because we had not completed the reclassification of positions.
. . . Reclassification had last been done in 1922."
[34] January 6, 1959, p. 11. (Printed edition.)

an interim basis, also elective and judicial positions, in some cases local and county, as well as state.[35] Although Pennsylvania's judges are generally elected, a great many at both the state and county levels are first elevated by gubernatorial appointment, to which post they are subsequently elected. The advanced age of many judges is one factor which increases the number of such vacancies. Both of Leader's successive attorney generals, Herbert B. Cohen and Thomas D. McBride, were appointed by Leader to the state Supreme Court, as was Judge Curtis Bok. Another cabinet member, Secretary of Revenue Gerald A. Gleeson, was appointed common pleas judge in Philadelphia by Leader in January, 1958.[36] Not only does this power to fill vacancies enable the governor to influence the character of the judiciary; it also imposes an additional political burden upon the governor.

A serious limitation upon the governor's power of appointment is to be found in the constitutional requirement that department heads and other "officers of the Commonwealth" (Art. IV, Section 8) must be approved by two-thirds of all elected members, or thirty-four of the fifty state senators. This particular constitutional provision is a great boon for senatorial minorities in opposition to the governor. For under this arrangement, seventeen sena-

[35] Pennsylvania Constitution, Art. IV, Sec. 8. Act of May 15, 1874, P.L. 205, extended these powers to include many county officers. District attorneys and county commissioners were excepted.

[36] Judge Gleeson was then elected without opposition in the fall of 1959 to the same position. McBride was defeated by Judge Michael Eagen in the 1959 primary election. Cohen and Bok remained on the court. See 92 *Pa. Manual,* p. 720 (on Cohen); Vol. 93, p. 283 (on McBride), p. 291 (on Gleeson), and p. 449 (on Bok). On the late Judge Bok, see also *Who's Who, 1960–61,* Vol. 31, p. 292. (Judge Bok died in May, 1962.)

tors can block a governor's program by refusing to confirm certain appointments.

It is customary for a governor, like the president, to have a freer hand in the choice of his own official family. Thus, in Leader's case, his initial cabinet appointments were approved promptly and unanimously by the Republican controlled Senate. However, eight other nominations which Leader submitted at the same time were laid upon the table in those early days.[37] In his first State of the Commonwealth Message, Governor Leader noted that his nominations to the new Fair Employment Practices Commission were still "being held in the Senate for confirmation." [38] As relations with the senate became more strained, the governor had increasing difficulty with the approval of his top appointments. On many occasions there were more than two hundred nominations awaiting senatorial confirmation. Some of these were for nonsalaried positions, such as State Teachers' College Boards. In those cases where a quorum was lacking the work of the board was seriously delayed.

Despite these "roadblocks" in the Senate, Governor Leader was sometimes able to reach an agreement with the senators directly concerned. Such a case arose in the spring of 1956, when Leader nominated Joseph Sharfsin for a vacancy in the Public Utilities Commission. The senate was not eager to confirm Sharfsin, who had been defeated as a Democratic candidate for mayor of Philadelphia in the 1951 primary. But remembering that the

[37] "GOP Confirms Leader's Cabinet," Philadelphia, *The Evening Bulletin* (January 19, 1955), p. 10B. "State Senators Stall Approval of Appointments," Harrisburg, *The Evening News* (January 25, 1955), p. 15.

[38] *Press Release* #490, January 29, 1956, p. 7.

term of Mr. P. Stephen Stahlnecker on the same commission was to end the next year, the Senate offered to confirm Sharfsin if Leader would agree to offer Stahlnecker another term. Stahlnecker, a Republican, had been executive secretary to Governor Pinchot, and had broad experience in the state government since that time, including a very liberal record as a member of the Utilities Commission since 1952. Thus Leader was delighted to make such a "deal," which gave him two desirable appointees.[39]

In Leader's case, the tremendous volume of appointments, high and low, represented not only a constant burden, but also a source of perpetual intra-party struggle. Many observers point to the tax question, the pardon controversy, and the appointment process as three of the major difficulties in Leader's administration. Despite these strains, Leader used his power of appointment to bring into state government better qualified employes. The higher personnel standards adopted even in the patronage sector constitute one of the important contributions of the Leader administration.

SELECTION OF CABINET

Leader's selection of highly qualified personnel was illustrated in the choice of his cabinet. The governor made a deliberate attempt to achieve a balance between the "political" appointees and those selected for nonpolitical professional reasons. Though there was some room for disagreement among observers in the classification of particular cases, it is evident that changes due to resignations, dismissals and replacements generally operated to increase

[39] Interview with David Randall, August 10, 1960. For biographies of Sharfsin and Stahlnecker, see 93 *Pa. Manual*, p. 294.

the number of department heads in the "nonpolitical" category.

On November 30, 1954, a few weeks after his election, Leader announced the appointment of his secretary, David Randall, and his first cabinet officer, Herbert B. Cohen, as attorney general. These choices were "political" in the sense that they were fairly close associates of Leader. Randall had already served as an aide to Leader in the final weeks of his campaign and Cohen, president of the York County Bar in 1954, had been a friend of the Leader family for years.[40] Leader's second cabinet appointee, Dr. William L. Henning, as secretary of agriculture, was not a "party organization man":

A political unknown, Henning has been a Penn State faculty member for 31 years and is currently head of its Department of Animal Husbandry. . . .

His appointment reflects Leader's campaign pledge to take the Department of Agriculture out of politics and name its Secretary from the ranks of working farmers.[41]

All observers interviewed have since cited Dr. Henning as one of the very able, professional, nonpolitical members of Leader's cabinet. He was retained as secretary of agriculture by Leader's successor, Governor Lawrence.

[40] Cohen had served four terms in the state House of Representatives, beginning in 1934, "during which time he served as both majority floor leader and minority leader. In these positions he played a key role in the development of the legislative program . . . of Governor Earle. Following this . . . he was Director of the Pennsylvania Legislative Reference Bureau." 92 *Pa. Manual,* p. 720. Also Philadelphia, *The Evening Bulletin* (November 30, 1954).

[41] *The Evening Bulletin* (December 17, 1954). The article quotes Leader as saying, "Dr. Henning is one of the nation's foremost authorities on animal husbandry and correlated farm and agricultural life." See 92 *Pa. Manual,* p. 722, Vol. 93, p. 286.

The day after Dr. Henning's appointment, the press learned that Governor-elect Leader had offered a cabinet post to James A. Finnegan, president of Council in Philadelphia and former Democratic city chairman. It was then rumored that Finnegan might be named secretary of the commonwealth, as he ultimately was, though that post was reportedly originally reserved for Patrick E. Kerwin, who managed Leader's primary campaign.[42] The position, secretary of the commonwealth, has been typically reserved for one of the kingpins of the party, and the writer has heard no criticism of Finnegan's appointment on the grounds that it was a "political appointment." [43]

The third and fourth cabinet members specifically announced, on December 21, 1954, were the following: former United States Attorney Gerald A. Gleeson, of Philadelphia, as secretary of revenue, and Mrs. Ruth Grigg Horting, of Lancaster, as secretary of public assistance.[44] Both of these appointees were long-term members of the party organization, which led support to some criticism that cabinet posts were being reserved for impor-

[42] *The Philadelphia Inquirer* (December 19, 1954), pp. 1, 3.

[43] A tradition initiated by Governor Mifflin in 1790. Harrisburg, *The Evening News* (January 7, 1955), p. 15.

[44] On Judge Gleeson, see *supra,* p. 89, footnote 36. Like Governor Leader, an active Lutheran, Mrs. Horting had been the first woman sent to the General Assembly from Lancaster County. She was a member of the state House of Representatives, 1936–38, when Pennsylvania's original Public Assistance Act of 1937 was passed. Long active in politics, Mrs. Horting had been vice chairman of the Democratic State Committee for eleven years, and a delegate to the Democratic National Committee in 1948 and 1952. After the merger of the Department of Public Assistance with the Department of Welfare in 1958, Mrs. Horting became head of the combined department, which was then the largest state administrative department in the country. *Infra.* p. 178ff. For Mrs. Horting's biography see 92 *Pa. Manual,* p. 727, Vol. 93, p. 291.

tant Democratic politicians. On December 30, 1954, Leader announced three more cabinet appointments: Patrick E. Kerwin, chairman of the Liquor Control Board, Robert Myers, secretary of banking, and Harry Shapiro, secretary of welfare. Kerwin was Dauphin County Democratic leader and had a special claim as Leader's primary campaign manager.[45] Myers, a Cumberland County banker and attorney "had not been active in politics for years. He was the attorney for the Department of Banking in the Earle administration and was selected on the basis of experience." [46]

Though Shapiro had been active in Philadelphia politics since before the New Deal, he was not, according to Leader, "a party wheel." Shapiro, whose age was announced as sixty-five, was known as the author of the state's Mental Health Act, and had been chairman "of a Senate Committee which investigated conditions at the Philadelphia State Hospital." [47] Senator Shapiro had been a trustee of Mount

[45] Attorney Kerwin resided in Lykens, near Harrisburg, which was also David Randall's home town. The *Bulletin* (December 31, 1954) wrote that his appointment to "the much-sought-after liquor board . . . [was] on the basis of personal and political ties with the Governor-elect." Aged forty-one, he practiced law in Harrisburg.

[46] Note received from Governor Leader, January 9, 1961. According to Philadelphia *Daily News* (December 30, 1954), p. 26, Myers, aged fifty-seven, was "understood to have had the support of Mayor David Lawrence of Pittsburgh for the cabinet post." He had also served as Secretary to Governor Earle in 1936. *Evening Bulletin* (December 30, 1954), under heading, "Kerwin Slated for Liquor Post," p. 17. On Myers, see also 92 *Pa. Manual*, p. 721, Vol. 93, p. 286.

[47] "Leader Names Shapiro Head of Welfare," *The Evening Bulletin* (December 31, 1954). According to this story Shapiro was "best known as a corporation lawyer," however. He was elected to the state Senate as a Republican in 1932, and the following two terms he was elected as a Democrat.

Sinai Hospital for thirty years and president of the board for the past five. Although he was one of five original cabinet members appointed from Philadelphia, Shapiro was not, according to the governor, originally recommended by Congressman Green's organization. Though Secretary Shapiro had long been politically active in his own right, his background certainly fitted him for the Welfare Department, where he was responsible for the operation of some twenty-one mental institutions, including an inmate population of over 47,000 persons in 1955. Shapiro became one of the stronger and more outspoken members within the cabinet. Some observers regarded him as the best secretary of welfare in Pennsylvania for many years.[48]

Leader's last two preinaugural cabinet appointments were Attorney Francis R. Smith, insurance commissioner, and Joseph J. Lawler, secretary of highways. Though these appointments were also "political," both of these men had had administrative experience in the federal service.[49]

[48] Though Shapiro was a vigorous fighter for the welfare programs in which both he and Governor Leader had a vital interest, the secretary repeatedly got into trouble with the Office of Administration and the legislature for overspending his budget. Like many a devoted specialist, Shapiro was impatient with bureaucratic regulations and eager to do a job for those in need, which temperament got him into difficulties. The merger of his department with Public Assistance was motivated in part by the desire of the legislature to retaliate against him and his operation. Leader recently praised Shapiro as "an aggressive humanitarian who drove ahead to eliminate human suffering." January 9, 1961 comment.

[49] Beginning as a United States marshal in 1941, Francis Smith, aged forty-three, had been appointed collector of Internal Revenue for the eastern district of Pennsylvania by President Roosevelt in 1945. 92 *Pa. Manual*, p. 721, Vol. 93, p. 285. Smith was also a member of the 77th Congress from Pennsylvania. 93 *Pa. Manual*, p. 1039. According to Governor Leader, Francis Smith and Gerald Gleeson were the two members of Congressman Green's organization ap-

As of January 1, 1955, ten of Leader's seventeen major cabinet posts still remained to be "nailed down." From the appointments already described, it can be seen how those liberals interested in seeing a shift from the old patronage system had at first some grounds for discouragement. Observers close to Leader, however, pointed out that, though some cabinet members were selected on a party basis, they also had professional qualifications in their particular fields. In fact, Leader himself issued a tribute to Jim Finnegan, when he returned after managing Stevenson's campaign, as the ideal combination of able politician and administrator, both at the same time.

Part of Leader's difficulty with appointments was a result of the abrupt party transition. In 1954, the Democrats did not have a large corps of administrators and bureaucrats, trained at the state level, upon whom to draw. Thus Leader's cabinet was a mixture of veterans from Governor Earle's "little New Deal" two decades before, Democratic city, county, and federal officials, plus a few intellectuals or "nonparty" men. Moreover, these new secretaries had the task of presiding over departments which had been run, in most cases, on a patronage basis under Republican auspices for at least sixteen years. As Leader himself

---

pointed to his original cabinet. Interview with Governor Leader, August 14, 1960.

Joseph Lawler, *supra,* p. 86 footnote 31, was even more of an "organization man," through his family. But his experience was also adequate. He served in Washington as third and, in 1949, first assistant postmaster general in charge of the Bureau of Postal Operations. In 1952 he became director of Internal Revenue in Scranton, but resigned in 1953 to become president of the Lawler Petroleum Company, also in Scranton. In 1936, he had headed a division in the state Public Utility Commission. 92 *Pa. Manual,* p. 723, Vol. 93, p. 301.

pointed out, it was unprecedented for a Pennsylvania governor to name three of his cabinet members from the opposition party, as Leader did.[50]

Friendly liberals, "reformers," and intellectuals were gratified to note the generous sprinkling of "eggheads" of their own type in Leader's original cabinet, and even more pleased to note later that the number of such persons increased, until they became almost a majority by the end of Leader's term. In the original cabinet these would include Dr. Henning, secretary of agriculture, Mr. Maurice K. Goddard, secretary of forests and waters,[51] Dr. B. F. Mattison, secretary of health,[52] Dr. M. A. Williamson

[50] Goddard, Mattison, and Boehm, described below, were Republicans.

[51] Professor Goddard brought to Leader's cabinet "an outstanding background in the field of conservation and allied endeavors." 93 *Pa. Manual,* p. 287. A professor at Pennsylvania State since 1935, he had been director of the School of Forestry since 1952, member of the National Council, Society of American Foresters, president of the Pennsylvania Forestry Association, and honorary vice-president of the American Forestry Association.

[52] Dr. Mattison, the first nonresident, and eighth department head to be named by Leader, was a physician in Buffalo, New York, where he had been county health commissioner for the past six years. Dr. Mattison had also been commissioner of Health at Yonkers, New York, and employee of the New York State Health Department, and a medical professor at the University of Buffalo. *The Evening Bulletin* noted that this appointment, like Dr. Henning's earlier, "appears to have been predicated solely on merit." January 4, 1955.

Later, Leader was scored by local "patriots" for appointing another man, William Batt, who was not then a resident of Pennsylvania, though he was a native of the Keystone State. Batt was another young intellectual, who had also been in the federal service (Department of Labor). His father, a republican, was former president of SKF Industries. Secretary Batt replaced Torquato, Cambria County Democratic leader, whom Leader removed as secretary of Labor and Industry. *The Evening Bulletin* (January 31, 1957), p. 3.

(Pennsylvania State's dean of engineering), vice-chairman of the Turnpike Commission, Dr. James C. Charlesworth (political science professor, University of Pennsylvania), as secretary of administration, and possibly also Senator Shapiro in welfare, Dr. Charles H. Boehm, superintendent of public instruction, and Mayor Lawrence's former secretary, John P. Robin, who was Leader's first secretary of commerce.[53] Four of these six or seven intellectuals or

[53] As noted *supra*, p. 20, Dr. Charlesworth had been Governor Leader's professor of public administration at the University of Pennsylvania. Trained at Harvard and the University of Pittsburgh, Dr. Charlesworth had published a textbook in public administration, and was president of the American Academy of Political and Social Sciences, in Philadelphia, in addition to his position as assistant director of the Fels Institute of Local and State Government. His appointment was strictly "non-political," and reflected Leader's interest in recruiting an administrative chief especially trained in that field. Dr. Charlesworth also had experience in federal administration. See *Evening Bulletin* (January 12, 1955), p. 3B on Charlesworth's appointment. Also, the tribute in *The Harrisburg Evening News* (August 30, 1956), Section 2, p. 1, on the occasion of his resignation.

The superintendent of Public Instruction enjoys a statutory term and is not removable by the governor at his pleasure. Dr. Boehm was not appointed to that position by Governor Leader until March 29, 1956, fifteen months after the resignation of Dr. Francis B. Haas. Long active in school administration circles both national and state, Dr. Boehm, aged fifty-three, had been assistant superintendent of schools in rapidly growing Bucks County, 1941–56. See *The Evening Bulletin* (March 29, 1956), and 93 *Pa. Manual*, p. 284. Dr. Boehm was reappointed to the same position in 1960.

John P. Robin, forty-two, was the youngest of the thirteen appointed to Leader's cabinet by January 12, 1955, according to *The Evening Bulletin* of that dateline (p. B 3). In 1946, Robin had been named young man of the year by the Pittsburgh Junior Chamber of Commerce, and when appointed by Leader, he was serving as executive director of the Pittsburgh Urban Redevelopment Authority. Generally known as a brilliant young intellectual, Robin has since

"eggheads" in Leader's original cabinet resigned before the end of their term. However, in their place Leader appointed persons equally eminent from the professional point of view, with the exception of Dr. Williamson's replacement.[54]

Joseph T. Kennedy, Leader's secretary of mines and mineral industries, had held numerous positions with the United Mine Workers of America, and he was reappointed secretary of mines by Governor Lawrence.[55] Finally, Lea-

---

continued as a speech-writer for Governor Lawrence, while serving as executive vice-president of the Old Philadelphia Development Corporation. Robin resigned as secretary of commerce September 13, 1955, to accept a more lucrative position, and was succeeded by William R. Davlin. 92 *Pa. Manual*, p. 727.

[54] Dr. Ferguson replaced Dr. Charlesworth, *infra*, p. 135. Dr. Wilbar replaced Dr. Mattison, and William R. Davlin replaced John P. Robin. See 92 *Pa. Manual*, p. 729, Vol. 93, p. 303.

Dr. Charles L. Wilbar, Jr., had been active in public health work in Hawaii since 1936, and was currently lecturing in the same field at the University of Pittsburgh. A native of Philadelphia, Dr. Wilbar had also had experience in pediatrics in Abington, Cincinnati, and Honolulu. He had been serving as deputy secretary of health when he succeeded Dr. Mattison on November 19, 1957. Dr. Mattison resigned from Leader's cabinet to become executive secretary of the American Public Health Association. 93 *Pa. Manual*, p. 289.

William Davlin moved up from his position as director of the Bureau of Industrial Development to become secretary of commerce. Mr. Davlin, forty-six, an industrial economist from the University of Wisconsin, had worked for the National Resources Planning Board (1938–42), the United States Commerce Department, Delta Air Lines, Inc., and the Commonwealth of Kentucky (1952–54). Thus, he was well qualified to handle Leader's industrial development program. 93 *Pa. Manual*, p. 292.

When Pennsylvania State's engineering dean, Dr. Merritt A. Williamson, resigned from his position as vice-chairman of the Turnpike Commission on October 1, 1957, he was replaced by Joseph J. Lawler. Leader's first secretary of highways. 93 *Pa. Manual*, p. 300.

[55] 93 *Pa. Manual*, p. 288.

der's adjutant general, Major General A. J. Drexel Biddle, Jr., came from a distinguished career, not only in the United States Army, since 1917, but also in mining in South Africa (1931–34) and in the diplomatic service.[56]

According to the *Pennsylvania Manual* Governor Leader's cabinet consisted of some twenty-three to twenty-six persons, though the exact number serving was subject to some variation. However, only seventeen of these are appointed by the governor to head major administrative departments.[57] There was considerable turnover in these seventeen positions. Altogether eleven or twelve replacements were made by Leader, four of which had just been described. One secretary was discharged (Torquato), one or two were transferred (Lawler, and later Rice), two died (Finnegan and Panati, who replaced Gleeson) and about six others resigned (Charlesworth, Cohen, Gleeson, Mattison, Robin, Williamson).[58]

[56] Biddle was minister to Norway, 1935–37, to Poland, 1937–39, deputy ambassador to France, 1940, and then ambassador extraordinary to various exile governments, such as Poland, Belgium, the Netherlands, Norway, Greece, Yugoslavia, and Czechoslovakia, 1941–44. 93 *Pa. Manual,* p. 285. He lived out at Indiantown Gap Military Reservation close to the governor's summer residence, where Leader also resided his last year in office.

[57] Others included the governor himself and the lieutenant governor, the secretary of internal affairs, who is elective, the secretary to the governor, and the Democratic state chairman (Senator Joseph M. Barr, under Leader).

[58] Charlesworth and Williamson resigned to return to their academic positions, from which they were on leave. Cohen, Gleeson, and Robin moved up to better positions in the judiciary or in private employment.

Omitted above was the January 3, 1956, appointment of John S. Rice as secretary of property and supplies to succeed William D. Thomas, forty-five, a Sharon, Pennsylvania, florist who served Leader only a short time. On July 18, 1957, Andrew Bradley, who had been

It is difficult, if not risky and sometimes unfair, to generalize about the relative qualities or qualifications of more than a score of persons involved in these substitutions. However Governor Leader and some of his close observers were convinced that on balance the cabinet was improving in quality as a result of these changes. At least two of the replacements, not yet discussed, produced men who were more experienced, and two other changes, mentioned briefly, placed in the cabinet men who were less identified with the patronage system.[59]

---

budget secretary since the beginning of Leader's term, replaced Rice in Property and Supplies. See *The Philadelphia Inquirer* (January 9, 1955), and 93 *Pa. Manual,* pp. 286, 970.

[59] Whereas Attorney General Cohen had been head of the Bar Association in York County (*supra,* p. 92), his successor, Thomas D. McBride, aged fifty-four, was at the time of his appointment chancellor of the Philadelphia Bar Association. McBride was widely known in the field of criminal law, and had helped to codify it as a member of Governor Duff's Crime Commission. He had also served as chief advisor to Mayor Dilworth, when he was District Attorney in Philadelphia. The *Evening Bulletin* (November 20, 1956) speaks of his vast "clinical knowledge" of cases and refers to his reputation, after twenty-five years of practice, as "a lawyer's lawyer."

The Department of Property and Supplies also received a more experienced if not better qualified secretary when John Rice and later Andrew Bradley replaced William Thomas, as just noted. Rice had been active in Democratic politics since 1932, when he was first elected to the state Senate. A member of Leader's Liquor Control Board 1955–56, Rice had also been Democratic nominee for governor in 1946 and, after Leader's administration, he succeeded Senator Barr, as Democratic state chairman. Widely known as a very able person, Rice was a trustee of Gettysburg College, and had a business in fruit growing and packaging. See 92 *Pa. Manual,* p. 722, Vol. 93, p. 286. Andrew M. Bradley, his successor in Property and Supplies, was also "political," but quite capable. He had served "five terms as vice president of the Young Democratic Clubs of Pennsylvania,

As a result of these changes, Leader secured for his cabinet some men of higher professional caliber. While friends of Leader generally applauded this shift to a somewhat less "patronage" basis, some Democratic leaders took the opposite view. Though this change within the cabinet was entirely consistent with Leader's concurrent drive for administrative reform, there was some feeling that the gov-

---

and headed the Negro division of the Democratic State Committee in every state-wide election since 1940. He served as a delegate to the Democratic National Conventions of 1948, 1952, and 1956." 93 *Pa. Manual,* p. 287. Mr. Bradley was also a CPA and a member of several other professional associations, in the fields of public finance, accounting and public administration. He too, was eminently qualified for the position, and was retained by Governor Lawrence.

Those notably less associated with patronage included William Batt, Jr. who replaced John Torquato in Labor and Industry, and Attorney Lewis M. Stevens, who replaced Joseph J. Lawler in Highways. Batt's professional background included some foreign service, not only in the military but also in lend-lease (under Harriman, 1941), and in federal aid under the United States secretary of labor. 93 *Pa. Manual,* p. 290. John Torquato, forty-six in 1954, had been active in Democratic politics since the Earle administration. Active in the Young Democrats in Pennsylvania, he had served as Democratic chairman of Cambria County seven terms since 1942. *Infra,* p. 104, also 92 *Pa. Manual,* p. 725. Torquato's appointment was originally a compromise after some dispute with union leaders, who had favored A. Allen Sulcowe. Torquato was appointed with the support of Senator Barr and Mayor Lawrence, according to *The Philadelphia Inquirer* (January 7, 1955), "Leader Names Labor Secretary."

Attorney Lewis M. Stevens, fifty-nine in 1957, when he became secretary of highways, was cofounder of the Greater Philadelphia Movement, which had an important role in securing the adoption of the new charter. A graduate of Harvard Law School, Stevens was a member of a prominent Philadelphia law firm, active in church, community, and public affairs. President of the boards of trustees of Lincoln University and the Fels Fund, Attorney Stevens had also been considered as a possible successor to Governor Leader. 93 *Pa. Manual,* p. 288.

ernor may have surrounded himself with too many "egg-heads," who were out of touch with party realities. However, most of Leader's final cabinet heads were retained by Governor Lawrence. Leader faced the problem of replacing a department head twelve times in four years, or an average of about once in every four months.[60]

USE OF REMOVAL POWER

The power to remove appointees also created political problems for Governor Leader. In constitutional language, the governor's power of removal has three aspects: (1) an unrestricted removal power conferred by the Constitution, Article VI, Section 4, (2) a ministerial removal power, based upon the same section, and (3) a qualified removal

[60] The chronology of replacements ran approximately as follows: (Those underscored were retained by Governor Lawrence.)

1. Davlin replaced Robin, 9/13/55.
2. Rice replaced Thomas, 1/3/56.
3. Ferguson replaced Charlesworth, 8/30/56.
4. McBride replaced Cohen, 11/30/56.
5. Batt replaced Torquato, 3/4/57.
6. Bradley replaced Rice, 7/18/57.
7. Stevens replaced Lawler, 10/2/57.
8. Lawler replaced Williamson 10/2/57.
9. Panati replaced Gleeson, 1/27/58.
10. Sulcowe (acting) replaced Panati, 4/3/58.
11. Harner, then Trout (acting) replaced Finnegan, finally 3/26/58. Then Rice, 6/9/58.

Governor Lawrence also retained: Myers, Horting, Kerwin, Wilbar, Boehm, Kennedy, Smith, Henning, Goddard, and Biddle.

This case held that an appointee can be removed without cause, except for the will of the appointing power. Moreover, the courts have held that the senate, which approves appointments, has no part in the removal power.

power, as defined by statute and by court decision. The governor's absolute power to remove officers whom he appoints, except judges or the superintendent of public instruction, was upheld in the case of *Commonwealth ex rel* v. *Likeley*, appellant, 276 Pa. 310. In the second category, elected officials can be removed "by the Governor for reasonable cause after due notice and full hearing, on the address of two-thirds of the Senate." [61] The third type of qualified removal power has been conferred by law upon certain officers with special status.[62]

Governor Leader was much criticized for his removal of certain specific officials.[63] One of these was Secretary Torquato from Cambria County. Secretary Torquato (labor and industry) was charged with using an administrative fund in workmen's compensation for hiring political favorites.[64]

---

[61] Article VI, Section 4. Section 15 of Article V, on the judiciary, provides a similar means for the removal of judges. According to Professor Burns, this ministerial power of removal has been rarely exercised. He cited only two occasions since 1874: the sheriff of Philadelphia County in 1887 and a common pleas judge in Allegheny County in 1885. 1887 P.L. 424, 1885 P.L. 310. Edward McNall Burns, "The Office of Governor in Pennsylvania." Unpublished M.A. thesis, University of Pittsburgh, 1927, p. 168.

[62] For example, 1887 P.L. 74 provided that the Board of Managers of Huntingdon Reformatory could be removed only for incompetence, neglect or malfeasance . . . after hearing and with charges. Similarly with the Lake Erie and Ohio River Canal Board, 1913 P.L. 654. Mine inspectors, who are also appointed by the governor, were to be removed only after the causes such as those just named were certified by the Court of Common Pleas. 1893 P.L. 73, 1921 P.L. 836. Burns, *op. cit.,* p. 168ff.

[63] Based on interview with John Calpin of the Philadelphia *Evening Bulletin,* June 23, 1960, and others.

[64] See Governor's Office *Press Release* #903 (January 23, 1957), #904, #905, #916, and also the transcription of Leader's *Press Conference,* January 17, 1957.

Another problem arose in connection with Leader's first secretary of property and supplies, William D. Thomas. Mr. Thomas, the florist and insurance man from Mercer County in the northwestern corner of the state, was included in the cabinet largely in order to achieve some geographical distribution. However, the governor felt that Thomas's administrative performance was not fully satisfactory. At the end of his first year, Secretary Thomas decided to resign for personal reasons.[65]

There were a few other removals which resulted in a certain amount of disaffection for the governor in party circles. One was Attorney William J. Lederer, deputy secretary of revenue, and another was Emmanual Weinberg, in the sales tax division of the same department. Many difficulties had been encountered in the administration and collection of this unpopular tax, which the governor had originally promised to veto. The problem was one of administrative difficulties rather than misuse of funds. There were also some personality problems. Finally, these two officials, who happened to be ward leaders in Congressman Green's Philadelphia organization, were asked to resign, which they did. Political critics of Leader took the attitude that not only were such removals bad for the party, but that adverse public opinion might arise, since the charges publicly announced by the governor were not very convincing. Leader actually offered Lederer another position as an attorney, which he declined.

In other cases Leader was obliged to make removals because of official misconduct or "irregularity." Two cases involved finances in connection with the state highway system. Pennsylvania's highways enjoy a somewhat privileged position, with independent earmarked funds from

[65] Based on interviews with David Randall and Governor Leader.

the gas tax and (in the case of the turnpike) from tolls. These operations are not subject to the same central fiscal controls as those departments which must live within their annual or biennial legislative appropriation. It must also be noted that the highway system is the largest source for state patronage at the county and local level.[66] Both of these circumstances serve to increase temptation, if not the exposure of the highway system to fiscal irregularity. A scandal developed within the state Highway Department, where it was found that thousands of dollars worth of cinders purchased by the state for icy roads were never delivered. Personnel removals were made and court action was undertaken, as soon as this misconduct was uncovered. The incident brought the Leader administration a bad press, despite the fact that the misconduct was discovered and exposed by the Highway Department itself, and also despite the fact that the governor took prompt and effective remedial action.[67]

Another scandal took place in a cognate activity, the Pennsylvania Turnpike Commission. There is an institutional connection between the independent Turnpike Commission, the secretary of highways and the governor, since the latter two serve as *ex officio* members of the commission. G. Franklin McSorley, an important Pittsburgh contractor and realtor, had been appointed to the commis-

[66] Pennsylvania has some 41,000 miles of state highways, one of the largest systems in the Union, if not in the world. See Joseph J. Lawler, "Aggressive Highway Program Planned," 28 *Pennsylvania Road Builder* (April, 1955), p. 6. See also Frank J. Sorauf, "State Patronage in a Rural County," 50 *American Political Science Review* (December, 1956), p. 1048.

[67] Secretary Lawler had developed a special investigations unit which was doing an audit of county records for the Highway Department. They found this irregularity to exist in several counties.

sion by Leader on February 19, 1955, and he became chairman on July 7, 1955. Late in 1956, it was found that McSorley had furnished a car and a chauffeur to former turnpike chairman, Thomas J. Evans, a Coaldale Republican, who had been indicted, along with his son, in connection with a turnpike scandal involving nineteen million dollars. Leader had removed Evans after learning of the fiscal irregularities which took place only a month or two after Leader took office. McSorley's favors to Evans raised the implication that both might have been involved in the financial shortages which were found.[68] In January, 1957, Leader suspended McSorley, pending disposition of his case in Dauphin County Court, where he was ultimately convicted of misconduct in office. His penalty was only a two-to-four month jail sentence and a $1,000 fine. Appeal was taken to the Superior Court, which finally on April 16, 1959,[69] voided his conviction and stayed his removal

---

[68] Evans had been appointed May 15, 1939 and reappointed June 4, 1945, by Republican governors. 93 *Pa. Manual*, p. 976. In 1956, the Supreme Court ruled that members of the Turnpike Commission could not be removed by the governor for political reasons. Evans, McSorley, and Torrance were removed from the Turnpike Commission's payroll. See *Press Releases* #917, #918, #919, January 25, 1957. In his State of the Commonwealth Message, Leader said: "In Lackawanna County five persons have already pleaded no defense against charges that they defrauded the . . . Turnpike Commission of approximately $500,000 . . . the grand jury investigation . . . led me to the conclusion that we faced the greatest public fraud of all time." *Press Release* #878, January 1, 1957, p. 6.

[69] The state failed to file an appeal to the state Supreme Court; so McSorley was legally reinstated, June 2, 1959. He collected $31,-752.16 in back pay for his twenty-nine months of suspension during the Turnpike trials. McSorley won his case on the ground that the State had failed to prove a "corrupt motive" in the automobile and chauffeur episode mentioned above. *The Evening Bulletin* (April 17 and July 9, 1959).

from the commission. Here the issue presented to the governor was not one of removing a Republican from an independent commission, since McSorley was a Democrat.[70] Nor was this another case of a ward leader who was an inefficient bureaucrat. Here was a case of possible misconduct in office, although some observers regarded McSorley as inept or incautious, rather than guilty of misconduct in office. In any case the governor's action was foiled, at least in part, by court action.

Governor Leader exercised his power of removal in another spectacular scandal, which was uncovered in the Joint Delaware River Bridge Commission. Here, as in the highway and turnpike cases, the most serious misconduct had been performed by appointees of the preceding administration. Leader's removal of two commissioners from the Pennsylvania side was based upon a preliminary investigation initiated by Joseph J. Lawler, secretary of highways. Further investigation by the Pennsylvania Department of Justice and a special House Committee revealed

[70] McSorley had served as a Democratic member of Governor Fine's Tax Study Commission. 93 *Pa. Manual,* p. 300.

The McSorley case (*McSorley* v. *Pa. Turnpike Commission,* 390 *Pa.* 81, 1957.) was a rather confused affair. The opinion of the court upheld the governor's power to remove or suspend members of the Turnpike Commission for willful misbehavior in office. Yet, in this case McSorley was (on appeal) found not guilty. This case had some importance for Pennsylvania constitutional law, because in earlier cases cited it has been held that the official conduct of the executive branch of the government "is not to be subjected to investigation by the judiciary." *In re: Investigation by Dauphin County Grand Jury,* June, 1938, 332 *Pa.* 289. In other words, the judiciary is limited in its power to inquire broadly into the functions of the executive branch, due to the principle of separation of powers. See *Purdon's Pennsylvania Constitution,* 1958 Pocket, p. 146.

spectacular misuse of toll bridge funds during the period 1953–55.[71]

PERSONNEL REFORMS

Leader's major institutional reform in the field of personnel was his establishment of the new Bureau of Personnel within the Office of Administration. Yet this bureau's position was somewhat ambiguous, because it was only one of three official units operating in the field of state personnel. The other two were the Civil Service Commission and the governor's personnel secretary, who operated within the Governor's Office but outside the Office of Administration.

Special problems arose here from the nature of the State Civil Service Commission, as well as from the heavy weight of tradition behind the patronage system. In fact, a combination of circumstances, historical, institutional, and political, resulted in a whole galaxy of interrelated personnel problems. The following were the most important, and will be discussed in succeeding pages:

1. Large amount of patronage and small amount of merit system coverage.

[71] Leader removed from the Commission Alexander R. Miller, treasurer of the Republican County Committee, Northhampton County, and R. Chapman Carver, Joseph R. Grundy's personal assistant, Bucks County. Leslie Brown, chairman of the Commission from Trenton, New Jersey, was removed by New Jersey authorities. Leader's press release described in detail the sumptuous facilities and entertainment provided Commission members and their guests at the Commission headquarters, unauthorized salaries of $84,000, extravagant expense accounts, fees, and similar matters. *Press Release* #508, February 14, 1956.

2. Inadequate support and unsatisfactory basis of the Civil Service Commission.
3. Incompetence and inadequacy of much of the state personnel.
4. Inequities and insufficiency of state salaries.
5. Inability to recruit or to hold able technical personnel.
6. Problems of supervision, standards, and morale.
7. Inadequate training and promotion systems.
8. Unsatisfactory condition of employee organizations, grievance machinery, merit ratings, and similar matters.

Paradoxically, this nexus of problems created such a situation that the Leader administration was able to strike some of its boldest blows in the field of personnel. In fact, Leader's personnel reforms may be one of his most lasting contributions. At the same time, personnel was one area where Leader got into his greatest difficulty with party leaders. Thus, many ascribe Leader's political downfall to his personnel program. There is irony in the fact that Leader was condemned by many county chairmen for not always playing the patronage game, while he was condemned by some civil service enthusiasts for yielding too often to political pressure. Here the governor was really on the horns of a dilemma. In so many cases, he was damned if he did and damned if he did not make a particular appointment.

In January, 1955, Pennsylvania had about 14,000 to 14,-500 persons under the merit system as opposed to some 51,000 working on the basis of political sponsorship.[72] Governor Leader placed about 10,000 of these patronage positions under civil service by Executive Board action, 1956

[72] The number varies, due to the large number of temporary or per diem employes, particularly on the state highways.

to 1958.[73] However, the Fish, Game, and Public Utility Commissions took the attitude that they were not bound by this Executive Board action, and their view ultimately prevailed.[74] With positions in these three agencies withdrawn, the net increase in civil service coverage amounted to approximately 9,000 persons under the Leader administration. The Civil Service Commission now services thirty-five agencies, as opposed to only eleven before the Executive Board action.[75]

Bills were introduced to provide a statutory basis for these civil service extensions, but were not passed. Most legislators, like many professional politicians in both parties, seemed reluctant to reduce the pool of state patronage, upon which they or their friends might draw, depending

[73] Executive Board civil service extensions began September 10, 1956; thirty-seven classes were added January 8, 1957, thirty-two position classes were added April 18, 1957, five more on May 16 and nineteen more on June 21, 1957. Source: Leader Papers. See also *Press Releases* #889 (205 positions added in the Welfare Department), #892 (100 bank examiners positions added), #915 (additional professional, technical positions added), and #935, February 8, 1957 (additional extensions).

[74] The Executive Board acted under their power over existing conditions of employment, according to Section 709 of the Administrative Code. Attorney General McBride issued an opinion holding that the action of the Executive Board, placing employees under the rules of the Civil Service Commission affected dismissal, as well as conditions of employment. Since the Fish and Game Commissions, for example, had special laws dealing with removal, these could not be altered by Executive Board action. See Official Opinion #4, September 12, 1957.

[75] Ralph Tive, "Pennsylvania Begins to Rejuvenate its Civil Service." 74 *Good Government* 5, pp. 48, 49. Mr. Tive is executive director of the State Civil Service Commission. See also *Annual Report* of the State Civil Service Commission (1957), *A Move in the Right Direction,* 22 pp.

upon which party was in power. Mr. Ralph Tive described the situation thus:

> Unfortunately, there was opposition to what was interpreted as the Governor's move to freeze recent appointees into their jobs—despite the facts that incumbents had to qualify by examination and they were almost equally divided between the two parties, with fifty-one per cent of one political affiliation and forty-nine per cent of another. An administration bill to write the Executive Board's action into law was permitted to die in committee while opponents introduced and passed a novel type of merit system legislation which was actually a tenure system in disguise. This met a gubernatorial veto.[76]

As a concession to public pressure for a genuine merit system, the legislature passed a resolution instructing its research arm, the Joint State Government Commission, "to study federal and state civil service systems and report to the 1959 session of the General Assembly."

At the beginning of Leader's term, state salaries were grossly inadequate and inequitable in their range and distribution. Before salaries could be raised, it was deemed necessary to develop an entirely new classification and compensation plan. To assist the Bureau of Personnel in this task, Governor Leader engaged the services of the Public Administration Service of Chicago.[77] After exhaustive study, a new classification plan was adopted, which reduced the number of position classes from 7,500 to 1,318. Then a new compensation plan established "forty-six overlapping pay ranges instead of obsolete rigid and unrealistic schedules with a host of specialized salary ranges." [78]

[76] Tive, *op. cit.*, pp. 48, 49.
[77] *Press Release* #94, March 10, 1955.
[78] Tive, *op. cit.*, pp. 48, 49.

The new pay plan, which took effect on August 1, 1956, provided no general cost of living increase, but each employe's pay was raised at least one half-step, or not less than two and one-half per cent over his old pay, except in those cases where such a raise would place a worker above the maximum for his grade.[79] The new plan also established regular increments within each grade for the first time. In a rather haphazard fashion, the old system had provided for increments of two to three per cent, up to a total range of ten to thirteen per cent within each grade. In accord with modern personnel practice, the new plan provided regular five per cent steps, with each employee eligible for five raises within his grade. Since each five per cent raise was based upon the year before, this permitted a total range within each grade of twenty-seven and one-half per cent. In practice, this new pay meant that nobody's pay was reduced and the average employe's pay plan was raised ten per cent.[80]

From 1956 to December, 1959, there were thirty-seven amendments to the pay plan by action of the Executive Board. Not all of these were salary increases, and some affected only a few positions, though altogether about a third of the classes were involved. Thus the total salary change from July, 1955, to December, 1959, amounted to an increase of thirty-four per cent for the average state employe. According to the Bureau of Personnel, such an increase kept up with the cost of living, though it was not granted specifically on that basis. Even with these increases, state salaries did not keep pace with the hiring rates in

[79] See *Press Release* #959, on the results of the personnel survey.
[80] Based on interviews with Mr. Russell Johnson, director of the Bureau of Personnel, December 3, 1959, and March 7, 1961.

private industry, in the federal government, and with some other states. State salaries under Leader were markedly better than under preceding administrations, and the Office of Administration expressed the conviction that they had done the best they could within the appropriations available.

Recruitment under the old system had been especially difficult in many professional and technical fields. For example, the survey of the State Highway Department by the national Automotive Safety Foundation revealed a deficiency of some 500 civil engineers. Preceding administrations had been unable to recruit any qualified engineers in recent years. Under the new personnel system, the Highway Department recruited about 200 graduate engineers, which was about as fast as they could be assimilated.

A similar situation arose with bank examiners, who were increasingly unwilling to look to political sponsorship for job security. In this area a training program was instituted with the cooperation of the banks, which proved to be a more satisfactory method of recruitment and training. There were still quite a few of these who shortly resigned from state service to work for the banks themselves, but the same thing happened in New York and other states. The Banking Department felt that if they were able to retain fifty per cent of the examiners trained, such was an improvement over the old system.

Recruitment of foresters was also improved under the new merit and compensation systems. Secretary Goddard, the former dean of the School of Forestry at Pennsylvania State University, was able to recruit all the foresters he needed, whereas in previous administrations, such had not been the case. Although the Bureau of Personnel had, in

1959, no firm statistics on turnover because of the difficulty of keeping such records, they knew that the rate was generally lower than before, particularly in certain categories.

Other aspects of personnel administration were also modernized and expanded under the Leader administration. Steps were taken to improve supervision, training, promotion, grievance and counselling services. For example, in many departments, there had been no regularly trained personnel officer to perform such functions. Personnel matters, like budget matters, were often handled by clerks attached to the secretary or the chief administrator. In the Leader administration, trained personnel officers were provided in many departments, and these persons collectively were formed into a Personnel Council, in November, 1956, which undertook to raise standards throughout the entire state administration. This Council was headed by a three-man steering committee composed of Russell Johnson, Robert H. Jones, and Ralph D. Tive, of the Bureau of Personnel, the Governor's Office and the Civil Service Commission, respectively. Chairmanship of the Council rotated every three months. This structure served to coordinate at least to some degree the operations of the three state personnel operations.

A Training Council was also established to work with the Bureau of Training in the State Civil Service Commission. As a result, training became much more important throughout the state government. Training had been one of the deficiencies found in a number of the departments by Governor Leader's Advisory Committee. One training program which received special attention was the seminar in administration set up for state administrators. This school for administrators was in line with recent executive development courses introduced in the federal government, in private industry, and in a few other states. Altogether about 100 deputy secretaries and department heads took this course, which met from October, 1955, to June, 1956. Five groups met for this first series taught by professors from four state-aided universities, Pennsylvania, Pittsburgh, Pennsylvania State and Temple. A second course, entitled, "Seminar in Administration and Management for Middle Management Personnel" was held in Harrisburg from February through April, 1958, and has been continued each year since then.

It was not the material that we taught them that was important. The important thing was the fact that they assembled to study government. Perhaps for the first time they sat down to get acquainted and to talk together, to understand and find out about, and to help solve their problems. We met weekly, and each week was devoted to evaluating the program of some particular department. We decided on the program in advance, and had it prepared for presentation. They had to do readings. At first it seemed strange that a Highway man would have to learn about Health. And, maybe at first they objected. But soon they caught on and seemed to take a great interest in this. I set up the program under the Office of Administration. . . . Here were busy people, taking time off from the job to go to school each week.[81]

Pennsylvania had no state-wide system of performance ratings before Leader, though they had been introduced in a few departments. In December, 1958, a state rating

[81] Interview with Dr. Charlesworth, who conducted the group consisting of deputy secretaries. Four groups of bureau heads met with Professors Blair, Martin, McGeary, and Short. See also, J. C. Charlesworth, "Pennsylvania's High Level Seminars in Administration." 29 *State Government* (April, 1956), p. 67.

system was inaugurated after many months of preparation, including the training of raters and supervisors. The Bureau of Personnel felt that this innovation was generally successful, although the rating system had not yet been integrated with the increment policy.[82] The Bureau of Personnel also worked up a revised method of handling grievances, which was ready for adoption towards the end of the Leader administration. For various reasons this scheme was left to the succeeding Lawrence administration for implementation.

One personnel policy which was not entirely successful is the matter of personnel complement control. Though the Office of Administration placed a great deal of emphasis upon this control device for budgetary purposes, it ran into considerable resistance on the part of line officials. To begin with, it proved most difficult to get agency heads to submit a firm figure as to their minimum or optimum complement of personnel. Secondly, many department heads resented the attempt of the Office of Administration to place ceilings upon specific categories of personnel. They felt that such centralized control over internal departmental personnel allocation interfered with the discretion needed for effective administration. Although steps were taken by the Office of Administration under Dr. Ferguson to ameliorate such detailed control over personnel, these plans were not fully realized by the end of the Leader administration, and thus the controls continued. Part of the problem was evidently a disagreement over what would constitute a desirable pattern of complement control.

In general state personnel was greatly improved during

[82] Interview with R. Johnson, December 3, 1959.

Leader's term. The number of positions under the merit system was almost doubled, which resulted in the recruitment of better qualified technical and professional personnel, many of whom would not even consider state service formerly. Secondly, the fact that the new Bureau of Personnel checked the qualifications of all patronage appointments resulted in higher standards within the noncivil service sector. Thirdly, Leader and some of his department heads undertook an energetic program of recruitment in certain key areas, such as in the health and welfare fields. This program, which was called "operation opportunity," was directed at the nation-wide labor market, and was, according to the governor, "enormously successful." [83] With the help of this new personnel certain departments, such as welfare and forests and waters, were infused with new blood. The number of persons in the state service with professional and technical training was vastly increased during Leader's term.[84] In certain departments the change was so great that if succeeding administrations can but hold the gains made, the state service will be tremendously improved.

On the other hand it must be acknowledged that despite energetic activity and even much solid accomplishment in personnel reform, the Leader administration still

[83] For the mental health program alone, about 1,300 professional workers were needed. *Press Release* #790, October 4, 1956.

[84] In the Department of Highways, for example, the persons in engineering positions who actually were registered as engineers or possessed an engineering degree increased as follows: January, 1955, twelve per cent; January, 1958, twenty-six per cent; and July, 1959 (under Governor Lawrence), thirty-two per cent. Information received from Pennsylvania Department of Highways, January 18, 1961.

bequeathed to its successors a number of unsolved or perhaps only partially solved personnel problems. Some of these were a legacy of the long neglect of state personnel in the past. Some observers regarded the continuation of an unintegrated system, part patronage and part merit, a basic unresolved irritant. Moreover, the improvement of personnel remains a continuing problem because of the decisive role of the personnel in any human organization. Permanent improvement will require not only institutional adjustment, but also much greater public awareness of both present and optimum conditions for the employment of state personnel. As William Penn remarked:

Governments, like clocks, go from the motion men give them.

LEGISLATIVE ACHIEVEMENTS

Governor Leader got much better results from his first, 1955–56, legislature than he did from the 1957 session. Although the 1955 session dragged on for seventeen months in dispute with the governor on the sales tax,[85] the rest of the governor's program fared rather well. Perhaps the legislators felt obliged to take action on other bills partly in order to justify their presence. There was also a political explanation for the strikingly different performance of these two successive sessions. In the 1955 session, the House was controlled by the governor's party, and the Republicans held the Senate with a majority of only two members. In the 1957 session, the Republicans con-

[85] Although the House passed Leader's classified income tax, the Senate refused to accept this measure. Ultimately, Leader was forced to accept a three per cent sales tax in order to secure necessary funds.

trolled both houses, with a majority of four votes in the
Senate and forty-three seats in the House.[86] With such a
shift in strength, there was also a change in the attitude
of the Republican legislative leaders. Whereas the Republicans generally went along with the basic outlines of
Leader's 1955 legislative program, they apparently decided, in 1957, not to give the governor anything more
than necessary. This may have been partly a design to
block Democratic achievement during the second biennium in order to recapture the State House in 1958. Although the Democrats captured the governorship again in
1958, their majority was much smaller than it had been in
1954.

At the close of the 1955 session, on May 22, 1956, Governor Leader said,

With the help and cooperation of aroused civic groups, the
Administration has succeeded in many of its efforts to bring
enlightened and humane government to the citizens of this
State. Although this was the lengthiest Session on record, it saw
more bills passed for the benefit of Pennsylvania's people than
any other meeting of the Assembly.[87]

Not only were more general laws passed than at any
other session in the history of the state, but the 1955 ses-

[86] The political division was as follows:

| | 1955 Session | | 1957 Session | |
	Republican	Democrat	Republican	Democrat
Senate	26	24	27	23
House	98	112	126	83
				(1 vacant)

Source: 93 *Pa. Manual,* p. 1020.

[87] *Press Release* #651, May 22, 1956. The session consumed 168
days. 93 *Pa. Manual,* p. 1023.

sion also granted more significant social and economic
legislation than any other session since 1937.[88]

At the close of the 1957 session Leader spoke quite dif-
ferently:

This year the Republican legislature has hamstrung, crippled, and in some cases sought to destroy the same laws which
it helped to write a year ago. It has refused to pass vitally
needed legislation which the administration has recommended
. . though much would not have cost a dime in new appropriations. . . . This was an irresponsible, Republican controlled legislature, so bad that it offended the decent instincts
of millions of responsible Pennsylvania Republicans. This was
a special-interest, do-nothing legislature, whose Republican
bosses cold-bloodedly turned their backs upon the needs of the
people and kowtowed to the whim of the big lobbyists. . . .
This was the worst legislature in Pennsylvania's history.[89]

One of Leader's greatest legislative achievements in the
1955 session was in the field of mental health. The Bureau
of Mental Health was completely reorganized under a new
mental health commissioner, who shortly became the second highest paid state official, second only to the governor.
The legislature appropriated $26,500,000 to hire more
skilled personnel to speed up the cure of mental illness,
plus additional sums totaling $47,000,000 for facilities for
mentally retarded children and others. The legislature also
established a Mental Health Foundation to put private
funds to work in state hospitals for research into mental
illness. Another measure authorized the setting up of spe-

[88] Interview with Henry Leader, the governor's legislative secretary, September 20, 1961, York, Pennsylvania.

[89] *Press Release* #A229, June 21, 1957 (for release Sunday, June
23).

cial education in the public schools for physically and mentally handicapped children. Mental health and welfare is the general area in which Governor Leader's accomplishments are best known to the public at large. The state Health Department had been reorganized and placed under civil service by Leader's predecessor, Governor Fine and Leader was able to continue and extend this reform in the health field administratively, without much additional legislation.

In the area of labor legislation, Leader managed after promotional efforts to secure the establishment of a Fair Employment Practice Commission, after some eleven years of failure on that issue, at Harrisburg. Unemployment compensation benefits were also raised, and the number of weeks of payment was increased. Pennsylvania's workmen's compensation laws were also liberalized in the same ways. Leader's first legislature also expanded public assistance, particularly for the disabled, blind, aged, and infirm, appropriating for example, $3,000,000 for nursing home care for disabled indigents, and increasing by $6,500,000 the state aid to the general hospitals.

The 1955 General Assembly also voted unprecedented sums to promote education in Pennsylvania. With $500,-000,000 of construction funds made available, the largest school building program in the history of the state was inaugurated. State aid to universities was increased by $14,500,000, plus an additional $12,500,000 for a building program at the Pennsylvania State University and $25,-000,000 for the state teachers colleges.

Other legislation was passed, pursuant to Governor Leader's pledge to assist economically depressed areas. This included a new $5,000,000 Pennsylvania Industrial

Development program, which the federal Department of Commerce later rated as the best in the nation. Additional sums were provided for anthracite mine drainage, coal research, and geological surveys, in order to restore and promote use of the state's mineral industries. Increases in the state matching funds for slum clearance made a total of $30,000,000 available for that type of urban redevelopment. This too was one of the largest programs in the nation.

Highway and turnpike authorizations and matching funds were extended; so that with the aid of federal funds, Pennsylvania embarked upon the largest highway construction program in the history of the state. Flood control, recreation programs, and state parks were also greatly expanded in Leader's first biennium. Other legislation was passed to deal with various aspects of juvenile delinquency. A new state boxing code was written, which it was hoped might serve as a model for all the states.[90]

Although there was relatively little new agricultural legislation, bills were passed to assure the quality of the feed and fertilizer the farmer buys, to authorize a state livestock show, and to exempt farmers from the tax on gasoline used on the farm.

PARDONS

The governor's power to grant pardons has created a great deal of controversy. Believing that the early governors had been too liberal in their exercise of pardons and reprieves, the drafters of the 1874 Constitution provided that the governor could not take such actions without the

[90] See *Press Release* #320 (September 8, 1955).

written recommendation of at least three of the four constitutional officers constituting the Pardon Board. The board consists of the lieutenant governor, chairman, secretary of the commonwealth, attorney general, and secretary of internal affairs. Since the first and last of these officials are popularly elected, no governor can grant a pardon recommended only by his own appointees.

The pardoning power is a form of executive clemency needed to provide some flexibility and a remedy for exceptional cases in the administration of justice.[91] However, in most states the pardon function creates administrative difficulties, since it includes "both archaic and contemporary features . . . in uneasy alliance." [92] The ancient practice of executive mercy has been increasingly combined, in part, with the modern device of parole. In Pennsylvania, for example, the Pardon Board carries out no extensive investigations on its own. Rather, it is obliged to depend upon reports prepared by agents of the Parole Board, by prison officials, judges, district attorneys, or others. In fact, in Pennsylvania,

. . . the Board of Pardons rarely releases a man; they only make him available for release by the Board of Parole, and the two Boards are administratively and functionally different bodies. The Governor has no authority to grant pardons or commute sentences without first receiving a favorable recommendation from the Board of Pardons. Moreover, the Governor is not bound by a favorable recommendation from the Board, for he has power to reject favorable recommendations

[91] Caleb Foote, "Pardon Policy in a Modern State." 39 *The Prison Journal,* Pennsylvania Prison Society (Philadelphia, April, 1959), p. 3.

[92] R. W. England, Jr., "Pardon, Commutation, and Their Improvement." *Ibid.,* p. 30.

and to refuse to grant clemency. However the Governor can do nothing about those cases refused clemency by the Pardon Board. It appears that the Board acts independently and without influence of any kind from the Governor's office, and the Governor acts independently and without interference of any kind from the Board.[93]

Here is a function carried out by three semi-independent groups of officials, the Pardon Board, the Parole Board, and the governor, no one of which is bound to take positive action by any other.[94] Such an arrangement defies the usual canons of administrative integration or unity. Granted that the chief executive of a large industrial state, such as Pennsylvania, does not have the time to grant every application the attention that it deserves, the above arrangement does not provide the governor with the quality of staff assistance or advice needed to do a really effective job. In the first place, there is no assurance that any of the members of the *ex officio* Pardon Board, with the possible exception of the attorney general, are professionally trained to deal competently with the penal-corrective problems involved.[95] In the second place, the board is a

[93] Marvin E. Wolfgang, "Analysis of Selected Aspects of the Board of Pardons." *Ibid.*, p. 9. See also *Appendix to the Legislative Journal*, 1957 Session, p. 4366, cited by Wolfgang.

[94] However, in a recent case the courts held that the power of the governor to grant pardons and commutations of sentence is exclusive. *Commonwealth ex rel Banks* v. *Cain*, 345 Pa. 581, 1943. A 1941 case held that parole at the expiration of minimum sentence does not violate the power to grant pardons upon recommendation of the Pardon Board. *Commonwealth ex rel Lycett* v. *Ashe*, 145 Pa. Super. 26, 1941.

[95] A recent chairman of the Pennsylvania Pardon Board has written that in his period most of the cases were disposed of by the Board in a rather cursory fashion. John C. Bell, "The Board of

part-time, amateur operation conducted by persons all of
whom carry full-time, or nearly full-time responsibilities
in other areas. It can be argued that it is also undesirable
to man a Pardon Board with two political appointees responsible only to the governor:

> The temptations leading a governor to misuse the power
> must not be underestimated. The most loyal followers any po-
> litician can have are the men he has helped "spring" from
> prison. He can count on their grateful and wholehearted sup-
> port at election time, together with the support of their fami-
> lies and friends. It is not too surprising that there have been
> governors unscrupulous enough deliberately to build up such
> a body of supporters.[96]

As Professor England points out, there has developed a
belief that "even governors can be reached" to release
prisoners, and thus, a pardon advisory board can act as
an important line of defense against political and criminal
pressures on the governor.

However, penal authorities now feel that pardon boards
can best be immunized against political pressures, not by
making them *ex officio,* but by manning these boards by
nonpolitical, full-time, professional personnel, chosen pref-
erably on a merit basis. Yet, the practice in the various

Pardons." 15 *Pennsylvania Bar Association Quarterly* (January 1944),
p. 113, quoted by England, *op. cit.,* p. 25. Other observers held that
such was not true of Leader's Pardon Board. Interview in Philadelphia, August 10, 1960.

[96] Attorney General's *Survey of Release Procedures,* Vol. III (Department of Justice, Washington, D.C., 1939), p. 143, quoted by
England, *op. cit.,* p. 26. Loose pardoning practices were involved in
the background of Governor Walton's impeachment in Oklahoma,
1923, topped only by "Ma" Ferguson's reported pardoning of 3,500
persons in two years, 1925–26. *Idem.*

states is so diverse that it is difficult to identify any dominant pattern.[97] In 1959, Professor England wrote that now,

> Only fourteen states continue to invest in their governors exclusive pardoning power; of these, six provide . . . no assistance. In the remaining eight they are aided by pardon attorneys, advisory officers or parole commissions. Thirty-four states have established boards within constitutional or statutory provisions which variously restrict gubernatorial power, ranging from nominal limitations to those of Idaho, Nebraska and North Dakota, whose governors are members of the pardon boards with voting power no greater than that of any other member.[98]

The pardoning power aroused considerable political controversy in the latter part of the Leader administration. In fact, this function came to be a kind of political albatross for Governor Leader, when the *Philadelphia Inquirer* continued for about three years to charge him with loose, excessive, if not partially corrupt pardons. Professional sources, generally friendly to the governor, observed that the press was completely unjustified in these charges, which were based not only upon a misstatement of facts, but also upon an orientation not in line with current thinking in the field of penology.[99]

[97] The matter is so complex that recent issues of the *Book of the States* do not carry comparisons of pardon boards in their biennial tables of executive and administrative organization. For the composition of pardon boards, in the various states, see *Index Digest of State Constitutions,* 2nd ed. Columbia University (1959), p. 340.

[98] England, *op. cit.,* pp. 23, 24.

[99] Based upon various interviews in Philadelphia, Harrisburg, and State College. The editor of *The Inquirer,* Mr. Walter H. Annenberg, may have been motivated in part by the fact that his father, M. L. Annenberg (*Inquirer* publisher, 1936–42), had earlier been denied a pardon.

Against the recommendation of some of his advisors, Leader chose to ignore these charges for months, which led some persons to believe they were true. Finally, in a Democratic state headquarters statement issued September 19, 1958, Leader explained that no pardons were, or can be granted except upon the positive recommendation of the Pardon Board. In the second place, the record and the recommendation for every pardon is duly reported to the General Assembly, and inscribed for public inspection in the *Legislative Journal*.[100] The facts indicate that Leader

[100] The cases which triggered such an uproar in *The Philadelphia Inquirer* over Governor Leader's pardons, involved three youths, convicted of armed robbery in Bucks County. A man had been killed in the incident and all three minors involved had been sentenced to death some six or seven years ago. One of these three, particularly, had important political connections, through his family, with the Democratic party. Upon the recommendation of the Pardon Board, Leader commuted all three sentences from death to life imprisonment, a result that had originally been favored by many, including some of the judges involved in the case. Leader pointed all of this out in his statement. See transcript of Leader's press conference, November 8, 1958.

Various persons acquainted with the facts said, in interviews with the writer, that *The Philadelphia Inquirer,* which conducted this campaign against the governor, had been offended by Leader and the Democrats on other grounds. Thus, the pardon issue was, in part, a public retaliation. The evident exaggeration of the facts by the press lends support to this interpretation. In any case there was a political motivation for these charges which were used by the opposition in Leader's 1958 campaign for the United States Senate. On the other hand, even friendly observers noted that Attorney General McBride, in his great concern for the "underdog" had apparently been pushing the Pardon Board to adopt a more liberal policy towards major offenders at a time when public opinion, particularly in Philadelphia, was much concerned about the growth of crime in the big cities. Based upon interviews in Philadelphia, August, 1960.

actually granted fewer pardons, in both absolute and percentage terms than had his recent predecessors:

. . . it cannot be denied that both the absolute number and the proportion of petitions granted during the past administration were low.[101]

The lowest year since 1915 was 1956, when twelve per cent of the petitions were granted. The highest years (since the Administrative Code of 1929) were thirty per cent in 1930 and thirty-four per cent in 1954, the year before Leader took office. In fact, the three-year moving average of Leader's administration, up to and including 1957 (1958 was not given), was 18.3 per cent, the lowest since 1946.[102]

Explaining that his Board of Pardons had been "the toughest in the recent history of Pennsylvania," Leader accused the Republicans of "deliberately trying to deceive the people." In his first three years, Leader granted 555 pardon applications, as opposed to 611 by Governor Duff and 883 by Governor Fine in their three lowest years. Of those Leader paroled, the record indicated that only eight per cent committed further crimes, as opposed to eighteen per cent recidivism by prisoners who served their full minimum sentence. As for term served for life sentence, Pennsylvania is "one of the toughest states in the Union— averaging eighteen years in Pennsylvania, as opposed to the national average of ten and a half years." Further, Leader noted that of the thirty-four United States cities of 250,000 or more population, twenty-five had a crime

[101] Wolfgang, *op. cit.,* p. 12.
[102] Source: Board of Pardons, Harrisburg. Table reproduced by Wolfgang, pp. 11, 12, 13. Also in Democratic State Headquarters statement (September 19, 1958).

rate higher than Pittsburgh and twenty-eight had a crime rate higher than Philadelphia. According to F.B.I. crime rates for 1957, Pennsylvania's crime was well below the national average (per 100,000 population) in every one of six major categories.[103]

Partly as a result of this controversy the General Assembly passed a proposed constitutional amendment dealing with the Board of Pardons. This 1957 resolution (J. R. No. 10) provided for a Board of five members, four full-time members appointed by the governor for eight-year terms, plus the lieutenant governor, who would continue as chairman.[104] When the Commission on Constitutional Revision issued their *Report* on March 9, 1959, still another arrangement was suggested. This body recommended:

> The Board of Pardons shall consist of the Lieutenant Governor, . . . chairman, the Attorney General, the chairman of the agency created by the General Assembly to administer paroles, and two members appointed by the Governor with the consent of the majority of the members elected to the Senate . . . [for six-year overlapping terms.] [105]

Neither of these proposals go quite so far in the creation of a professional Pardon Board, as has been recommended by specialists in this field. However, both proposals would represent an improvement over the present *ex officio* type of Board. It should be noted that the 1959 pro-

[103] Democratic State Headquarters statement (September 19, 1958).

[104] *Report of the Commission on Constitutional Revision*. Harrisburg, 1959, p. 26. There was also a legislative investigating committee, which drafted these recommendations. Wolfgang, *op. cit.*, p. 8.

[105] Class 1 Changes, *Report of the Commission . . .* , p. 25.

posal goes a step further in making an institutional connection between the pardon and parole operations. Whether a more "professional" or a more "judicial" type of board might have prevented the kind of embarrassment Governor Leader experienced in the operation of the pardon function remains a hypothetical question. It seems likely, however, that such a board might have been less open to the charge of "political determination." [106]

[106] Governor Leader also appointed a Commission on Penal and Correctional Affairs, whose final report was issued on January 16, 1959. (Governor's Office *Press Release* #A970). This Commission recommended increasing the Parole Board from three to five, increasing salaries of Board members, changing its name to the Board of Probation and Parole, and increasing slightly its jurisdiction. Reported in 2 *State Government News* (Council of State Governments, February 1959).

CHAPTER IV

PROGRAM EVALUATION—LEADER'S
MOST NOVEL ADMINISTRATIVE REFORM

ORIGINS OF THE PROPOSAL

One of the most novel aspects of Governor Leader's administrative reform was the Bureau of Program Evaluation, the sixth bureau within the Office of Administration. This bureau was added by Governor Leader to the original Economy League plan for the Governor's Office upon the recommendation of his advisors. One significance of this bureau is that it represented in the eyes of its sponsors a new and somewhat revolutionary approach to the function of administrative policy making.

Since most of their time is devoted to primarily political matters, few governors have much opportunity to consider their administrative operation in terms of major social goals. Thus, the provision of a special agency to evaluate the status and adequacy of programs throughout the various departments, and to provide some coordination among them was regarded as an important type of administrative innovation. Such program research was designed to provide the governor with a more rational and factual basis for administrative policy making. Pennsylvania's Bureau of Program Evaluation can be regarded as an experiment in gubernatorial staff organization, as well as a new technique for high level policy review and initiation. The object was to avoid the type of situation described by Homer E. Scace:

Lack of systematic study of impending problems has often led a governor to move from crisis to crisis, making decisions with conscientious good faith, but with too little time to check into basic facts. Sometimes a good alternative to a suggested course of action will crop up later to embarrass the governor; sometimes a whole problem area will be missed by the governor and exploited successfully by the opposition party.[1]

The Bureau of Program Evaluation was consistent with Governor Leader's conception of his office, his program of administrative reform and his strategy of action. Though the idea of such a bureau was first suggested to him by his preinaugural Advisory Committee, Governor-elect Leader saw in this proposal another way to help him keep track of a whole panorama of highly complex administrative operations. Leader knew from his training and brief experience in the state legislature that he needed the help of full-time, skilled, and informed advisors. He thought that such a bureau would provide a specially desirable place to use specialists in government whose knowledge and skills he so much respected.

Four persons were primarily responsible for putting the breath of life into the idea of a separate bureau for the function of program evaluation. These persons were Dr.

[1] "The Governor Needs Staff." 40 *National Municipal Review* (October, 1951), p. 464.

Stephen B. Sweeney, Dr. Harold E. Alderfer, Dr. William G. Willis, and Dr. James C. Charlesworth, all of them original or subsequent members of the Governor's Advisory Committee. In their initial discussions with Leader, the first three of these persuaded the governor-elect to add such a bureau to the Economy League Plan, and after a few weeks of hesitation, Leader accepted this advice, partly out of respect for these persons and the institutions they represented.

Dr. Charlesworth put his views on the subject of program evaluation into writing as early as 1951. In that year he published a textbook on *Governmental Administration,* Chapter XXX of which is entitled "Appraisal; Program Evaluation." Many of the ideas for the new bureau, which was originally known as the Division of Program and Policy Research, were also drawn from Chapter XIV, in the same work, entitled "Administrative Planning." [2] In part, Dr. Charlesworth's conception of administrative planning, and ultimately of program evaluation, are logical extensions of the generally accepted definition of the staff function:

> The dominant voices in the science of public administration agree . . . that a staff officer is one who specializes in research, observation and study, and who draws up plans and proposals for approval by the top executive, to whom he is attached collaterally.[3]

[2] Dr. Sweeney's letter transmitting the prospectus for the Bureau to Governor-elect Leader refers specifically to pages 297–298 and 303–306, both on administrative planning in Chapter XIV. See those pages in *Governmental Administration* by J. C. Charlesworth (New York, 1951).

[3] *Ibid.,* p. 296.

On the next page, Dr. Charlesworth outlined the functions of his proposed research and policy unit in the following terms:

The research and policy unit should have a free hand to study what it wishes, and should have access to information anywhere in the entire organization, whether confidential or not. It should have no routine duties whatever, such as submitting production reports to the top executive. Its personnel should be intellectually curious, humble, and imaginative, and the unit should schedule its work so that there is time for speculation and inquiry.

At least two elements of this description appear repeatedly in later proposals for the Bureau of Program Evaluation. One is the freedom from administrative or line operations, and the other is the quality of personnel, equipped to deal with important facts and ideas, and free for speculation and inquiry.[4]

[4] Thus, the four successive directors of Program Evaluation were all professors, the first three in the field of political science, and the fourth in the field of American history. They were as follows:

Dr. William C. Seyler, February, 1955–July, 1955.

Dr. John H. Ferguson, July, 1955–September, 1956.

Dr. Harold F. Alderfer, September, 1956–September, 1957.

Dr. Robert Christie, September 1957–February, 1959 (at which time he became also acting director of Management Methods. These two Bureaus were later combined. Executive Board resolution, February 10, 1960).

However, there was actually far more continuity in the bureau than this list of successive "king's tasters" indicated. For one thing, Dr. Alderfer had been a colleague of Dr. Ferguson's at Pennsylvania State for many years, and the two continued to work closely together after the latter replaced Dr. Charlesworth as Secretary of Administration. In other words, many of Dr. Ferguson's major concerns as director of the bureau were now continued in his new position. Likewise, Dr. Christie served as assistant to Dr. Alderfer a full year before he replaced him as director of the bureau.

When Governor Leader came to organize his new Office of Administration, the Bureau of Program Evaluation was included as one of the five major units under Secretary Charlesworth. In February, Leader secured the services of a young political scientist at the University of Pittsburgh as first director of progam evaluation, Dr. William C. Seyler.[5] Although Dr. Seyler resigned from the Bureau in July, less than six months after the birth of the bureau, for a more responsible position as deputy secretary of internal affairs, a position which he still holds (1963), his appointment served to give the new bureau some professional stature. Those first six months were something of an experimental period when a number of activities were begun, but few were carried to completion. Thus, the more permanent work of program evaluation did not really get under way until the regime of Dr. Ferguson. Dr. Seyler shared the conviction of his superior, Dr. Charlesworth, that the theory of program evaluation was sound and that it represented a potentially significant function in the state administration. He defended this point of view in two speeches in the spring of 1955, one to the Pennsylvania Political Science and Public Administration Association, on April 22, and the other to the meeting of the Tax Institute, also in Harrisburg, on April 5. He expressed the prevailing viewpoint of all proponents of program evaluation when he said,

[5] Dr. Seyler received his Ph.D. in political science from Duke University in 1952, and had been teaching at the University of Pittsburgh since 1946. *Directory of the American Political Science Association,* 1953, p. 168. For several years Dr. Seyler has edited the *American Political Science Review*'s annual roster of doctoral dissertations in political science in progress at American universities. In 1959–60, he was president of the central Pennsylvania (Harrisburg) chapter of the American Society for Public Administration.

One of the great weaknesses of American public administration it seems to me, is its emphasis on efficiency for efficiency's sake. We become so involved in instituting modern accounting systems [he told the Tax Institute] that we forget the fact that accounting is a tool and not an end in itself.

. . . We frequently get ourselves into the same dilemma with respect to personnel, centralized purchasing, and other so-called administrative efficiency operations.

What I am driving at is that Program and Policy Research . . . should have its main job the task of making certain that the substance of the Commonwealth's program is not lost in the forest of efficient procedures. Very often, we must stop and ask ourselves . . . "should the program be continued at all."

In these same speeches, Dr. Seyler gave a prospectus for the work of the bureau in the following terms:

1. We plan to make studies of the major economic and social trends within the Commonwealth with special reference to the effects of these trends on the programs of the various Commonwealth departments.

2. We expect to develop, in cooperation with the Management Research Division, a form on which each agency under the Governor's jurisdiction will describe and evaluate its past, its current, and its future programs.

3. We plan to study and evaluate the major program developments in those states whose problems are comparable to Pennsylvania.

4. We plan to provide information for the reorganization surveys which will result from the enactment of the reorganization bill.

5. We expect to provide continuing studies of the functions performed by Commonwealth agencies with a purpose of reviewing the appropriateness of the program and the element of duplication of programs.

6. We hope to assist and coordinate the activities of depart-

mental research units which may be established in the operating departments.

7. We expect to consult with and advise the statistics gathering units of the operating agencies in order that these units may provide meaningful data which will be available for policy formulation.

The young director admitted that these objectives represented "an ambitious undertaking," but expressed the view that such analysis should be of more than passing interest to those concerned with raising the "wherewithal to support public programs."

The bureau early acquired an assistant director, two or three program analysts, a clerk, and a secretary. As particular jobs undertaken by the Bureau required additional services, such personnel was "borrowed" on a rather informal basis from various of the regular departments. There was also considerable interchange of personnel among the various bureaus of the Office of Administration.

The Bureau of Program Evaluation shared both the benefits and the handicaps of the Office of Administration in its early days. The office lacked a specific statutory basis. Even more important was the fact that for about a year there was no money specifically appropriated for the Office of Administration. According to Dr. Charlesworth, "We lived on furniture, spare supplies and people scrounged from other departments." [6] Though the bureau had this problem of establishing itself as a legitimate operation in the eyes of some of the older departments, it

[6] Interview in Philadelphia, September 8, 1959. "This was a situation like Dawes, trying to establish the prestige of the Budget Office in Washington," Dr. Charlesworth noted. "When Dawes came in as Budget Director and tried to work with the older departments, people would say, 'Who are you?' "

never faced any overt hostility on the question of its legality. More serious, however, was the resistance to the bureau in some quarters because of its "brain trust" or "egghead" quality or character. Party leaders on both sides would understand and accept the appointment of a collection of "party hacks" at the outset of any new administration. What was new and curious about the Office of Administration and its constituent bureaus, was the importation into the state service of a number of college professors and eager young college graduates, or "eggheads" as they were called. According to various party leaders recently consulted, such new employes were not objectionable people, *per se*. Rather, they were resented because they lacked political experience and were less ininclined to play the usual political game. The "egghead" issue was heard throughout the Leader administration, not only among party officials, but also in the lower levels of the bureaucracy, in the legislature, and to some extent in the press. A recent example of this attitude can be found in a letter from a member of the state legislature, appearing in the Harrisburg *Evening News,* January 15, 1960. This legislator alleged that the Civil Service Commission (in this case) was "in the hands of unqualified, self-seeking, self-providing, alleged academic experts . . . who perpetuate mediocrity." [7] Moreover, according to Dr. Elmer Gra-

---

[7] The letter continued with caustic references to the "bright young men . . ." responsible for qualifying exams and in-service training. These exams, it was asserted, are not fitted to the job, and tend to undermine the agencies . . . by disregarding faithful men . . . "for bright young graduates from some alleged school of public administration." Dr. Graper, who cited this letter, added that he presumed he was not one of the "bright young men," since he is the retired chairman of the Department of Political Science from the University of Pittsburgh.

per, chairman of the Civil Service Commission, such an attitude is still held by "an appreciable percentage of those in the General Assembly."

At other times, the Office of Administration was resented because it was run by "the P.A. boys," meaning the experts or specialists in public administration.[8] Such hostility was not an entirely impersonal objection to academic people as such. There were a number of personality clashes within Leader's new Office of Administration, some of which had most unfortunate repercussions upon the relations between the central staff and the line agencies. On one occasion, Dr. Charlesworth gave a speech to the Federation of Community Councils in Philadelphia on the subject of "Responsiveness *vs.* Efficiency in Government." It was a speech on governmental improvement, such as might be received with interest if not applause by any gathering of political scientists. The speech contained one or two points which could be, and were exploited by persons critical of the "egghead" leadership of the Office of Administration. Such critics seized upon Dr. Charlesworth's question, "Is it not time that we consider a competence test for voters?" and made quite a tempest out of it. They particularly resented the implications of the speaker's suggestion that "the illiterate, the indifferent and the cynical" should not vote. The outcry became so loud that even leaders of the gov-

---

[8] Presumably private business is justified in employing any kind of financial, marketing, or administrative expert needed to promote its product, its efficiency or its operation. However, the state government, since it is the public's business, is often assumed to be reserved for amateurs who may have acquired some claim to political favoritism or largesse. Such a vested interest in mediocrity, when stated, at least in such extreme terms, is on the decline. For one thing, taxation pressures have forced the people to demand higher quality service for their money.

ernor's party introduced and passed a resolution of cen-
sure in the General Assembly.[9] Such episodes as these had
their effects upon the work of the Office of Administration,
and upon many of its constituent bureaus, in the early
days when the units were just becoming established at
Harrisburg.[10]

[9] House Resolution 1952, Serial #174, "deploring the tenor of
remarks, denying the right of suffrage to certain citizens." Pennsylvania *Legislative Journal,* 1955 session, p. 5854. Dr. Charlesworth
had also recommended fewer and better qualified legislators in his
address.

[10] Despite some difficulty with his own party, Governor Leader
defended his secretary of administration in press conferences and
statements. In the first place, he issued the full text of Dr. Charlesworth's speech as an unnumbered press release (February 2, 1956).
Then the governor heartily defended Charlesworth's right to speak,
adding, "I don't necessarily agree with what he said." *The Harrisburg Patriot* (Friday, February 17, 1956).

The headline of *The Pittsburgh Post Gazette* represented the
governor's attitude in even bolder terms: "Leader Backs Advocate
of Vote Curb," with the subtitle, "Defends Right of Charlesworth
to Air Theme." (February 17, 1956.)

On the same day, the governor told his press conference that Dr.
Charlesworth "is one of the greatest political scientists today and is
making a great contribution to this administration. . . . What he
said has no relationship to what we are planning to do in this
administration. . . . I wanted creative conflict . . . stimulating view-
points. . . . I could have had an easy dreamy type of government,
as we had in the past, when people did little else in high jobs but
sign their names and shuffle along." Moreover, Leader pointed out
that "A number of other states require literacy tests of their voters,"
adding that Charlesworth knows because he ". . . holds top honors
in his field." See typescript of *Press Conference,* February 16, 1956,
pp. 7–9.

When Dr. Charlesworth finally resigned to return to his academic
duties some six months later, *The Harrisburg Evening News* on
August 30, 1956, printed a most eloquent tribute in its leading editorial:

"WE DOUBT if Pennsylvania soon will see the likes again of a
Dr. James C. Charlesworth in a position of major power and in-

The Office of Administration and its constituent bureaus faced their most serious resistance when they touched upon patronage, particularly in matters of personnel. Any survey or reform which involved the selection or retention of state personnel, or such matters as the placement of state contracts was apt to draw rapid fire from political leaders and other interests both inside and outside the legislature. Such opposition to a new bureau or activity is a normal expectation when administrative reorganization and reform are undertaken.[11]

CONCEPT OF PROGRAM EVALUATION

We have described Leader's Bureau of Program Evaluation, the sixth unit within the Office of Administration, as the most novel of his administrative reforms. This novelty rests superficially upon the fact that neither Pennsylvania nor any other state ever previously had a central bureau with exactly that name. More important is the question whether the function was also a new one. On this point the professors responsible for the origin of the bureau did not claim that the function was necessarily new or peculiar to this agency. Their concern was, rather, to restructure, identify, isolate, and dignify a function which they felt had too often been inadequately staffed or pushed into the background by the pressure of other duties at the governor's chair. As one of the originators put it, nobody doubts that a governor must have some means of evaluat-

---

fluence in its state government. . . . He leaves here in Harrisburg a governmental system which has been improved and made far more efficient because of what he was able to contribute to it."

[11] On the sabotage of reform in Philadelphia, see James Reichley, *The Art of Government, Reform and Organization Politics in Philadelphia* (New York, 1959).

ing his various programs. The only question is how or by whom such study and observation should be done.

One difficulty about the concept of program evaluation is that it straddles the traditional distinction between policy and administration. On the one hand, the governor cannot adequately perform his responsibility as chief administrator unless he has timely, accurate and relevant information on the various programs under his jurisdiction. On the other hand, such administrative data is also of prime importance for the governor's role as policy maker. Program evaluation thus occupies a kind of *terra incognita,* or no man's land, whose title is constantly shifting between the policy makers and the administrators. Such a dual position might have been banished as illegitimate in the days of the rigid dichotomy between politics and administration.[12] It is now generally conceded that not only the chief executive, but also most of the executive branch—at least all of the higher administrative officials—are involved in policy formation as well as policy execution. In fact, in any dynamic organization or ongoing human activity, the processes of deciding and of acting upon decision are so interwoven at points as to become part of a seamless fabric or web.[13]

[12] Politics is used here in the political science sense of "the formation of public policy." Wallace S. Sayre outlined the major landmarks of the post-war dissent from the politics-administration dichotomy in his paper, "Trends in the Study and Teaching of Public Administration," included in Stephen B. Sweeney, ed., *Education for Administrative Careers in Government Service,* pp. 37–43, at p. 40.

[13] This unity is one of the basic assumptions of Harold Stein's case-book, *Public Administration and Policy Development* (The Inter-University Case Program, New York, 1952.) The analysis of public administration in the Introduction is one of the clearest of this synthesis. (See page xvii.)

Most of those associated with the formation of the Bureau of Program Evaluation did not regard its function as primarily managerial. They thought of it as primarily an aid to the governor in his role as a major policy maker. Yet Governor Leader was not one to reach policy decisions and then give little thought to their implementation. He kept in touch with a vast amount of administrative detail. Thus his staff was always close to the pulse of daily operations. It was a constant problem for the Bureau of Program Evaluation to keep from being drawn into the vortex of administrative problems. The exalted position of "policy only" is always difficult to maintain, and this proved to be the case for the Bureau of Program Evaluation as well as for the governor. The record indicates, however, that the creation of a unit in the Governor's Office to study the substance rather than just the method or procedure of particular programs was of help to a governor such as Leader, who was constantly initiating or promoting new programs. The Bureau of Program Evaluation and the many *ad hoc* advisory groups working with it helped both to spearhead and to regularize Leader's initiative in many fields. Such a unit concerned with "what" rather than "how" represented an innovation in Pennsylvania government, as it would in many other jurisdictions.

Some of the originators of the bureau regarded program evaluation as one of the basic administrative processes. They believed such evaluation to be a necessary prelude to any effective program planning, as well as an indispensable guide for the formation of top policy. They had observed that the pressure of events upon a chief executive required that he have a regular, full-time staff to sift out program data, evaluate current operations, and weigh new program proposals. Only with such special help, they believed, could any governor decide upon relative priorities.

The argument for a separate bureau to do this job was based partly upon logic and partly upon strategy. Granted that existing staff groups might also evaluate various state programs, a separate agency was recommended in order to fix responsibility for program evaluation and keep it distinct from other functions. Program analysts could develop special skills and achieve the detachment needed to coordinate the information or "findings" of the various departments for the governor. A special agency for program evaluation would help to identify and clarify the function, as well as to emphasize its importance to the entire state governmental organization.[14]

The argument for supplying the governor with this type of staff arm was both a quantitative and a qualitative one. From the quantitative point of view, the sheer burden of the state administrative job is so overwhelming that new and special channels are required to reduce the bulk to manageable size. There was also the qualitative argument. No governor, mayor, or president can himself possess all the knowledge, skills and information needed to make wise and fully informed decisions on all the matters that clamor for attention. It was believed that a distinct staff for program evaluation might possess qualities not found in other agencies. One originator, for example, saw the need for a unit in the state government, where the political scientist could work as such, bringing to the administration not the viewpoint of a bureaucrat, civil servant, or practicing politician, but the perspective of a mature scholar trained in the larger problems of govern-

[14] Dr. Stephen B. Sweeney, interview, Harrisburg, August 25, 1959.

ment and society. Unlike the line official, he would be free from routine operations, able to view and reflect upon either particular programs or the total state operation from the viewpoint of public need. The concern of such an agency would thus not be limited to what the state was presently doing, but could also include some consideration of what the government ought to be doing.[15] In other words, a special agency could help the policy makers to direct their fire at substantive program matters. Its central location was particularly important for many of the public affairs concerns of the governor involving interdepartmental, if not interdisciplinary, activity.

Budget analysts presumably evaluate all programs as a part of the budgetary process. However, they start from the perspective of dollars, and usually face the problem of cutting, trimming or fitting various programs into their financial limits, ceilings, or priorities. Without denying the necessity for such fiscal operations, the sponsors of the bureau felt it was important to have others on the governor's staff who looked at programs on their merits, and who tried to develop priorities on the basis of public need, rather than first from the viewpoint of the budget-maker.[16] In other words, budget review usually stresses the efficiency with which a particular end is to be achieved, rather than the adequacy, the desirability or the wisdom of the object

[15] Dr. Harold F. Alderfer, interview, Philadelphia, October 6, 1959. This idea resembles what March and Simon have described as an "innovating" unit. James G. March and Herbert A. Simon, *Organizations* (New York, 1958), p. 184ff.

[16] Some twenty years ago, Dr. V. O. Key pointed to the same problem: "On what basis shall it be decided to allocate X dollars to activity A instead of activity B?" "The Lack of a Budgetary Theory." 34 *Amer. Political Science Review* (1940), p. 1138.

itself.[17] In this connection it is important to note that Leader's Bureau of Program Evaluation made an important contribution in the field of budgeting by helping to develop Pennsylvania's first genuine program budget.

Organization and methods analysts also examine administrative programs. They are supposed to ask what, when, where, how, and why about every program, but they are generally so busy drawing charts and mapping the where and how that they rarely, if ever, seriously raise the question "why" a certain program is undertaken.[18] The federal Bureau of the Budget has a special unit for legislative clearance. However, Leader's Buerau of Program Evaluation undertook to do something more than analyze legislative proposals. It was designed to conduct a "continuing review of program" from the viewpoint of advisable public policy.[19] Such a review differs from those undertaken solely in the interest of economy, efficiency, legality, or sound organization. It involves an exploration of the public policy consequences of present and possible future programs. These ideas by no means represented the total rationale for the Bureau of Program Evaluation, but they represented a basic core or cluster of purposes and assumptions to which many other ideas and concepts related.

METHOD

On the question of method, the bureau was launched before its founders had reached any consensus as to how

[17] Dr. John H. Ferguson, interview, State College, March 25, 1959.
[18] Dr. James C. Charlesworth, interview, Philadelphia, September 8, 1959.
[19] Based upon a discussion with Dr. Sweeney and Dr. Ferguson in Washington, D.C., September 10, 1959.

program evaluation should be done. One of them reported, "Our idea was to have a small unit, specially staffed, concerned with 'program' in the broadest sense of the word." [20] Thus part of the method was to secure as a director a mature person, knowledgeable in Pennsylvania government, and if possible, in comparative state administration as well. However, there were others who felt it was more important for the head of such a unit to have experience in the state administration than simply academic knowledge. One hoped that the new bureau might do research into the programs of other states in order to provide perspective on Pennsylvania's activities in various fields.[21] Another proposal was that as the bureau got under way, its staff might eventually specialize according to the various major program areas, such as social welfare, the regulation of economic activities, conservation, finance and other matters.[22] The bureau did not develop in this way, partly due to inadequate budget and staff, and partly due to the pressure of other problems to which it was assigned, as noted below in Chapter V.

One of the founders of the Bureau of Program Evalu-

[20] Dr. John H. Ferguson, interview, March 25, 1959.

[21] Dr. Charlesworth's view, as reported by Mr. David DeLong, a former program analyst, interview, Harrisburg, December 3, 1959.

[22] Dr. Thomas J. Davy, "How is Administrative Performance Measured." *Strengthening Management for Democratic Government,* American Society for Public Administration, Digest of National Conference (1959), p. 113. In his task force report to the Chesterman Committee (January, 1953), Dr. Charlesworth had made a similar proposal. Later, the Pennsylvania Commission on Governmental Reorganization proposed that the governor appoint six administrative assistants "to function as coordinators of related departments and agencies." *Recommendations to the General Assembly* (March, 1957), p. 12.

ation admitted privately that he really did not have a method for program evaluation, but expected the new unit to "play it by ear" to some degree.[23] One aspect of method which greatly affected the nature and scope of the agency was the question whether the bureau should do most of the program evaluation with its own staff, or whether it should concentrate on directing such activity by departmental personnel. During his term as director of program evaluation, Dr. Alderfer once suggested a decentralized operation, which suggestion was never fully implemented.[24] Thus the bureau was never actually able to embark upon a comprehensive evaluation of the entire state operation, such as might be implied in its mandate

[23] However, the files of the Office of Administration reveal the fact that various procedures for program evaluation were proposed, and ultimately some of these were adopted:

    (1) Establish a priority system for programs to evaluate.
    (2) Assemble available information on each [one chosen].
    (3) Establish a relationship with the program administrator and other interested parties concerned.
    (4) Establish a means for continuing program evaluation.

Undated memorandum to Dr. Ferguson, Leader Papers, c. July, 1957.

[24] His July 8, 1957, memorandum to Dr. Ferguson, Secretary of Administration, suggested, "That the Bureau . . . have an official contact in each department . . . through which it would work. This person shall be designated by the Secretary of the Department or the Executive Head of the agency as the Program Evaluation officer. He . . . would be mature enough to understand the workings of the department . . . and would help work on evaluation surveys made. In this way our staff of four could get more coverage." From the files of the Bureau of Program Evaluation, Harrisburg, under *Duties of the Bureau.* (Another memo in the same file indicated the major departments had been divided up for program purposes among three of the analysts of the bureau.)

to help establish "relative program priorities." [25] However, by means of a questionnaire the bureau secured some data for evaluation of all the departments and agencies under the governor's jurisdiction.[26] Moreover, the bureau's activities in the area of departmental reporting, including

[25] According to 93 *Pa. Manual*, p. 308, "The Bureau of Program Evaluation is responsible for providing the information and recommendations needed to determine relative program emphases. To do this it reviews the services provided by the Commonwealth, analyzes their objectives and purposes as well as the consequences of increasing or decreasing expenditures for each service. It suggests and evaluates proposals for new programs, making recommendations in relation to need and fiscal requirements. It also attempts to prune activities which have lost their usefulness and rearrange or eliminate activities that are out of balance with the overall objectives of the various agencies. One important phase of its function is to coordinate programs involving interdepartmental policies and activities and represent the Office of Administration in the work of special citizens' committees appointed by the Governor to study and develop program and policies in specific fields."

[26] *Program Evaluation Questionnaire* (from bureau files):

1. Cite fully constitutional, statutory authority for program.
2. Describe program clearly and concisely. (See '57 Budget.)
3. What are the objectives of this program?
4. What measurable units do you use to determine extent of this program: people served, forms processed, licenses, etc.?
5. What progress have you made toward achieving the objectives of this program especially during the last and present bienniums?
6. What unmet needs should be served by this program?
7. Any circumstances that will diminish need for this program?
8. Effect upon the welfare of the people of the Commonwealth if this program were to be abandoned or curtailed?
9. Statutory, administrative or other changes to strengthen this program: explain.
10. If program receives federal aid, can it be increased by state action?
11. Are there any new programs the state ought to inaugurate?

its study of state publications and statistics, its activities involving governmental reorganization, plus a number of its interdepartmental activities, all served to expand the influence of the bureau beyond what would seem likely in view of its limited staff.

Any attempt to formulate in advance a rigorous methodology for program evaluation (purely on the basis of *a priori* judgments concerning its proper role and function) might have been an unsettling and unsatisfactory experience. What the bureau did was to feel its way as problems arose to which it was assigned. Purists in the so-called "principles" approach to organization theory might be appalled by such a pragmatic approach to this new operation. However, recent writers, such as Herbert Simon, who emphasize careful description of administrative situations as a prelude to theory, would likely be more sympathetic to the bureau's pragmatic approach. This is another way of arguing that though the bureau's activity was novel, it was not doctrinaire, and for a picture of its method we must look at the activities of the bureau (Chapter V).

Part of the bureau's "method" was a function of its position in the hierarchy. The director of program evaluation participated with the other five bureau directors in the weekly staff meetings conducted by the secretary of administration. This gave him some picture of the difficulties encountered by the other staff arms. Thus in certain problem areas the Bureau of Program Evaluation was called upon to assist these coordinate units, such as budget and management methods, in the performance of their managerial functions. On other occasions the Bureau of Program Evaluation was asked to work on a problem in which the governor was particularly interested. Some of these were questions of top policy in areas such as migrant labor, correctional industries, forestry camps, education, or milk control. Other assignments can be described as more operational or administrative in nature, such as the reform of publications, statistics or biennial reports. Sometimes the director of program evaluation became the secretary of administration's specialist on program and policy proposals which were submitted to him by the governor. Other assignments originated with the secretary of administration, or on rare occasion, with the director of program evaluation himself, after clearance with his superior.

Program evaluation was not chiefly a library operation. It usually involved direct contact between the program analyst and the line departments involved. Another "method," if it can be called such, was employed in those cases where the bureau was serving chiefly as home base or coordinator for the various advisory committees and commissions. This activity was extensive throughout the Leader administration and of such significance that the serving of these groups alone would seem to be sufficient for such a unit within the Governor's Office.

ORGANIZATIONAL LOCATION

What is the validity of having such a special staff unit or position within the Governor's Office? Program evaluation could be and should be done to some extent by every line administrator. Why then a central staff for this function? In the preceding section it was argued that a special staff could reap the advantages of identification, specialization, direction, and detachment. There is, however, the question raised in the literature on the British cabinet secretariat and elsewhere whether such a staff unit creates problems of "layering." That is, did department heads feel that this bureau created an undesirable or unnecessary layer between them and the chief executive? Though a large evaluation bureau might raise this question, Governor Leader's Program Evaluation staff was so small that this problem did not generally arise. Department heads continued to have direct access to the governor on matters of importance to them. In a few cases where department heads became restive about an "outside official" investigating their programs, it was possible for the Secretary of Administration to send in budget examiners, whose role was better accepted—perhaps to gather some of the same information. If this had been done in many cases, the distinction between program analysis and budget examination would have been sacrificed, however.

The question of an appropriate staff for the governor must always be related to the immediate situation or to the governor's peculiar needs. Since the Leader administration was pioneering in so many program areas, special services were needed to staff such administrative energy and initiative. In such times when the temper is not one of stability, consolidation, or even retrenchment, there is urgent need for such specialized program and policy research.[27] As a member of Governor Rockefeller's staff in New York recently indicated, the proper staff for policy formation and program review varies with ". . . the character of the Governor, the administrative environment

[27] Viewpoint expressed by Dr. Sweeney, August 25, 1959.

within which the staff must operate, the competence of the personnel and other factors." [28]

EXPERIENCE IN OTHER STATES

Leader's experience with program evaluation is in line with, if not somewhat in advance of similar developments in other progressive states. In the nearby but somewhat smaller state of New Jersey, recent governors have preferred not to develop a large central staff. When Governor Meyner felt a need for specific program or policy research he simply called upon people in the department concerned.[29] On the other hand, the recent recession prompted Governor Meyner to establish an *ad hoc* group, known as the Governor's Economic Watch-dog Committee, composed of officials drawn from such agencies as the treasury, labor and industry, economic development, and employment security. Other subcommittees of the cabinet were established to deal with such problems as faculty salaries, juvenile delinquency, or problems of the aged. There was, thus, in New Jersey, no development of a regular program and policy staff within the Governor's Office, such as Governor Leader had. In fact, in many states the term program evaluation is not even known to the governors, and they

[28] Mr. Milton Musicus, "Staffing the Governor's Office for Program Planning and Review." Unpublished paper presented to American Society for Public Administration, Los Angeles, April 13, 1960.

[29] Mr. Ronald Zweig, assistant to Governor Meyner. Panel remarks on "Establishing Administrative Services for the State Executive," Fels Institute, October 6, 1960.

are not aware of the possible existence of such staff resources.[30] Thus in general,

> . . . state concern with over-all program evaluation at the
> top executive level is of comparatively recent origin, and we
> are still in the process of adapting state administrative struc-
> ture to the task.[31]

New York State has gone further in establishing a central
staff for program evaluation within the Governor's Office.
The secretary to Governor Rockefeller supervises three
staff units—the Program Section, the Reports Section, and
the Administration Section:

> It is their function to develop, review and recommend pro-
> grams to meet the needs of the state government, both as to
> policy and structural organization. They review existing pro-
> grams which cross departmental lines to insure proper coor-
> dination and eliminate overlap of functions. They serve as
> an effective linkage or relay station between departments and
> the Governor's Office. They analyze reports and data received
> from departments and are within easy reach of the Secretary
> and the departments to answer inquiries emanating from ei-
> ther direction.[32]

[30] Mr. John A. Donaho, unpublished paper presented to American
Society for Public Administration meeting, Los Angeles, April 13,
1960, representing John A. Donaho & Assoc., Baltimore.

[31] Mr. Marvin Meade, assistant director, Governmental Research
Center, University of Kansas. Panel remarks at the same meeting.
Unpublished typewritten copy on file at the Fels Institute.

[32] Mr. Milton Musicus, panel address on "Program Planning and
Review in New York State," at the same Los Angeles meeting. Mr.
Musicus is assistant secretary to the governor for administration,
State of New York, Albany.

The Program Section resembles Leader's Bureau of Program Evaluation. In addition, Governor Rockefeller has utilized program study groups or "task forces" composed of cabinet members, citizens, and specialists in various fields. Some forty of these were in operation in Albany in 1959 and their work contributed to many of the approximately one hundred seventy administration bills, about 140 of which passed the legislature. Governor Rockefeller relied also on his counsel, the lieutenant governor, the attorney general, the budget director and his staff, department heads, legislators, political leaders, and personal advisors for additional program and policy advice and review, as do most governors. Thus, even in a state such as New York which has a more elaborate central staff than most states, there is expressed the conviction that the advisory function cannot be institutionalized too far. On particular issues different groups of persons may be involved or consulted.

In some states program and policy review is treated as a part of management improvement and handled either by budget or by management methods personnel. Even New York's governor, who has a Program Section in the office of the secretary to the governor, delegates much of the more specific aspects of program review to the eleven management examiners located in the Budget Division's Administrative Management Unit.[33] Connecticut also has a Management Section, consisting of some eleven persons

---

[33] According to a comparative study prepared by the Budget Bureau, Department of the Treasury, State of New Jersey, *State Government Management Improvement Programs* (Trenton, 1958), p. 8.

under the budget director. However, it is reported that this unit does not concern itself with program and policy review except in response to a specific request for an opinion.[34] In California, the management improvement staff consists of thirty-nine persons, known as an Organization and Cost Control Division under the director of finance. This "central unit reviews programs and policies of state agencies and recommends legislative action when appropriate." [35] This unit is not a close parallel to the Bureau of Program Evaluation because it is not located within the Governor's Office and because it is cost-oriented, chiefly concerned with program and policy matters as they relate to legislation.

Ohio has a similar pattern with a Management Division within the Department of Finance, consisting of seven systems analysts and a secretary. North Carolina and Kansas have smaller administrative or management analysis units, which are apparently just getting underway. North Carolina's is located within the Department of Administration, while the Kansas unit reports to the budget director. Apparently the new units in these three states analyze methods and procedures from the point of view of efficiency, rather than programs and policies from the viewpoint of wisdom, adequacy or desirability, though Ohio claims to do some of the latter.

Though none of these states have a special bureau devoted to program evaluation as such, Pennsylvania's experience can be regarded as in line with the general trend to strengthen the governor by increasing his staff. By 1960,

[34] *Ibid.,* p. 30.
[35] *Idem.*

Pennsylvania had one of the largest governor's staffs in the union, consisting of more than one hundred persons, approximately eighty of whom were in the Office of Administration.[36] Pennsylvania is also currently in the forefront of the states by virtue of the large and fairly comprehensive scope of its Office of Administration. The Bureau of Program Evaluation was noted for its particular purpose and function, rather than for its size. It never had a complement much larger than five or six persons on its staff.

The Bureau of Program Evaluation represented a rather new idea in state administration. Management aids, such as the executive budget, fiscal, and personnel units, have long been accepted as essential to effective administration. Organization and methods units have also been regarded as an essential in all large scale organizations. However, the idea of establishing a special bureau in the Governor's Office concerned with the worthiness or desirability rather than management efficiency in the operation of programs was original with the Leader administration. Leader also utilized, as do other governors, judgments made by other line and staff officials, legislators, judges, politicians, recipients of service, newspapers, pressure groups, political parties, and by the informed public. Though many such views filter up to the governor on any heated issue, there remains, from the governor's viewpoint, the problem of balance and objectivity, plus other difficulties resulting from the prevailing political climate and the varying visibility of different state services or programs. Altogether, the theory of program evaluation was based upon the conviction that,

[36] Panel presentation by Mr. David R. Baldwin, Pennsylvania's budget secretary and deputy secretary of administration, at the Fels Institute, October 6, 1960 (Tape-recorded.)

. . . most important is a clear conception of objectives. Fuzzy-mindedness on the part of a chief executive and his key aides concerning objectives leads to endless confusion and frustration.[37]

Although the governor needs the best advice he can get for making these judgments, the selection and operation of such an advisory staff is not easy. Wisdom is not easily recruited, as Plato noted in his *Republic*. It was the conviction of the founders of the Bureau of Program Evaluation that such a "small and select staff headed by a broadly trained, mature and wise director . . . can do much to set the tone for the Governor's administration." [38]

Moreover, there is evidence that the general literature on public administration is pointing in this direction, as numerous observers, research agencies and scholars become more engrossed with the forces and procedures of decision-making.[39] Governor Leader's Bureau of Program Evaluation stands properly on the frontiers of this research, as an experiment in the procedures of decision-making. Here was an attempt to institutionalize some of the processes in the Governor's Office which bear upon top policy decision. Here was also an attempt to increase rationality at the apex of the state's political and administrative processes, by factoring some of the elements of decisions into systematic program data.

There are parallels here to the President's Council of Economic Advisers, which was established by the Full

[37] Panel remarks by Dr. John H. Ferguson at the 1959 A.S.P.A. convention noted above. (Los Angeles.)

[38] *Ibid.*

[39] See Paul Wasserman and Fred S. Silander, *Decision Making, An Annotated Bibliography.* (Ithaca, 1958.)

Employment Act of 1946.[40] However, this group was specialized in the sense that it dealt with only the economic area. Its scope was the condition of the national economy, rather than the adequacy, the wisdom, or the desirability of any particular governmental program—though this was also included in some of its findings and recommendations. Other parallels can be drawn at the federal level to the National Security Council and the former National Resources Planning Board. These two specialized in the areas indicated in their titles. There were other differences, such as the fact that the former council is an *ex officio* body consisting mainly of department heads. Program Evaluation was not an *ex officio* body, nor was it an economic research agency to prepare the governor's annual message on the economy. Nor does it seem likely that program analysts will soon become a new professional group, as the planners have become. The fact that the national planners were debudgeted in 1943 (except possibly for national defense purposes) is an indication of the risks of pushing too far the machinery for executive decision-making without a corresponding growth or acceptance of the idea in legislative circles.[41]

[40] See Stephen K. Bailey, *Congress Makes a Law* (New York, 1950), Corinne Silverman, *The President's Economic Advisers,* Inter-Univ. Case Program #48 (1959); and Edwin G. Nourse, *Economics in the Public Service: Administrative Aspects of the Employment Act* (New York, 1953).

[41] Pennsylvania has a legislative agency which makes some evaluation of state programs, at the request of and for the use of the legislators—The Joint State Government Commission, created in 1937. This agency, which corresponds to the legislative council in other states, has a staff of some forty-eight persons, most of them at the professional level. This agency made an extensive evaluation of the *School Health Services* (title of report, 39 pp.) for the 1955

The origin and rationale of the Bureau of Program Evaluation probably has much more in common with the Executive Office of the President, which was created in 1939, following the 1937 studies of the President's Committee on Administrative Management. That is, both the bureau and the Executive Office of the President were created in response to current thinking on the problem of executive leadership. Further evidence of such thinking can be found in other structures or experiments at both the federal and state level, which are beyond the scope of this book. It has been sufficient to indicate that the theory of program evaluation was in line with similar thinking on the problem of executive leadership at both federal and state levels.

---

legislative session. The report included a thorough evaluation of the present program, recommendations for change, with legislative proposals which were presented and adopted at the next session. This agency did not duplicate the work of the Bureau of Program Evaluation, since its work was limited to legislative inquiries. Interview with Mr. Guy W. Davis, counsel and director, Joint State Government Commission, Harrisburg, October 4, 1960.

CHAPTER V

MAJOR ACTIVITIES OF THE BUREAU
OF PROGRAM EVALUATION

The experience of the Leader administration with program evaluation can best be explained by looking at the specific activities undertaken. The activities of the Bureau of Program Evaluation were diverse and disunited. For present purposes they can be classified under five major headings:

1. In the area of departmental reporting.
2. In the area of governmental reorganization.
3. Substantive program appraisals.
4. Investigating proposals.
5. Matters of interdepartmental concern, including intergovernmental relations.

1. ACTIVITIES IN THE AREA OF DEPARTMENTAL REPORTING

The physical end product of most of the work of the Bureau of Program Evaluation took the form of reports.

Biennial Reports

When Governor Leader's preinaugural Advisory Committee made a survey of the major state departments, the inadequacy of departmental reports was specifically noted in twelve out of sixteen departments. Such reports as there were frequently were insufficient to permit an adequate appraisal of the department's objectives, programs or performance.[1] The Bureau of Program Evaluation undertook to systematize and improve these reports by prescribing a uniform outline to be followed by all departments and agencies under the governor's jurisdiction. New forms were prepared and supervised by persons in the bureau who were trained in governmental research. The purpose of this reform was to identify and present the program objectives and accomplishments of each department. The new forms began with a definition of the programs and services of each unit, followed by data on organizational changes, fiscal and personnel management. The latter part of each department's report was to deal with accomplishments in improving management methods and planning.[2]

[1] Biennial reports to the governor are required under Section 504 of the *Administrative Code,* and had been rather perfunctorily published as *Departmental Reports,* since about 1900. Recent editions of this series had consisted primarily of case decisions in workmen's compensation. In general, this series was quite unsatisfactory for purposes of administrative reporting.

[2] The outline for the new Biennial Reports was as follows:

    I. PROGRAMS AND SERVICES

        List programs and services carried on during the biennium which were authorized prior to the current biennium.

        List programs and services . . . authorized during the current biennium.

        State the objectives of each program and service mentioned above.

    II. ORGANIZATION

        Indicate organization changes made in the Department during the biennium and date of authorization.

    III. FISCAL MANAGEMENT

        See attached charts.

This new procedure resulted in reports which were much more valuable to the governor and his staff, aiding them in spotting lagging agencies and marginal units throughout the entire state administration. Such improve-

IV. PERSONNEL MANAGEMENT

See attached charts.

Describe personnel action taken during this biennium in recruitment of professional and technical assistance.

Explain the personnel action taken to improve supervision by bureau and division heads during this biennium.

Indicate action taken by your agency to initiate in-service training programs.

Describe the goals which you have for increasing or decreasing the number of employes and the amount of compensation during the coming biennium.

V. MANAGEMENT METHODS

Indicate what has been done in your agency during this biennium with respect to each of the following. Mention also the officer specifically charged with responsibility for each:

a. Developing forms control
b. Records management
c. Allocating space
d. Analyzing flow of work
e. Developing written procedures
f. Mechanizing procedure
g. Controlling supplies and property
h. Developing standards for work measurement.

Indicate what studies or plans are being conducted at present in your agency to improve methods.

VI. PLANNING

How successful have you been in achieving the objectives set forth for each of your programs and services?

Give your recommendations for improving the administrative organization and management methods of your department during the next biennium. Give your recommendations for improving your programs and services during the next two years (1957–59).

During the years 1959–63.

During the years 1963–67.

ment was essential if the governor was to be the chief administrator in fact as well as in name. These departmental reports not only provided the governor with raw materials needed for checking upon program performance; they also enabled him to make better judgment on matters of program priority. This matter of improving departmental reporting was part of the official mandate of the Bureau of Program Evaluation.[3]

In some cases, the bureau's program analysts actually sat down with line officials and helped them to identify and define their programs. This procedure helped to make the reports more comparable and of greater use to the governor. The bureau's next step was to compile, from these departmental reports, a general report tracing the objectives and the accomplishments of the administration during its first biennium:

In 1957, the Bureau gathered material from agency submission and wrote a *Biennial Report* on the policies and aims and their accomplishment in the Leader administration, as manifested in the activities of the agencies under the Governor's jurisdiction.[4]

Improved reporting was intended to serve not only the chief executive, but also to provide line administrators

[3] See the staff report, "Role of the Office of Administration." August, 1958: The objective of the Bureau of Program Evaluation is "To assist in developing programs and ensure that the programs of state agencies are mutually consistent and directed toward the achievement of the goals of the Administration." Of the eight "Duties" that follow, #7 is "To prepare general reports of programs and activities for the Secretary of Administration and the Governor."

[4] From a staff report, entitled "Accomplishments of the Bureau of Program Evaluation: 1955–1958" item #15. This thirteen page report lists fifty-three activities of the bureau.

with a broader perspective on their operations and to serve as a self-evaluating technique. This reporting reform also contributed materials for three other activities of the bureau—program appraisal, interdepartmental coordination, and the transition to the program budget. Each of these is discussed below.

The activity of the bureau in the field of departmental reporting went beyond the annual and biennial reports. It included a comprehensive survey of all the statistics and publications of the commonwealth. State publications and statistics represent special types of reports, which are designed for a much larger audience. The bureau was concerned with these, both as a service to the departments and to the public.[5]

STATISTICS

It became obvious to the bureau in the summer of 1955 that some evaluation of the statistical series of the commonwealth was needed. There had developed a great deal of duplication, since several departments were publishing

[5] The staff report on the Bureau's "Accomplishments . . . 1955–58" described this activity in the following terms:

#30. *Statistics and Publications.* In a joint venture of the Bureau of Program Evaluation and a Statistical Council appointed by the governor, commonwealth statistics have been subjected to thorough scrutiny. A Statistical Index was published in 1957 for the first time in many years in cooperation with the Department of Internal Affairs. The bureau has also had a hand in a comprehensive review of state publications. As a result of these activities, statistics will be more reliable, and publications more attractive and readable, and economies are expected to be made in both fields. Bureau personnel have also helped to compose publications to be distributed by the state on general information about Pennsylvania.

statistics about the commonwealth with little or no co-ordination, control review or supervision. Various departments simply issued a statistical bulletin when the time for the next issue became due. In many cases there were no qualitative standards, no revision of the mailing list for ten or twenty years, and no survey of the reaction of the users.[6] Consequently, with the help of the bureau, a Governor's Advisory Council on Statistical Information was established in the summer of 1955, "to study, review, analyze and improve the statistics of the Commonwealth." [7] This council was composed of some thirty-five specialists drawn largely from business circles, but also from some of the large universities, unions, and state and city departments. In announcing a meeting of this council for December 14, 1955, Governor Leader pointed out that many of the commonwealth's present statistical reports are prepared "without apparent rhyme or reason," and moreover, "no one uses many of them." The governor presented these five topics for the Council to discuss and make recommendations upon:

1. How useful are the statistics now assembled . . . to the public?
2. What statistical services and reports should be discontinued or consolidated?
3. How can statistical services and reports be improved?
4. What new statistical services and reports are needed?
5. How can . . . statistical services be better coordinated within Commonwealth agencies and with similar services of private parties?

[6] Interview with Dr. Ferguson at State College, Pennsylvania, March, 1959.

[7] *Press Release* #438, December 13, 1955, p. 1.

In preparation for this meeting, an index detailing some 120 separate commonwealth sources of statistics had been printed. According to the governor, this was the first such index printed since 1940. The index was then taken over and continued by the Department of Internal Affairs, which, under Section 1205 of the Administrative Code, has statutory authority to collect and prepare statistics and information.[8] In compiling the index of statistical sources, it was found that the state then employed 279 full-time employees in statistical activities, and that more than 1,300,000 separate releases were distributed by the state each year. The basic job was to see whether some of this volume of printed information could be consolidated, eliminated, reduced in content, and at the same time, improved.

However, after the Governor's Statistical Council had met and made their recommendations, the question arose as to whether the Director of Program Evaluation, as the agent of the governor, would have the legal authority to review, reject or approve the statistical publications of some of the statutory departments. It was felt by the governor that this bureau was the logical place for such review and coordination to be done. However, to man a continuing analysis, an additional staff of statisticians would be required, able, for example, to evaluate and coordinate the population statistics issued by the Departments of Health, Commerce, and Public Instruction. Ultimately, it was believed, there should be established within the bureau a coordinator of statistics, as well as a chief publications

[8] See *1960 Index of Statistical Sources for Pennsylvania,* 4th ed. Department of Internal Affairs, Bureau of Statistics (March, 1960), 12 pp. with index.

officer for the commonwealth, which, in fact, was the larger problem that the bureau now moved into.[9]

State Publications

On August 8, 1957, Dr. Ferguson, then secretary of administration, directed a memorandum to Dr. Harold Alderfer, his successor as director of program evaluation, asking for a "list of all publications of the Commonwealth accompanied by the following information:

1. Frequency of publication.
2. Number on the mailing list (and type of clientele).
3. Cost.
4. Recommendations for curtailment."

On September 3, Dr. Alderfer returned such a list, based upon a questionnaire which he had sent to all departments and agencies. In his covering letter, Dr. Alderfer said that it appeared Section 2406–J of the *Administrative Code* was not being followed, and that if it were, "a great deal of savings could be made." [10] Dr. Alderfer made these additional findings and recommendations as a result of his publications survey:

[9] Many sources on state government decry the deficiencies in state reporting and statistics. See W. Brooke Graves, *American State Government* (1953), p. 491.

As for the untidy character of criminal statistics in the states, see Thorsten Sellin, "The Uniform Criminal Statistics Act." *Journal of Criminal Law and Criminology*, Vol. 40, No. 6 (March–April 1950), pp. 679–700.

[10] This section provides that the Department of Property and Supplies shall sell all documents costing over ten cents. Other subdivisions of Section 2406 grant that Department broad powers to compile, edit, and distribute various publications, which authority had not been fully utilized. See also Tanger, Alderfer, and McGeary, *Pennsylvania Government, State and Local* (1950), p. 128.

1. Savings could be achieved by running mimeographed materials on both sides, though heavier paper would then be required.
2. Many persons on various Commonwealth mailing lists do not read the data sent to them. In a random check, . . . only one in ten did.
3. Data handed out to capitol tourists is mostly discarded.
4. Standards were needed to evaluate the usefulness of departmental publications.
5. A small subcommittee of our Interdepartmental Committee on Publications might well undertake the job of evaluation.[11]

The evaluation of publications continued to be an active concern of the bureau and of the Office of Administration for more than a year. At the governor's suggestion a committee consisting of the attorney general, the secretary of property and supplies and the secretary of administration picked up this problem and submitted a "Report on Publications" on July 10, 1958. This fifteen-page report included a scheme to eliminate duplicate or superfluous publications, by coding them into these four classes:

I–Should be continued in . . . the present or equivalent form.
II–Should be embraced in consolidated, or departmental report . . .
III–Should be discontinued.
IV–Subject to further justification.

[11] Memorandum to Dr. Ferguson, September 3, 1957, Leader Papers. Attached to this memorandum was a copy of the questionnaire sent to all departments. Other communications in the file to and from Mr. Randall show that the publications survey was of direct interest to the governor. Part of one message was in Leader's handwriting.

The secretary of administration circulated this report to the heads of all departments and agencies under the governor for their comments. This step stirred up considerable controversy in some departments, whose officials felt they were in a better position to appraise their publications than were members of the committee or the staff of the Office of Administration. However, since this evaluation had the strong support of the governor, changes were made in a number of the commonwealth's publication series. Moreover, steps were taken to establish publication standards, along the lines of the recommendations of the report.[12]

This work of the Bureau of Program Evaluation in

[12] The major recommendations of the Committee on Publications were as follows:

1. Every department and agency should submit an annual report to the Governor and the General Assembly, whether or not required by law. . . . Moreover, all purely quantitative reports now issued by . . . subdivisions should be confined to the annual report where possible.
2. Every report issued to the public should be basically educational in purpose, and should . . . set forth the reason for publication. . . . Statistical information should be subordinate. . . .
3. Reports should not contain names and pictures of officials, only official titles.
4. A Publication Officer should be established in the Governor's Office . . . to approve . . . reports reaching the public.
5. This officer should control . . . format, kind of paper, price, number of copies . . . but not the substance, purpose or style of reports.
6. . . . Maximum use should be made of state-owned reproducing machines. Also the needs of small agencies should be combined. . . .

Source: *Report on Publications (Circulated by Agencies Under the Governor)*. Commonwealth of Pennsylvania, July 10, 1958. (Mimeographed.)

helping to refurbish the commonwealth's statistics and publications is a good example of the function for which the bureau was created. Though such investigation and reform aroused some opposition within segments of the bureaucracy, it did result in lasting improvements in state information.[13] Most of the work of the Bureau of Program Evaluation in the area of departmental reporting was ultimately taken over by the departments themselves, as was true of many of the bureau's activities. Such a shift does not nullify the significance of the reform initiated by this central staff unit.

2. ACTIVITIES IN THE AREA OF GOVERNMENTAL REORGANIZATION

George Leader, like Gifford Pinchot, brought to the governorship a burning interest in governmental and administrative reorganization. Leader's preinaugural Advisory Committee had found ten or eleven of eighteen departments and agencies examined in need of basic changes in internal structure. When Leader took office top level reorganization began at once, beginning with the Governor's Office, as described in the preceding chapter. Some of this reorganization could be done by executive order, whereas other steps required legislation. Leader had considerable success with both types of reorganization— administrative and statutory.

[13] Particularly valuable is the new *Pennsylvania Statistical Abstract,* which was published for the first time in 1958 by the Department of Internal Affairs and has continued since on an annual basis. The same Department now publishes also a *Directory of State Publications,* periodically, in addition to its monthly bulletin, *Internal Affairs,* which was in its twenty-seventh volume in 1959.

The Reorganization Act of 1955

Leader's first message to the General Assembly, within a week of his inauguration, on January 24, 1955, was on the subject of reorganization.[14] His first administration bill, introduced into the General Assembly (H.B.1), was passed and became known as the Reorganization Act of 1955.[15] There was some controversy over the constitutionality of Leader's reorganization bill, which was patterned after the federal reorganization legislation. However, the legality of the bill was vindicated in a nine-page letter from Attorney General Herbert B. Cohen.[16]

On February 8, 1955, Governor Leader proposed a twelve-man commission to carry out the provisions of the proposed Reorganization Act, a plan which was also authorized.[17] Dr. Charlesworth served as executive director

[14] *Press Release* #10, January 24, 1955. See also the *Legislative Journal,* 1955 Session, on that day.

[15] Act #81, July 7, 1955. This Act authorized the appointment of a Commission on Governmental Reorganization, which was authorized to submit interim reports to the governor, in addition to a report to the General Assembly . . . proposing constitutional amendments, legislative enactments and administrative actions . . . See "Executive Recommendations #1–7," directed to Governor Leader, Commission on Governmental Reorganization, Commonwealth of Pennsylvania (undated, c. 1955), 7 pp., mimeographed. On November 15, 1956, the Commission submitted "Legislative Recommendations #1–11," 10 pp. (Mimeographed.)

[16] *Press Release* #30, February 2, 1955, contains the letter.

[17] Act of July 7, 1955, P.L. 256. The late Adjutant General Anthony J. Drexel Biddle, Jr. served as chairman of the commission, which included members of the Senate and the House, department heads, the governor's legislative secretary, a political scientist, and representation from the State Chamber of Commerce and the Joint State Government Commission.

of the commission and much of the staff work was done by persons connected either with the Governor's Advisory Committee or the Bureau of Program Evaluation. In fact, three of the four persons who ultimately became directors of program evaluation served as expert consultants to this commission.[18]

With the help of this commission and the Office of Administration, which served as its headquarters, a great deal of reorganization was accomplished during Leader's first biennium. The governor submitted eight reorganization plans to the 1955 General Assembly, during its long seventeen-month session. The legislature approved numbers 1, 2, 5, 6, and 8 and disapproved plans 3, 4, and 7.[19] The major changes were as follows:

Plan #1—Transferred the State Planning Board from the Department of Commerce, where it was created in 1949, to the Governor's Office. (Adopted June 7, 1955. 1955 *Pennsylvania Statutes* 2045.)

---

[18] Dr. Sweeney, original chairman of the Governor's Advisory Committee, served as principal consultant. Twelve additional consultants served also without compensation, and prepared reports on special fields in the summer of 1956. Dr. Ferguson, then director of program evaluation, prepared a "Report on Regulation of Milk," and other reports on agriculture and public utilities. Dr. Alderfer, his successor at the bureau, prepared a seventy-four-page "Report on Local Government" for the commission, and his successor, Dr. Christie, then at Lafayette College, prepared a thirty-one-page "Report on the Department of Labor and Industry." Other consultants, three of whom had also served the Governor's Advisory Committee, prepared reports on such fields as public health, welfare, recreation, education, conservation, public information, records, and fiscal administration. Mimeographed copies of all of these task force reports are located at the Fels Institute of Local and State Government.

[19] Plans 3, 4, and 7 were disapproved by the Senate, but only #7 was disapproved by the House. See *Purdon's Pennsylvania Statutes*.

Plan #2—Transferred certain functions of the Department of Public Instruction to the Department of State. (Adopted December 12, 13, 1955. 1955 *Pennsylvania Statutes* 2047.)

Plan #5—Transferred prison inspection from the Department of Welfare to the Department of Justice (a change which had been recommended by the Governor's Advisory Committee). (Adopted December 12, 13, 1955. 1955 *Pennsylvania Statutes* 2048.)

Plan #6—Transferred the State Athletic Commission from the Department of Revenue to the Department of State. (Adopted January 17 and February 4, 1956. 1955 *Pennsylvania Statutes,* 2049.)

Plan #8—Transferred the Surplus Property Disposal Division from the Department of Public Instruction to the Department of Property and Supplies. (In its new position, this operation was greatly expanded.) (Adopted January 30 and February 14, 1956. 1955 *Pennsylvania Statutes* 2051.)[20]

The director of program evaluation, as well as the secretary of administration, devoted a great deal of time and attention to the work of this commission. Reorganization plans were also cleared for form, content and strategy with such persons as the attorney general, the governor's legislative secretary and the departmental personnel involved. Reorganizations not requiring legislation were made in such departments as highways and public instruction. A major departmental reorganization took place in the latter part of Leader's term. This was the merger of the Departments of Welfare and Public Assistance, as described below (pages 173–180).

[20] Source, *History of Senate Bills and Resolutions,* 1955 Session. Later, the housing and redevelopment functions of the State Planning Board were transferred back to the Department of Commerce. P.L. 477, April 12, 1956, 1955 *Pennsylvania Statutes,* 1449, 1458.

To give further study to those reorganizations which would require constitutional amendments, Governor Leader secured legislative approval for the establishment of a fifteen member Commission on Constitutional Revision. This commission, chaired by Superior Court Judge Robert E. Woodside, and containing members of both political parties, functioned throughout the latter year and a half of the Leader administration. Its final report was issued in the early part of the Lawrence administration on March 9, 1959.[21]

Departmental Organization

The staff of the Bureau of Program Evaluation had less to do with the structural changes or proposed reorganizations on a grand scale, affecting the executive branch as a whole, than with matters of internal departmental organization:

The Bureau has played a signal part in the careful study that has been given the organizational structure of each agency

[21] See *Report of the Commission on Constitutional Revision.* Harrisburg, 1959, 226 pp. Also, Act of July 15, 1957, P.L. 927. Without waiting for the report of this Commission, some seven constitutional amendments were proposed to the 1957 session, of which two can be regarded as "reorganizations" in the broad sense of the term:

1. To make the attorney general elective.
2. To regulate the membership, powers, and duties of the Board of Pardons.
3. To provide for annual legislative sessions.
4. To liberalize the residence requirements for voting.
5. To increase the borrowing capacity of certain school districts.
6. To provide for the election of Supreme Court judges at large.
7. To lower the franchise to age eighteen.

of the Commonwelath. New organizational charts showing necessary revisions have been prepared for nearly all agencies and
approved by the Executive Board. With modern organization
the departments, boards, and commissions are in a better position to supply leadership and direction for their many important programs. Besides such overall guidance, the Bureau has
from time to time considered administrative changes in con-
junction with given agencies of even the smallest units, with
the aim of better operation in mind. For example, in the Department of Public Instruction various small groups who were
working on different facets of safety education were combined
into a new and comprehensive Division of Safety Education.[22]

The bureau operated in this field to provide the governor
(and his secretary of administration) information and
advice on problems of departmental organization, one of
the major responsibilities of a chief executive. No governor
in charge of an enterprise like the commonwealth of Pennsylvania can give adequate attention to the organizational
problems of such a vast structure without regular and
substantial staff assistance. Human organizations are of
such a nature that reorganization can never be done once
and for all. It is part of a continuing process, because governmental structures must be constantly fitted and adjusted
to changing needs and conditions.[23]
　　There were many problems of departmental organization which were joint concerns of the Bureau of Program
Evaluation and the Bureau of Management Methods,
though the latter unit was more apt to enter the problem
at a later stage, when an entire management survey was

---

[22] "Accomplishments of the Bureau . . . ," *op. cit.,* #2, p. 2.
[23] See Herbert Emmerich, *Essays on Federal Reorganization* (University, Alabama, 1950).

requested and authorized. The latter bureau also tended t
follow the more orthodox procedures developed by specia
ists in methods and procedures (O and M). The fact tha
various bureaus within the Office of Administration too
an interest in problems in particular departments mad
it difficult for the Bureau of Program Evaluation to estab
lish its separate identity. Thus, though many of the prob
lems tackled by program evaluation, such as the merger
were very important, few people in Harrisburg knew of th
bureau as such.[24]

The Merger

The merger of the Departments of Welfare and Publi
Assistance represents one of the major administrativ
reorganizations of the Leader administration, and its de
tails are still being worked out under the Lawrence ad
ministration. Welfare and public assistance were two o
the largest state departments, and their merger created on
of the largest state administrative departments in th
United States. A great deal of preliminary work was don
on the merger by Dr. Alderfer as director of program
evaluation and by Dr. Ferguson as secretary of adminis
tration.[25] Ultimately, the merger of two departments em
ploying more than 18,000 persons involved the time and
attention of many persons and groups outside the Bureau

[24] Based upon interviews in Harrisburg with Mr. Donald K. Pro
bert, assistant director of management methods, August 25, 1959
Dr. Seyler, April 8, 1960, and others.

[25] Dr. Alderfer worked on the merger for about six months. For
some time daily meetings were held with representatives of the two
departments and the Office of Administration. Interview with Dr
Alderfer in Harrisburg, December 3, 1959.

)f Program Evaluation. After the legislature had taken up
his question and created a Merger Committee, the bureau
continued to provide staff services and liaison among the
ecretary of administration, the legislative committee, and
he departments involved. The merger activity was so
comprehensive that it is difficult to extract from the record
:he question of the bureau's contribution or influence
upon the total operation. However, the fact that many
persons outside the bureau undertook the substantive
:ask of working out the merger does not invalidate this
subject as an example of program evaluation. Even though
the center of gravity of this activity shifted to other loci,
:he bureau made a conceptual contribution, particularly
at the preliminary stages.[26]

The idea that these departments should be consolidated
had been expressed in various places for some time. To
begin with, very few other states maintained separate departments for welfare and public assistance.[27] The most
concrete explanation for two departments in Pennsylvania
was that under federal law public assistance had to be

[26] From a practical point of view, no one would expect a small
bureau of five or six persons to handle all the negotiations for such
a vast undertaking.

[27] It was frequently asserted in the merger discussions that Pennsylvania was the only such state. However, Leader's secretary of
welfare, Mr. Harry Shapiro, indicated (in an interview with the
writer in Philadelphia, October 13, 1959) that two states had separate departments—Pennsylvania and Illinois.

According to *Book of the States, Supplement* II, July, 1959, separate departments are maintained by Illinois, Kentucky, and possibly
Oklahoma. (Two agencies are named, but not two directors.) However, unification had been recommended in Illinois by the Commission to Study State Government, *Report to the General Assembly*.
(Springfield, Illinois, December 1950), p. 10.

under the merit system. Most of the Department of Welfare was not under the merit system until after the merger had taken place. Since Pennsylvania's organization was somewhat unique, there was always the presumption that waste and duplication might be avoided if these two departments devoted to meeting the needs of persons and families were consolidated. At least persons concerned with administrative improvement were quick to point out the advantages that might be gained from an integrated management. Dr. Charlesworth and the Chesterman Committee, for example, had specifically recommended such a merger in 1949 and 1953. However, it was one thing to have a particular change recommended for some years, and quite another thing for the governor to decide to act upon such a recommendation, with all the political implications which might be involved. It was in this area between "recommendation" and "policy decision" that the bureau first played an important role.[28]

Preliminary work was undertaken by the bureau to investigate the program, policies, and desires of the departments involved—in order to anticipate areas of agreement and areas of potential conflict. One of the problems, for example, was to reconcile the interests and claims of the mental health groups with those of the welfare groups. Thus, at the outset, the biggest questions were conceptual. After a basic ideological framework for the merger was hammered out in these sessions with the bureau, it then became a problem of securing acceptance and implementation of the recommendation. Later, there were problems

[28] Interview with Dr. Ferguson at State College, Pennsylvania, December 12, 1959.

of organization, personnel, equipment, field offices, records, budget, accounts, supervision and other matters, which in some areas are still being worked on in 1960.[29]

Quite independently of these discussions, a merger bill was introduced into the 1957 session of the General Assembly, which had an interesting history. The original House Bill 1572 was introduced by members of the party in opposition to the governor, with some malice, to deliver a crushing rebuke to the secretary of welfare, who had offended the legislators (chiefly on budgetary and personnel matters) on several occasions. This bill would have abolished the Department of Welfare and would have distributed its functions among three or four other departments. After many changes, involving at least five different printings, the merger bill passed the house and went to the senate, where it was reported out of committee. According to the governor's legislative secretary:

We observed this, and felt it might pass the Senate and have to be vetoed. Yet, we felt a veto should be avoided. . . . Recalling that many citizens felt that Welfare and Public Assistance were related and should be joined, we decided to consider shifting this bill, to effect such a merger. . . . We asked the secretary of administration to call all citizens' groups involved, to see if they were interested. They were, so we got together and created a new bill—actually in the form of an amendment, although we crossed out every line.[30]

[29] Interview with Dr. Christie in Harrisburg, August 25, 1959. Dr. Christie added that one way the bureau assisted in the merger was in "helping the departments to identify and define their program goals."

[30] From an address given by Mr. Henry B. Leader at the Fels Institute, University of Pennsylvania, November 12, 1959. (Tape-recorded.)

The substitute bill was then turned over to a member of the Department of Justice, who happened to be a Republican, to explain to the senate. It was accepted as an amendment, and with the concurrence of the house and the governor, it became the law. House Bill 1572, which had been simply a "ripper bill," was completely changed in the process. The new bill was appropriately enacted as a part of the Administrative Code. Moreover, the new bill provided for an official committee to work out the merger in a systematic way, whereas the original bill undertook to merge the various functions summarily. The merger law is a brief authorization without any crippling provisions or limitations.[31]

Pursuant to this act, a Merger Committee was appointed by Governor Leader in the fall of 1957.[32] This committee had available several evaluations of the situation in welfare and public assistance over the last twenty-five years or more. They consulted, for example, the reports of:

1. The Goodrich Committee on Public Assistance on Relief, December 31, 1936.
2. The Special Advisory Committee on Medical Care, June 15, 1936.

[31] See Act 390, 1957 Session.

[32] The committee consisted of twenty-seven prominent citizens under the chairmanship of Mr. Thomas B. Harvey of Philadelphia and the vice-chairmanship of Dr. Stephen B. Sweeney. See *Press Release* #A385, October 13, 1957. The committee prepared a Statement of Mission on December 3, 1957, and submitted a plan for implementing the merger by June 1, 1958. See its *Interim Report* submitted to the governor on April 1, 1958. This report was reprinted in two *P.C.A. Reports,* Pennsylvania Citizens Association for Health and Welfare, April 14, 1958. The next issue (April 28) carried Appendix A of the interim Report, "The Allocation of Functions Among Major Organizational Units." Additional data on the merger appeared in subsequent issues over the next two years.

3. Kenneth Pray's "Survey of Fiscal Policies of State Sub-sidies to Private Charitable Institutes," December, 1922 (one of Pinchot's reports).
4. The Sterling Report (Joint Legislative Committee on Finance), 1934.
5. A University of Pennsylvania faculty study on Institu-tional Medical Care, January, 1957.

The Merger Committee also indicated in its final report that it gave "careful consideration to a preliminary report prepared by a staff group representing the merged depart-ments and the Governor's Office of Administration." [33] The Governor's Committee apparently retraced some of the ground already covered by the Bureau of Program Evaluation. It explored in detail the functions and pro-grams of the departments to be merged, and finally pre-pared a new organizational chart, together with a descrip-tion of the responsibilities of every major unit within the new Department of Public Welfare.[34]

Finally, the Merger Committee recognized that the job of evaluation and reorganization was by no means com-

[33] *Report* of the Governor's Committee on Merger of the Depart-ments of Welfare and Public Assistance, February 9, 1959, 40 pp., at p. iv.

[34] The committee's *Report* was divided into two phases, the first dealing with the organization of the new department, and the sec-ond dealing with the "Policies and Programs Needed to Complete the Merger." The committee also specified "changes in practice in the two . . . departments" necessary to complete the merger. This section included recommendations dealing with personnel, fiscal matters, hospital and medical services, boards, committees and com-missions, reassignment of functions, and local administration. Strik-ing among these proposals was the advocacy of a "Department-wide" merit system (which was adopted), and also the proposed transfer of "ten state-owned hospitals . . . to local ownership." See *Report* . . . , pp. x, 24ff.

pleted when it closed its books in the spring of 1959. It recommended to the legislature a "codification of the State's various welfare laws," together with specific changes, including the establishment of "a public commission . . . to prepare a plan for the decentralization of responsibility for welfare services." The *Report* also advocated "an advisory committee for each major program area and an advisory board for the total department," to replace a number of separate "boards, committees, and commissions now attached to the central headquarters of the Department." [35]

From this brief survey of a very complex matter, it can be seen that the merger activity represented not only administrative reorganization, but also program evaluation, as defined by those responsible for the establishment of the bureau. The merger required a comprehensive survey of the policies and the programs of two fairly large departments, followed by "retooling," in order to fit these diverse activities into a new organizational structure. The Bureau of Program Evaluation did preliminary work on the conceptual basis for such a reform, and continued to provide some staff and liaison services for the Merger Committee. However, the assignment was too large and too complex to be completed by the bureau under its own steam. After legislative approval was obtained, new interdepartmental

[35] *Report* of the . . . Merger Committee, pp. 30–40, and "Summary," p. x. One reason the merger was so complicated is that the new department embraces six major programs, all of which are somewhat different. There was some dispute over the question of establishing regional offices. Such branch offices were finally authorized but few were in operation by 1960. Address by Mrs. Ruth Horting, secretary of the new Department of Public Welfare, at the Fels Institute, April 21, 1960.

and *ad hoc* structures were created to carry the work forward. The function of program evaluation proved to be larger than could be handled by the bureau, but it served as an initiator and a home base for the whole operation. The bureau's role embraced, alternately, two different functions: policy advice to the governor and staff assistance to the line agencies. In actual practice, these two were often interrelated.

3. SUBSTANTIVE PROGRAM APPRAISALS

In both of the preceding categories, administrative reporting and reorganization, the appraisal of substantive programs was required. We consider now some examples of such appraisal for its own sake, rather than as a part of a larger reorganization program. Such activity is embraced in two of the specific duties included in the official mandate of the Bureau of Program Evaluation:

#. To analyze and evaluate existing and proposed program plans, capital improvement plans, and program performance in terms of legislative requirements, administrative goals, current needs, personnel, material and financial requirements, available resources, and administrative propriety.

#4. To direct, coordinate or conduct studies of specific program areas at the direction of the Governor, or the Secretary of Administration, or at the request of agency heads.[36]

Although the Bureau of Program Evaluation never had the staff resources and time needed to undertake an evaluation of all the commonwealth's programs, a number of them were analyzed. The bureau undertook, either on its

[36] "The Role of the Office of Administration," staff report, August, 1958.

own or with the aid of outside consultants, investigations of the commonwealth's programs, for example, in the following areas: milk control, insurance, education, recreation, migrant labor, correctional industries, industrial development and forestry camps. We consider first the case of milk control.

MILK CONTROL

For various historical and political reasons, Pennsylvania has an independent Milk Control Commission, just as it has special commissions for the protection of fish and game. Pennsylvania's Milk Commission fixes and controls both wholesale and retail milk prices.[37] The three-member commission is usually manned by persons of agricultural background who are also politically prominent. The consumer's interest has no special representation. A study by the Bureau of Program Evaluation disclosed a rather wide price disparity among eighteen or nineteen regions for no apparently valid reason.

Shortly after a drought in 1957, the commission granted a further increase in price, which created a minor administrative crisis in Philadelphia. Pennsylvania milk was now so much higher than that of surrounding states that the federal government threatened to cancel its marketing

[37] First established on a temporary basis in 1934, the commission was made permanent in 1937 (Act #105, P.L. 417, as amended 1941, 1943, and 1947). Thus, by Leader's term, the commission enjoyed broad powers to "supervise and regulate the entire milk industry of the Commonwealth, including all matters pertaining to the production, manufacture, processing, storage, transportation, disposal, distribution and sale of milk and milk products . . . for the protection of health and welfare." 93 *Pa. Manual*, p. 358.

agreement in the greater Philadelphia area. Such a step seemed certain to have a negative effect upon the Leader administration. Aside from the economic loss, such a breakdown of intergovernmental cooperation would have been an embarrassment to the governor.[38] It would provide political ammunition for the rurally dominated Republican Senate, whose members would probably note that two of the three milk commissioners were Leader's democratic appointees. This case illustrates how what is presumably an administrative routine or detail can suddenly become an important policy question with political implications, upon which the governor needs authoritative advice. Ultimately, the state prices were lowered enough to satisfy the federal authorities, so the immediate crisis was averted.

The subject of milk control was sufficiently important to be given attention by the Governor's Advisory Committee, by the Commission on Reorganization, and by two bureaus in Leader's Office of Administration—the Bureaus of Program Evaluation and Management Methods.[39] Program evaluation was the first of these bureaus to take up

[38] Although Pennsylvania is usually regarded as an industrial state, it is also an agricultural state, and milk is an important part of its economy. Over a third of its agriculture income is from dairy products, a field in which Pennsylvania ranks fourth in the nation. See E. S. Deatrick, *The Pennsylvania Citizen* (New Brunswick, New Jersey, 1958), p. 146.

[39] The milk industry has also presented important questions of constitutional law, such as the limits of interstate commerce, the limits of the police power of the states, and, at one time, the doctrine of "business affected with the public interest." See *Nebbia* v. *New York*, 291 U.S. 502 (1934), *Hood* v. *DuMond*, 336 U.S. 525 (1949), and in the case of Pennsylvania, *Milk Board* v. *Eisenberg*, 306 U.S. 346.

the milk problem, and its activity was summarized in a staff report in the following terms:

A research project of appreciable scope was carried out by the Bureau to make possible a stable base for milk prices in the state. Various state agencies, as well as several departments of the Pennsylvania State University, were consulted. The Bureau is presently serving as liaison with the Commonwealth's permanent consultant on milk problems.[40]

Here, as in other cases, the bureau utilized the services of various experts and consultants beyond the resources of its own limited staff. For example, shortly after the price-fixing crisis in the Philadelphia area, Governor Leader set up a North-Eastern Pennsylvania Committee on Milk Marketing, which at the outset operated directly out of the Governor's Office.[41] After the dispute with the federal authorities was settled, Dr. Christie of the Bureau of Program Evaluation, arranged committee meetings and reported the findings to the governor through the Office of Administration. Various milk marketing experts at Pennsylvania State University met with Dr. Ferguson, representatives of the bureau and the governor to discuss advisable changes in the state's milk prices. These discussions raised the policy question as to whether it would be better to discontinue retail price-fixing, retaining such controls only over wholesale prices. Despite the possible merits of such a step from the technical or substantive point of view, it was decided to continue both types of control partly for political reasons. Farmers, who were well represented in the Senate,

[40] "Accomplishments of the Bureau . . . , 1955–58," *op. cit.,* #20.

[41] Mr. Mark Robinson, a dairy farmer from Northeastern Pennsylvania, served as chairman of the committee.

would certainly object if retailers were decontrolled, while control of the producers was continued.

In this case, the substantive or technical advice prepared or collected by the governor's staff, and by the bureau had to be tempered with political considerations. Yet one result of the bureau's exploration of the milk control program was the activation of the Milk Commission's Advisory Committee. This committee was composed of fourteen producer representatives and fourteen dealer representatives. Members of the governor's staff were quite eager to have this committee do an effective job, and were apparently not disappointed.[42]

The fact that Leader himself was a farmer may have resulted in greater attention to this type of problem than would otherwise have been the case. Agricultural problems were discussed in several of his speeches to the General Assembly, and milk price-fixing became the subject of two or three of Leader's press releases during the first biennium.[43]

Other substantive aspects of milk control were also investigated by the bureau. For example, on October 4, 1957, representatives of the Governor's Office were conducting a survey by making field purchases of milk, presumably

[42] See 93 *Pa. Manual,* p. 358.

[43] Leader's General Assembly speech of March 28, 1955, *Press Release* #125, and his State of the Commonwealth Message, January 11, 1957, *Press Release* #878, both dealt with farm problems. His message to the legislature of January 16, 1956, was entirely devoted to farm problems. See *Legislative Journal,* 1955 Session, or *Press Release* #480, analyzing some ten agricultural bills recently introduced.

Press Releases #118, 195, and 258 (March 24, May 19, and July 6, 1955) discuss the milk problem, particularly as related to the price paid by state institutions.

to compare prices.[44] Subsequently the Milk Control Commission invited the secretary of administration to make a comprehensive management survey. The survey was made late in the Leader administration. As a result of all these activities, carried out under the auspices of the Office of Administration, the policy issues involved in milk control were clarified, and the commission's regulatory program was better handled.[45] Steps were also taken to aid the industry by promoting the consumption and sale of milk. With the active support of the Governor's Office, automatic milk dispensers were installed in state government offices, schools, and elsewhere throughout the state. This milk marketing program was also reported to be successful.

INSURANCE

Insurance is another area where considerable program evaluation was done under the Leader administration, and where, as a result, important changes were made. Most of this appraisal involved the commonwealth's own insurance practices and coverage, rather than the regulatory operations of the Department of Insurance, as such. Just as the milk control operation received special attention partly because Governor Leader was himself a farmer, so the area of insurance received special attention partly because Dr. Sweeney, one of the originators of the Bureau of Program Evaluation, was formerly a professor of insurance at

[44] Leader Papers, subject file #63, under Ferguson, a communication to the governor on the milk survey. Further data on the milk problem also appears in the Committee–Commission Report compiled by the Bureau of Program Evaluation in the spring of 1958. See "Accomplishments of the Bureau . . . ," *op. cit.,* #21.

[45] Based upon several interviews in Harrisburg, with both the bureaus involved, August and December, 1959.

the University of Pennsylvania, and saw in the appraisal of insurance practices a proper example of the function for which the Bureau of Program Evaluation was created. The state's insurance policies came to Dr. Sweeney's attention by way of the Governor's Advisory Committee, of which he was chairman. As Dr. Sweeney later characterized the matter:

> We who had been in the insurance field just felt that the whole system was bad—much favoritism, dealing with a handful of local agents at high fees, providing separate coverage for each automobile. . . . Several of us just saw the whole program as unsound and unsavory.[46]

The work of evaluating the state insurance program was done largely by persons recruited by Dr. Sweeney for the Advisory Committee's Subcommittee on Insurance Practices, including the late Dean Kulp of the Wharton School, Dr. Howard Teaf of Haverford College, Mr. Clayton E. Moul, and others with whom Dr. Sweeney had been professionally associated for many years.[47]

The work on insurance practices got under way very early in the Leader administration, partly because Governor Fine had failed to designate the brokers, as had been the practice, in the month of December, 1954. Thus, according to the press, Leader inherited a "substantial nest egg" of insurance commissions to be designated.[48] The

[46] Interview at Washington, D.C., September 10, 1959.

[47] See Clayton E. Moul's report, "Insurance and Bonding Program of the Commonwealth of Pennsylvania," 25 pp., undated and unpublished, in the files of the Governor's Advisory Committee, Fels Institute.

[48] "State Cuts Fees on Insurance to Favored Few." Philadelphia, *The Evening Bulletin* (June 5, 1955), article by Duke Kaminski, pp. 1, 2.

subcommittee on insurance worked rapidly and issued a sixteen-page "Report and Recommendations" on May 31, 1955, just a little more than four months after Leader took office.[49] The extent of this study was not generally known, since the report was confidential. In scope, the report covered the state's automobile liability insurance, fidelity bonds, and fire insurance (for the State Liquor Control Board). Complete data was presented on the statutory requirements, present coverage, types of contracts, bidding practices, companies patronized, premiums, commissions, cost to the state, and recommended changes. A new insurance program, resulting from this study, was then prepared, cleared with the secretary of administration, the attorney general, and approved by the governor early in June, 1955.

As announced to the press on June 4, the new insurance program was estimated to save the State approximately $200,000 per year.[50] A major part of the savings resulted from a reduction in brokers' commissions, which had been handed out on a patronage basis since the Martin administration, and were reported to have run as high as twenty-five per cent in recent years. Leader decreed that no contract should allow commissions in excess of fifteen per cent. Moreover, considerable savings resulted from consolidating the policies and the coverage, so that whereas more than a dozen companies received the business before, the new plan called for about four companies "to handle

[49] See Insurance Advisory Committee, *Report and Recommendations,* May 31, 1955 (Confidential). This was a condensation of a forty-five-page typewritten report, which also appears in the files of the Governor's Advisory Committee, at the Fels Institute.

[50] Governor Leader indicated that subsequent insurance reforms resulted in even greater savings. Interview in Dover, August 14, 1960.

the whole deal." [51] The insurance appraisal continued throughout Leader's term, along the lines already indicated. For example, two years after the initial study, another report was sent to the governor on insurance practices by the Office of Administration. According to this report of March 14, 1957:

The Commonwealth is now purchasing employee fidelity bonds at less than a quarter of the annual cost before 1955, and the coverage has increased tenfold.

Before 1955, the state purchased individual bonds of the faithful performance type for about 3,000 employees, most of them for the minimum coverage of $1,000 or $1,667. By 1957, the state was purchasing a single blanket fidelity bond, covering some 40,000 employees, each for at least $10,000, and the cost to the state was only 25.9 per cent of the former cost.[52]

The insurance study and reform illustrates the possible significance of program evaluation when done under competent auspices. At least one of the bureau's founders describes this activity as an example of program evaluation pursued with considerable rigor by persons who could be regarded as outside consultants or professional experts for

[51] Philadelphia, *The Evening Bulletin* (June 5, 1955), p. 1. A saving of about $135,000 was to result from buying casualty insurance on some 9,000 state vehicles on a fleet basis. Another $28,000 was to be saved yearly by securing blanket coverage of state employee security bonds. Other savings of $30,000 yearly were to result "from reshuffling the fire insurance policies of the State Liquor Control Board." *Ibid.*, p. 2.

[52] Unpublished report of March 14, 1957, in the files of the Insurance Advisory Committee, at the Fels Institute. The premium cost was $53,768 in 1954, as opposed to $13,910 in 1957, according to this report to the governor. See also *supra*, p. 59.

the Bureau of Program Evaluation. Since the bureau itself lacked the resources for such an appraisal on its own, the work was done for the bureau and for the governor by way of volunteer or citizen participation. The bureau preserved the records and findings of this group and made them available to the secretary of administration and to the governor.[53] The bureau also helped to prepare some press releases on aspects under the province of the secretary of administration.

EDUCATION

Governor Leader and his principal aides took great interest in the state's educational programs at all levels. It should be recalled that George Leader had prepared for a teaching career in his undergraduate work at the University of Pennsylvania. This gave the governor some specialized knowledge of the educational field. More important, as governor, Leader had surrounded himself with a "brain trust" of college and university men from the very beginning.[54]

The Leader administration went into the evaluation of the commonwealth's educational programs in a quite comprehensive way. This appraisal was described as long overdue, since Pennsylvania had for some time lagged behind

[53] See files of the Bureau of Program Evaluation, under Insurance, 1955–59. Also, see the unpublished Committee–Commission Report, prepared by that bureau in the spring of 1958. Both of these are now located in the newly consolidated Bureau of Program and Management.

[54] Note particularly the academic persons attached to the Governor's Advisory Committee.

other states in such matters as teachers' salaries, recruitment and training, school construction, and school district reorganization. There was also need for curricular revision and for special classes for handicapped children. All of these problems received special attention by the Bureau of Program Evaluation and by various educational advisory bodies whose work the bureau coordinated.

The Bureau of Program Evaluation undertook an evaluation of the educational situation in at least a dozen different program areas. For example, soon after his appointment as director of program evaluation, Dr. Ferguson prepared and sent to Henry B. Leader, the governor's legislative secretary, a memorandum outlining Pennsylvania's rank among the forty-eight states in per capita expenditures in fifteen major areas, including several categories of education, welfare, public assistance, highways, and natural resources. This study showed that Pennsylvania ranked thirtieth among the states in general expenditures for education, seventeenth in average salaries for classroom teachers, twenty-seventh in state contributions for current expenses and capital outlay for education, and forty-fifth in per capita expenditures for state institutions of higher education, in the year 1954.[55] Such a comparison of Pennsylvania's standing among the other states was one of the specific purposes for which the Bureau of Program Evaluation was established.

The bureau also "made an extensive study of ways to improve the effectiveness of the Bureau of Special Services in the Department of Public Instruction."[56] That bureau

[55] Leader Papers, File #63, under Ferguson.
[56] "Accomplishments of the Bureau . . . ," *op. cit.,* #53 (p. 13).

supervises the instruction of handicapped children, which was one of Leader's major program emphases. The Bureau of Program Evaluation helped to provide qualified staff for the handicapped program by furnishing job specifications modifying the administrative structure, and by giving some program direction in this area.

Such work with the Department of Public Instruction was but a part of a much larger program to improve the lot of the handicapped in many areas. Here again, personal experience brought this need to the governor's immediate attention, since one of his own children was slightly handicapped. Pointing out that "one out of every five children suffers from some kind of mental or physical handicap," Leader pressed repeatedly for more special classes for these children.[57] In support of this program, the governor took to the stump repeatedly, and appealed for the handicapped in more than forty speeches during the next two or three years, all of which were released to the press. In Philadelphia, for example, Leader told Labor's League for Political Education to "put the blow torch on the General Assembly" on half a dozen subjects, one of which was the handi-

[57] The governor provided the facts and figures in his address to the Pennsylvania State Education Association, *Press Release* #873, December 28, 1956, pp. 6, 8. Leader pointed out that in less than two years he had increased the number of special classes for the handicapped from about 1,000 to 1,845, serving at that time about 67,000 children. The number of mentally retarded children receiving special training was increased from one-fifth of those in need to about one half of those in need since he took office in 1955. Leader said, we still "need 1,307 teachers for the mentally retarded . . . 135 speech and hearing teachers . . . 64 for the physically handicapped, 21 to teach the blind and 32 to teach the deaf. These are our rock-bottom . . . requirements."

capped children, whom the governor now described as "victims of Old Guard, Republican obstructionism." [58]

In response to this pressure, the General Assembly passed a law making special classes mandatory for the first time, and provided state reimbursement for the cost of such training. The legislature also authorized the General State Authority to establish three new institutions for retarded children, in western, central, and eastern Pennsylvania. Each of these was expected to cost about ten million dollars and to provide about one thousand beds apiece. Another law[59] enabled the Department of Public Instruction to employ professionally trained personnel to assist with the expanded program for handicapped children. In April, 1956, Leader proclaimed "Free School Week," declaring that now the commonwealth was going to provide free schooling for every Pennsylvania child for the first time.[60] The next year, Leader followed up this program by appointing a Governor's Committee for the Handicapped, which subsequently served as a focal point for a number of these efforts. This advisory committee, like many other similar ones, operated as an adjunct to the Bureau of Program Evaluation.

In December, 1957, Leader told the State Educational

[58] Speaking of the "26-man roadblock in the Senate," the governor remarked, "You can't do business with dinosaurs. . . . They are powerful, but not renowned for brain power! . . . We've got too many of them in our legislature. . . ." *Press Release* #519, February 26, 1956.

[59] H.B. 1641 (Act 429), March, 1956.

[60] Address to the Pennsylvania Association for Retarded Children, Inc., Harrisburg, May 18, 1956, *Press Release* #645, 7 pp., *passim. Cf.* Leader's address the year before to the Pennsylvania Society for Crippled Children, *Press Release* #198, May 20, 1955.

Association that the state "now has roughly 100,000 children in classes for . . . the visually handicapped, the hard of hearing, the physically handicapped, the handicapped in speech." [61] This included programs in sixty-one of the sixty-seven counties, and embraced about twice as many as had such training four years earlier, when only three counties maintained such classes. However, Leader said the job was still only half done, since it was estimated that Pennsylvania must have some 200,000 children in need of such facilities. The legislature also authorized $1.3 million for special training facilities in the state teachers' colleges, to train the teachers, therapists, school psychologists, and others for this special education program.

Such a rapid expansion of the state's program in the field of special education required a great deal of research into the commonwealth's present and past program, its adequacy in terms of the total need, the extent to which such facilities are provided in other states, and the administrative, legislative and fiscal implications or requirements for a more adequate program, at the state, county and local level. Such a comparison of what the state "does do" with what it "should do" is held to illustrate program evaluation in its purest form.[62]

The careful attention given to this program area produced some results. In the closing months of his term, Governor Leader issued a special commendation for ten counties, which had developed outstanding programs for special education. Leader characterized their work as "ter-

---

[61] Yet the governor complained that the 1957 legislature had cut his request for special education from $14.5 million to $12,150,000. *Press Release* #A482, December 27, 1957, p. 11.

[62] Charlesworth, *Governmental Administration*, p. 667.

rific progress . . . for human need," adding that this education program represented "the most gratifying achievement of my administration." [63]

It was also for the education of the handicapped that the staff of the Bureau of Program Evaluation undertook on its own a survey of the total situation at the state-operated Scranton Oral School for the Deaf. If this study had embraced only the administrative practices and the efficient management of the school, it might have been an appropriate assignment for the Bureau of Management Methods. However, according to Dr. Ferguson, something quite different from a management survey was undertaken in this case. What the Bureau of Program Evaluation did was to inquire into the program content, to determine whether timely and appropriate methods of instruction were being used. As a result of this appraisal, a number of staff changes were made at this institution, and the entire program emphasis of the school was changed.[64]

Closely related to Leader's interest in education for the handicapped was his program to secure employment for the handicapped. This program started "right at home," and a great many qualified but partially disabled persons were hired by the state government itself. The services of many conscientious persons were thus secured—persons who would otherwise have difficulty competing in private industry. In fact, some six weeks before the end of his term, the governor issued two executive directives to the

[63] *Press Release* #866, released September 22, 1958.
[64] See "Recent Improvements at the Scranton State Oral School for the Deaf," unpublished document in the Leader Papers, Subject File #63 under Ferguson. The governor returned the report, with his comment, "Good" in pencil.

various state departments and agencies, concerning their employment of the physically handicapped.[65] Early in his term, Leader had issued two press releases urging citizens to employ the handicapped, who were otherwise qualified.[66] In June, 1957, Leader set up a Committee on Employment of the Handicapped, to explore this problem further, and fifteen months later, this group arranged a Governor's Conference on Employment of the Handicapped, which stimulated further action on this program.[67] Both of these groups were serviced by the Bureau of Program Evaluation. This humane concern for the handicapped of all ages thus became another program emphasis for which the Leader administration was known and appreciated by many persons of all political persuasions.

So comprehensive was the governor's concern about all aspects of education and welfare, that these programs sprouted a whole range of cognate activities, ranging into juvenile problems, vocational rehabilitation, problems of the aging, labor camps, higher education, probation, parole, classification of offenders, police activities, and many other matters. Persons close to the Leader adminstration were frequently amazed at the energy and drive with which the governor and his staff aides thrust themselves into these many substantive program areas.

To provide additional perspective on the state's position in one of these areas, the Bureau of Program Evaluation prepared a report on the administration of vocational edu-

[65] *Executive Directives* #105 and #110, October 9 and December 1, 1958.

[66] *Press Releases* #105, #110, both in March, 1955.

[67] *Press Releases* #A210, June 6, 1957, and #A853, September 11, 1958.

cation in Maryland, Nebraska, Pennsylvania, Texas, and Vermont. Later, the governor had the pleasure of dedicating a new $8 million State Vocational Rehabilitation Center at Johnstown, Pennsylvania, which is said to be one of the outstanding institutions of its kind in the nation.[68]

MIGRANT LABOR

The Pennsylvania Department of Labor and Industry is responsible for a program on behalf of seasonal farm labor in the state. The law which set up this program was regarded, by 1955, as inadequate and the regulations under which it operated as antiquated. Farmers utilizing such labor frequently failed to provide adequate facilities. Administration of migratory labor programs in Pennsylvania involved problems of health, housing, sanitation, child care, wages and hours, child labor, education, transportation, safety, unemployment, and public assistance. These problems involved other state departments—such as public instruction, public assistance, health, welfare, the Bureau of Motor Vehicles, and the State Police. To deal with these problems, Governor Fine had appointed in 1952 an Interdepartmental Committee of State Agencies dealing with migratory labor, and the Department of Labor and Industry had commissioned Dr. Morrison Handsaker, chairman of the Department of Economics and Business Administration at Lafayette College, to make a study of the problem.[69]

[68] *Press Release* #A929, October 26, 1958. The center was begun under Governor Fine, however.

[69] See *Seasonal Farm Labor in Pennsylvania* (Lafayette College, Easton, Pennsylvania, 1953), 243 pp.

There had been some citizen interest in getting stronger governmental control over the treatment of migratory labor, particularly by persons connected with Lafayette, Bucknell, and other Pennsylvania colleges and universities. Dr. Ferguson was among those particularly interested in the problem, and one of the first things he did when he became director of program evaluation in 1955 was to make inquiries in the Department of Labor and Industry about this program. Dr. Charlesworth also agreed that the matter needed attention, and authorized the Bureau of Program Evaluation to set up a number of interdepartmental meetings with the various agencies involved. One attempt was made to revitalize the program by proposing its transfer to the Department of Agriculture, which the legislature refused to do. Other bills were introduced to deal with the health, welfare, and child labor aspects of the problem, but these were also unsuccessful. Then it was discovered that the Department of Labor and Industry had sufficient authority to change many of the regulations under existing law. These changes were made with the help of the interdepartmental committee, coordinated by the Bureau of Program Evaluation. One of these changes involved the licensing of crew leaders of seasonal farm laborers.

As a result of the interest generated in this problem, Governor Leader appointed a Governor's Committee on Migratory Labor. After further study, Governor Leader and William L. Batt, Jr., the secretary of labor and industry, went to Washington and pleaded for federal legislation on migratory labor. After Dr. Ferguson became secretary of administration, Dr. Christie in the Bureau of Program Evaluation continued to work on the problem, with the Governor's Committee and with his legislative secretary.

Program evaluation also helped to formulate the new code of regulations, and later a management survey of migrant labor program was conducted by the Bureau of Management Methods. Further efforts for legislative action were made in the early part of the Lawrence administration.

RECREATION

State programs in the field of recreation have been very limited in Pennsylvania. However, with the population explosion, the automotive expansion, and the increased leisure time for many persons, the demand for recreational facilities in the state has multiplied. Recreational work and planning have come into their own, both as a specialized profession and as a customary or expected function of government. The Departments of Highways, Forests, and Waters, and others had made studies bearing upon such matters as the adequacy of recreational offerings in Pennsylvania, the demand for additional state parks, highway picnic tables, rest stops, camping sites, swimming pools, and community recreational programs. Some of the highway facilities could be and were added, particularly on the turnpike, at very little added expense. The provision of camp sites, state parks, or public pools required considerably more long-range planning, and in some cases involved additional problems of land acquisition, effective demand, seasonal usage, and other matters.

Recreation experts attached to the State Department of Forests and Waters found, for example, that Shawnee State Park in Bedford County had as many as 85,000 persons using its facilities on Sundays in the summertime, and that sixty-five per cent of these persons came from the Pittsburgh area, a distance of 110 miles. Such findings indicated that the state was low in park facilities in the Pittsburgh region. As a result, by 1960, the department was adding state parks in Green, Cambria, and Butler Counties, all on the fringe of Allegheny County.[70]

Governor Leader took particular interest in the state park program, and was able to announce in his Final Message:

We are moving closer every day to our goal of a State park within 25 miles of every Pennsylvanian. Four new parks have already been built, and another six are under construction.[71]

A total of fifty-nine state parks in 1955 had been increased to sixty-four by 1959, and the department hoped to have seventy-four parks open to the public by 1960. The use of the state parks had increased nearly fifty per cent over 1954, making a total of over twenty-one million park users in 1959. Such a figure was reported to represent the second most heavily used state park system in the nation. Additional attention was given to such things as expansion of existing parks, development of historic sites, clean streams, water resource development, and general conservation, partly in the interest of other types of open country recreation.[72]

[70] "Evaluating the Program and Organization of a State Department of Forests and Waters," panel address by Mr. Harry Griffiths (the department's administrative officer), at the Fels Institute, May 19, 1960. (Tape-recorded.)

[71] *Op. cit.*, January 6, 1959, p. 11. The governor added that in the related field of conservation, the Department of Forests and Waters had been able to achieve the best professional direction since the days of Gifford Pinchot. One of the new state parks was named in his honor.

[72] Supplement to *Final Message* by Maurice K. Goddard, secretary of forests and waters, pp. 45, 46.

The Department of Forests and Waters believed that they could not evaluate the significance, priority, or status of all these various recreational and conservation programs without the aid of specific check lists and manuals of procedure. These were completed by the department in 1959, in cooperation with program analysts from the Office of Administration. The check list covered the department's work in parks, stream clearance, forestry, and even certain administrative procedures.

Though such activity was described as program evaluation by the department in question, it differs in two respects from the other examples which have just been presented. First, a greater portion of the evaluating was done by departmental or line personnel themselves, rather than by persons attached to the Bureau of Program Evaluation. Secondly, such techniques as manuals of procedure are more often associated with management improvement, or efficiency work, rather than broad-gauged evaluation of the appropriateness, relative significance or priority of the operation in question. The forms developed did inquire, however, into such matters as "the basic purpose and intent of the program," which is a key aspect of any broad-gauged evaluation. Moreover, departmental spokesmen claimed to consider such other criteria as Pennsylvania's standing in particular programs in comparison with other states, and professional standards, such as those employed by the United States Army Corps of Engineers.[73] One sig-

[73] They appeared to make no clear distinction between this broad-gauged evaluation in terms of national or professional standards, or in terms of public need, and the more customary "bread-and-butter" type of evaluation, which is primarily a kind of efficiency study. He spoke, for example, of personal inspections of field offices by division chiefs and of additional inspectional terms of technical and administrative personnel.

nificant result of the evaluation program undertaken largely by the department itself was a shift in the emphasis of the state park program from central Pennsylvania, where population is relatively sparse, to eastern and western Pennsylvania, where there is much greater demand for recreational facilities.

Further research conducted under the supervision of the Office of Administration revealed that Forests and Waters Department was by no means the only one concerned with the state recreational program. It was found that twelve state agencies were providing some recreation service in 1956. However, these services were unrelated and many were unknown to the people who might wish to use them.[74] Several of the specialized studies by the Bureau of Program Evaluation dealt with existing or proposed programs of recreational value, including the program for young historians, the proposal for an information center for visitors at the capitol, an "open house" for the public by all state agencies and the celebration of "Pennsylvania Week" by the public schools.

The participation of so many state agencies in some form of recreational service presented problems of interdepartmental coordination and planning. There was no state agency for relating all these recreational services to the requirements of a balanced program. No one had

[74] The Soil Conservation Commission of the Department of Agriculture, the State Farm Show Commission, the Department of Commerce, the Pennsylvania State University, Department of Public Instruction, Historical and Museum Commission, the Capitol Park, and various aspects of the state health, welfare, public assistance, and correctional programs were included. "Report on Recreation for the Commission on Governmental Reorganization" by Charles B. Cranford, Philadelphia deputy commissioner of recreation, Consultant, 19 pp. (undated, c. 1956), at pp. 11–13.

evaluated the various programs with respect to the larger problem of the wiser use of leisure time for purposes of crime prevention, mental health and good citizenship. The variety of uncoordinated offerings resulted "in a waste of money, physical resources and skills which might otherwise have been useful." [75] To provide such coordination, central insight, and planning, the Governmental Reorganization Commission's consultant on recreation recommended the establishment of a state Department of Recreation, independent of all other departments and directly responsible to the governor.[76] This recommendation was not adopted, partly for budgetary reasons. Instead the full commission recommended the creation of an Advisory Board on Recreation within the Department of Public Instruction. There was also consideration of a citizens' advisory committee on recreation, to include representatives of all sections and of various recreational interests within the state.

Recreation illustrates the shift of matters formerly regarded as marginal and of no concern to the state. Recreation is now an important problem of an urban civilization, a new industry with tremendous promotional possibilities, and a new frontier for governmental, as well as commercial, activity.[77] The exploration of such areas is a good ex-

[75] Charles B. Cranford, *op. cit.,* p. 11.

[76] *Ibid.,* p. 4. The Cranford Report found that of some 2,765 political subdivisions within the state, only 151 of these had year-round recreational programs with full-time professional personnel. Some additional 800 communities had summer programs. Most of these programs were limited to "athletics for boys and playgrounds for children," rather than well-planned activity for all ages. *Ibid.,* p. 14.

[77] According to the Cranford Report, recreation ranks third among the state's major industries and provides an annual income of about

ample of what is meant by program evaluation. In this case, however, the total job was not undertaken by the staff of the Bureau of Program Evaluation. Some evaluation was done by departmental or line personnel. The more comprehensive job of evaluating the state's total recreational offerings and needs was done by a consultant to the Commission on Governmental Reorganization. The work of this commission was coordinated, however, by the secretary of administration, and various areas were studied by persons then or later in charge of the Bureau of Program Evaluation.

CORRECTIONAL INDUSTRIES

The Bureau of Program Evaluation undertook to appraise the program of the Division of Prison Industries in the Department of Justice. There were a number of problems involved in this operation. One was the policy question of the extent to which useful, productive activity should be introduced or expanded within the various adult correctional institutions. From the standpoint of modern penology and rehabilitation, the industrial program should be expanded. On the other hand, various business and other pressure groups with political influence had protested such expansion.[78] In Pennsylvania, only

---

$600 million per year. With adequate promotion, he estimated this income might be trebled. Recreation has an even greater economic value when one considers its contribution to the prevention of delinquency and crime, institutional care of the sick, accidental death and injury, labor absenteeism, and anti-social behavior.

[78] The case for expansion is well presented by Richard A. McGee, "Saving Prison Waste," 293 *The Annals of the American Academy of Political and Social Sciences,* pp. 59–69, which is a description of California's prison industry program.

about 1,700 prisoners were engaged in non-maintenance work out of a prison population of 6,911, on September 1, 1954.[79]

That amount of correctional industry represented a considerable expansion over conditions prior to the Devers reform in 1953, when the state prisons were removed from the Department of Welfare and placed under a new Bureau of Correction in the Department of Justice:

> For some twenty years before the Bureau was set up, there had been no substantial change in the number of prisoners put to work. Only some 700 prisoners were engaged in non-maintenance work. This number has been increased to about 1700 and further increases are to be expected.[80]

The question of prison industries was still an active one in the early days of the Leader administration, and Dr. Ferguson of the Bureau of Program Evaluation was asked to give the governor policy advice on this question. Correctional industries were further expanded, although there was some vocal opposition to this expansion on the part of various interests who feared that they might be adversely affected.[81]

Closely related to correctional industries was the pro-

[79] *Bureau of Correction,* Department of Justice, descriptive pamphlet (p. 17) printed at the Pennsylvania Industrial School, Camp Hill, Pennsylvania, October, 1954, one year after that bureau was established, by legislation known as the Devers Package, July 29, 1953. See *Follow-up Report of the Devers Committee,* the Governor's Office, Harrisburg, November 19, 1954.

[80] Thorsten Sellin, consultant to Governor Leader's pre-inaugural Advisory Committee, "Report on the Bureau of Corrections," January, 1955, p. 9. (Unpublished, Consultant's Report, Governor's Advisory Committee, at the Fels Institute.)

[81] See materials in the Leader Papers on Correctional Industries.

posal to set up forestry camps for juvenile offenders. With the governor's approval, some of these were set up by Commissioner Arthur T. Prasse of the Bureau of Correction, and with the technical assistance of the Department of Forests and Waters. Dr. Charlesworth, secretary of administration, supplied policy advice on some aspects of this program. Later, Dr. Christie of the Bureau of Program Evaluation gave counsel and provided liaison to the Division of Prison Industries, on procurement problems and matters of purchasing procedure. Program evaluation staff also helped to develop an in-service training program for employees of that Division of the Department of Justice.

MISCELLANEOUS

In a number of other departments, program and policy questions came to the attention of the secretary of administration and the governor. There were so many changes taking place at Harrisburg at one time, and so many new areas being tackled, that the governor had frequent need for a staff arm capable of doing research on many of these problems. Governor Leader himself said that in the early part of his administration, he regarded program evaluation as one of the most important bureaus of his office. Whatever administrative problems arose requiring study were submitted to that bureau for research and recommendations.[82] He found these services of great importance for "trouble-shooting" many purely departmental matters, as well as for interdepartmental matters, involving sometimes more general reorganization. In fact, one difficulty with the bureau's experience, acknowledged by all concerned,

[82] Interview with Governor Leader at Dover, August 14, 1960.

is that it was so busy dealing with these "trouble-shooting" assignments, that it could never undertake a systematic evaluation of the entire commonwealth program, in terms of relative weight and priority, as had been envisioned. It had also been hoped by members of the Governor's Advisory Committee responsible for setting up the Bureau of Program Evaluation that eventually various members of the bureau's staff "might specialize according to major program areas, such as social welfare or economic regulation." [83] The pressure of other problems plus financial limitations prevented the bureau either from specializing in that way, or from undertaking an evaluation of the total state administrative program.

However, particular studies were made by the bureau in many other program areas too numerous to elaborate upon. For example, after William Batt became secretary of labor and industry in March, 1957, it was decided to make a number of changes in the operation of that department's Bureau of Mediation. The new secretary called upon program evaluation personnel to offer recommendations in connection with that reorganization.[84] The governor also called upon the bureau at one point to evaluate the effectiveness of the new Industrial Development Authority, which had been established under the Department of Commerce to stimulate the economic growth of the state, particularly in various depressed communities. Directors of that program within the Department of Commerce

[83] Thomas J. Davy, panel reporter, "How is Administrative Performance Measured," *Strengthening Management for Democratic Government*, Digest of American Society for Public Administration, National Conference, March, 1958 (Chicago, 1959), p. 113.

[84] Interview with Dr. Ferguson at State College, December 12, 1959.

had been pointing with pride to the large number of new industrial plants, whose location they claimed to have been induced by their program.[85] The important question was how many such plants might have been expected as a part of normal economic change or expansion, and how many could be specifically traced to the commonwealth's new program. The Bureau of Program Evaluation, it was believed, might give a more unbiased interpretation of the claims than the department in question.

Other evaluations were undertaken in the educational field, in cooperation with the Department of Public Instruction. Aside from Leader's interest in providing special classes for handicapped children, his administration had placed a major emphasis upon raising teachers' salaries, attracting more teachers, improving their preparation, constructing new school buildings, improving the curriculum and classroom instruction, securing federal aid, and reorganizing school administration. In many of these programs, members of the Bureau of Program Evaluation served as the representative of the Governor's Office, in working with the departmental personnel concerned. Moreover, it was found that when it became known that the Governor's Office was taking particular interest in a program, action was stimulated and results were sometimes forthcoming much more promptly. In many situations, then, the Bureau of Program Evaluation served less as a source of policy advice for the governor than as his alter ego, or as a catalyst for stimulating departmental action.[86] In such cases, the bureau was operating as one

[85] See *Press Release* #180, May 7, 1955.

[86] Based upon interviews with Dr. Ferguson and with George Mohlenoff, assistant director of program evaluation, December 3, 1959.

means of extending the governor's influence at various points within the administration.

4. INVESTIGATING PROPOSALS

During his campaign for election Governor Leader had recommended the establishment of a consumers' council, to represent the consuming public in various administrative determinations. Dr. Ferguson was asked by the governor to evaluate this proposal even before Ferguson came to Harrisburg as director of program evaluation. The experience of other states with such an agency was found to be such that the governor was given a negative recommendation, at least for the time being. Civil defense was another area which was beginning to receive a great deal of attention in other states, such as New York, particularly in the days following the Korean War and the development of the hydrogen bomb. There was federal encouragement for the state to undertake rather far-reaching shelter, training and educational programs. Here was another area where the governor needed information and expert advice on the situation in Pennsylvania. Ultimately, it was decided not to undertake heavy spending for civil defense, at least until the matter was somewhat clarified. Instead, the industrial development staff under Leader decided to advertise Pennsylvania's mountainous terrain as an enticement to defense industries to locate within the state, under cover of the natural mountain barriers.[87] The policy question on civil defense participation went beyond the Bureau

[87] Governor's Office *Press Release* #205, May 25, 1955. The commonwealth did, however, cooperate with various national civil defense tests. See *Press Release* #223, June 7, 1955, and *Executive Directives* #26 and #94.

of Program Evaluation, and involved at one time a study of New York State's program by a subcommittee of the cabinet.[88]

Shortly after he became director of program evaluation in July of 1955, Dr. Ferguson saw a research report by Dr. Carl D. Morneweck of the Department of Public Instruction indicating that Pennsylvania's colleges would be faced with doubled enrollment, according to present trends, by 1970. Since Dr. Ferguson was a college professor as well as a state official, he was much impressed with the implications of such a projection. Apparently nobody in state government had given this prediction any special attention. A short time later, the governor was asked to make a speech to the Pennsylvania State Educational Association, which assignment was turned over to Dr. Charlesworth and ultimately to Dr. Ferguson for suggestions. Dr. Ferguson gave considerable study to the question of the state's total responsibility for education, an area in which he had been working throughout his professional career. Finally, he wove into the proposed speech a suggestion for community colleges. Dr. Charlesworth was not sure about this, but after some discussion decided to leave it as a "trial balloon," and the governor included that suggestion in his address to the educational association.[89] The newspapers picked up the idea, and it caused considerable public discussion. To explore the matter further, Leader announced that he planned to appoint an advisory Com-

[88] *Press Release* #95, March 10, 1955.
[89] *Press Release* #352, September 29, 1955, contains the speech.

mission on Higher Education, which was announced on November 23, 1955. Composed of prominent educators throughout the state, the chairman of this commission, which was announced the same day as another Commission on Public Education, was President Paul R. Anderson of Chatham College.[90] Although these two educational advisory commissions were composed of different persons, Dr. Ferguson served on both in his capacity as director of program evaluation. The Bureau of Program Evaluation supplied staff services and helped to prepare the final report of both commissions.

Partly in response to this activity and the public interest which it both stimulated and channeled, a number of bills were introduced into the General Assembly to establish, or to provide subsidies for, "community colleges, junior colleges and technical institutes" as advocated by Governor Leader. Three house bills were introduced during the 1957 session, providing for such community colleges under the supervision of the public school authorities, all of which bills died in committee, while four bills in the senate dealt with the same subject, along with other bills dealing with scholarships, medical college construction, and other higher education matters, such as the boards of trustees of state owned or aided colleges. The community college proposal died in the Senate, though some other educational bills were enacted.[91]

Meanwhile, the launching of the Soviet sputniks added further fuel to the governor's campaign for more and

[90] *Press Release* #414.
[91] HB 1585, HB 1590, HB 1134, SB 410, SB 680, SB 681, SB 682, were all junior college or community college bills. See *History of Bills and Resolutions,* 1957 Session.

better education, and specifically to his plea for federal aid to education. In the spring of 1957, the Department of Public Instruction formed a twenty-two member advisory Commitee on Science and Mathematics "to study what could be done." [92] This was followed by a fourth official advisory body in education, the State Curriculum Commission.[93] At the governor's direction, the Department of Public Instruction also conducted a survey to get further data on the effective demand for higher education in various parts of the state. This survey disclosed

. . . that in the south central area only one student out of three applying for admission as a freshman at a group of representative colleges actually stands a chance of being accepted

because of the capacity limitations of those eight private colleges in central Pennsylvania.[94] Though the community college program originally suggested to the governor by Dr. Ferguson did not become a reality during the Leader administration, the idea was revived in the next legislative session, though such a measure had not yet been enacted by 1960.[95] Pennsylvania did, however, participate in the federal scholarship program known as the National De-

[92] *Press Release* #A491, January 3, 1958. The governor said, "This is one of the first moves any state government has taken to explore the many problems. . . ."

[93] Leader spoke of these four educational advisory groups in his speech to the Conference on Improvement of Instruction in Pennsylvania Schools, Harrisburg, January 28, 1959. *Press Release* #A524, p. 10.

[94] *Press Release* #A147, May 10, 1957, p. 1. Leader followed this with a series of luncheon meetings at the Executive Mansion with educational leaders. Three such meetings were to be held by the governor that week, according to the same press release.

[95] HB 1940 and SB 854, both introduced June 15, 1959. See *History of Bills and Resolutions*, 1959 Session.

fense Education Act of 1958, and the Leader administration took credit for being one of the first states "to submit plans for utilization of the Act." [96]

Pennsylvania also participated in strength (nearly 100 persons) in the White House Conference on Education, which was convened in Washington, D.C. on November 28, 1955.[97] Preparations for this conference at the state level began early in the Leader administration, before the governor had formulated his educational program in any detail. Yet he felt that persons representing the state should have some direction from the governor, indicating at least something about the administration's educational philosophy and program. This assignment went to Dr. Ferguson in his early days as director of program evaluation. Ultimately, he prepared a letter which the governor sent to all the Pennsylvania delegates urging them to support federal aid for education.[98] Though such a recommendation was not binding upon the delegates, the letter was one of the steps in the formulation of the Leader administration's educational philosophy and program, an assignment which was treated as in the province of program evaluation.

The Pennsylvania delegation to the White House Conference decided they would like to have a continuing body

[96] Dr. Boehm, superintendent of Public Instruction, said, "The Department is in full activity preparing . . . to use $23,250,000 of federal funds in the next four years." (In Pennsylvania, both public schools and higher education are under the same Department.) Supplement to *Final Message* of Governor Leader, January 6, 1959, p. 99. (Report of the Department of Public Instruction.)

[97] *Press Release* #416, November 23, 1955, contains the names of the delegates appointed by Governor Leader.

[98] Based upon an interview with Dr. Ferguson in Washington, September 10, 1959. The governor's letter is also reprinted in *Press Release* #416.

to evaluate the state's educational program. Consequently, Governor Leader subsequently appointed seventeen of them to serve on his Advisory Commission on Public Education, already mentioned.[99] In its final report, the White House Conference recommended the calling of a similar conference on higher education. Instead of having the second group convene in Washington, President Eisenhower appointed a Committee on Education Beyond the High School, which met in the various states. The work of this group was facilitated in Pennsylvania by the fact that Governor Leader had already established an active Commission on Higher Education.[100]

Many of the educational topics tackled by these various advisory groups were also active concerns of the Department of Public Instruction and, in several instances, also of the Bureau of Program Evaluation, which became now the headquarters for all the Governor's Advisory Committees and Commissions, and the place for both the discussion

---

[99] *Press Release* #629, May 14, 1956. Dr. Marion R. Trabue, dean of the College of Education at the Pennsylvania State University was now appointed chairman of this commission. Governor Leader set forth the mandate of the Commission on Public Education in the following terms:

1. Methods of school financing
2. Local school district consolidation
3. County school district consolidation
4. Teacher recruitment
5. Teaching methods
6. Educational program
7. Pupil classification
8. School building design
9. School buildings needed
10. Specialized education . . . for the retarded or handicapped.

[100] Committee for the White House Conference on Education, *Report to the President* (Washington, D.C., 1956), p. 7. Based also upon an interview with Dr. R. Matthews, School of Education, University of Pennsylvania, February 3, 1960. Dr. Matthews was an alternate delegate at the White House Conference.

and the formulation of many of the final reports. The governor had set a one-year target date for the Commission on Higher Education, but their final report was submitted at the end of fifteen months in February, 1957. This report did not particularly feature federal aid, as the governor had, but did support many other points which became key items in the governor's program for higher education. Noting that Pennsylvania colleges

. . . received a smaller percentage of support from state and local governments than any of the adjacent states and than the United States average. . . .[101]

the commission encouraged the commonwealth to "develop a cohesive, sound, long-range policy for higher education," which subsequent recommendations indicated would include a "scholarship and loan program," new "junior colleges, community colleges and technical institutions," higher faculty salaries, more physical facilities, as well as a permanent State Commission on Higher Education, to improve coordination, planning, financing, and so on.[102]

All of these findings represent examples of program evaluation of proposed future needs and programs, done in this case with the assistance of citizens' committees who

[101] *Higher Education in the Commonwealth,* Report of the Governor's Commission on Higher Education, February 1, 1957, at p. 25, quoting figures from *Higher Education in the Forty-Eight States* by the Council of State Governments.

[102] *Ibid.,* pp. 29, 31, 34, 44, 45, 54, 55ff. On the question of projected enrollments, this commission predicted a 1970 college population 112 per cent higher than 1955. Such was based upon expanding college-age population plus increased interest in college study. The former alone would indicate only a 55 per cent increase by 1970. *Ibid.,* p. 17.

The commission consisted of eleven members plus a research assistant.

serve as if they were expert consultants to the Governor's Bureau of Program Evaluation. The job of these commissions, however, was to go beyond the present administrative program, to consider its adequacy in the light of present and projected future need, in comparison with other states, and also with respect to other professional standards. Program evaluation was here a service to the governor and to the people on the matter of desirable public policy in the field of education.[103]

ADVISORY COMMITTEES AND COMMISSIONS

Far too many state administrations, it is often alleged, have "bungled along" not knowing either where they were or where they were going. Governor Leader had resolved from the very first not to operate in that fashion. His pre-inaugural Advisory Committee was one indication of his determination to get the facts and take "soundings" before launching his ship of state. As a result, Leader felt that he was one of the few recent Pennsylvania governors who was really "on top" of the situation throughout his administration from the moment he took over.[104] However, most of the consultants' reports to his Advisory Committee were not merely "soundings" of the submerged

[103] Dr. Ferguson feels that this activity in the field of higher education was an example of program evaluation at its best. Interview in Harrisburg, August 25, 1959. Dr. Charlesworth maintains in his book, *Governmental Administration*, p. 667, that education is the field where professional standards for program evaluation have probably been most systematically developed for a considerable period of time. Such resulted in part from the process of school accreditation.

[104] Interview with Governor Leader at Dover, August 14, 1960.

terrain, but also agenda for action. Shortly, Leader faced two additional problems. The first was how to keep up-to-date and keep track of those agenda as his program got moving, and the second was how to generate the public support needed to carry his program forward by legislative or administrative action or both. The governor needed eminent and qualified protagonists who would help to "carry the ball" through the blocking of inertia, fending off also the heavy tackle of interest groups adversely affected.

For this purpose Leader set up, not simultaneously but as the need arose, nearly a hundred different advisory committees and commissions—more than any recent Pennsylvania governor. The governor was constantly issuing press releases announcing the formation, appointment, meetings, recommendations, or final reports of these various advisory committees and commissions.[105] These citi-

---

[105] Some illustrations are as follows:

1. Governor Leader's preinaugural Advisory Committee announced 12/31/54.
2. Expanded, permanent Governor's Advisory Committee announced in February, 1955.
3. Meeting of the Governor's Advisory Committee in Philadelphia, 9/27/56, *Press Release* #779.
4. Advisory Committee on Governmental Reorganization, 2/10/55, *Press Release* #48.
5. *Executive Directive* #5 on Advisory Committee publicity, 1/24/55.
6. New Statutory Governmental Reorganization Commission, 5/17 and 23/55, #638, #642.
7. Committee to determine workable flood insurance program, 11/10/55, #398.
8. Appointment of eleven-man Flood Disaster Committee, c. 1/20/56, #483.

zens groups met, generally under the aegis of the Bureau of Program Evaluation, to study, confer, and recommend action in specific program areas. Some of these commissions—such as those on higher education, public education and penal affairs—the bureau was instrumental in estab-

---

9. Appointments to 48th Annual Conference on Taxation, 10/5/55, #363.
10. Appointment of seventeen-member Advisory Committee on Public Education, 5/14/55, #629.
11. Eleven-man study group on compulsory auto insurance appointed, 11/17/55, #408.
12. Governor's Advisory Council on Statistical Information meets, 12/13/55, #438.
13. Two-man fact finding board to study Westinghouse Electric strike, 2/12/56, #507.
14. Leader signed HB 1687 setting up Advisory Board on Older Workers, 4/11/56, #582.
15. Governor's Committee on Children and Youth selected, 5/11/56, #626.
16. Advisory Commission on Penal & Correctional Affairs appointed, 5/20/56, #646.
17. Speech to the Governor's Committee for Refugees, 6/1/56, #661.
18. Commission on Tax Problems and Pennsylvania Finance established, 7/27/56, #701.
19. Nine members appointed to State Council of Education, c. 7/31/56, #708.
20. Governor's Advisory Committee on Recreation, 9/10/56, #753.
21. Appointment of Citizens' Study Commission, 10/5/56, #792.
22. Formation of Governor's Commission on Rehabilitation, 10/19/56, #803.
23. Appointment of N.E. Pennsylvania Dairy Farmers Committee, 10/24/56.
24. Volunteer Committee on Hungarian Refugees, c. 12/3/56, X846, 830, 849, 833.
25. Appointment of new Study Commission for Philadelphia Area, 11/27/56.

lishing, partly in order to extend its own resources of expertise. In other cases—such as the Committee on Older Workers—members of the bureau served as representatives of the Office of Administration on the committee, to give direction and some coordination with the governor's pro-

---

26. Governor's Traffic Safety Council to Meet, 11/29/56, #840.
27. Committee on Children and Youth and Juvenile Delinquency, 12/11/60, #850.
28. Conference on Problems of Education in nine regions, 2/2–15/57, #895.
29. Consultants on enforcement of the three per cent sales tax, 2/8/57, #938.
30. Creation of the Deans' Committee on Mental Health, 2/14/57, #944.
31. Governor's Commission on Higher Education, 3/1/57, #968.
32. Remarks to Pennsylvania Health Council Meeting, Harrisburg, 3/8/57, #973, #981.
33. Meeting of the Governor's Committee on the Aging, 3/20/57, #1004.
34. Meeting of Tax Policy Advisory Committee, 3/29/57, #A15 (postponed, #A24).
35. Pennsylvania Welfare Forum, Harrisburg, 3/28/57, #A14.
36. Conference on Water and Resource Problems, c. 4/2/57, #A27.
37. Report of Commission on Public Education, 4/29/57, #A115.
38. Advisory Board on Revision of Regulations for Labor Camps, 5/15/57, #A150.
39. Report of Governor's Committee on Children and Youth, 5/17/57, #A159.
40. Governor signs HB 1489 creating Commission on Constitutional Revision, 7/15/57, #A256.
41. Conference on Improvement of Instruction in Pennsylvania Schools, 1/28/58, #A524.
42. Automotive Safety Foundation begins study of Department of Highways, 1/31/58, #527.

gram.[106] Early in 1958, the Bureau of Program Evaluation compiled a report on the activities and plans of the many citizen committees set up to deal with specific problems. Some of them had already expired or been superceded. Thus, it was the bureau's job to keep the administration *au courant* with the status of these groups, some of which ceased to exist because the particular legislative action or session had now been concluded.[107]

Members of the Leader administration noted a striking parallel here with the "hundred days" of President Franklin D. Roosevelt. Similar energy and activity was personified not only by Leader's own enthusiasm, but also by this remarkable congeries of citizen study groups, which descended upon Harrisburg during his first legislative session. One of the benefits of that long seventeen-month session was that it gave the governor time to build fires of support for many of his proposals. While the session dragged

---

43. Governor signs FEPC bill, thanking groups who helped, 10/27/55, #388.
44. State Education Association endorses higher education program, 5/24/57, #A177.
45. Report of nonpartisan Committee on Housing, 5/31/57, #196, 197.
46. Committee on Employment of the Handicapped, 6/6/57, #A219.
47. Hospital Study Commission, first meeting, 9/10/58, #A856.
48. Day-long Conference for Youth and Parents, 9/19/58, #A868.
49. Group to investigate quality of study in schools, 9/19/58, #A867.
50. Governor's Conference on Fitness, 11/7/58, #A942, A927.

[106] "Accomplishments . . . ," *op. cit.,* items #29 and #26.

[107] *Ibid.,* item #21. This "Committee–Commission Report" was not published, but is collected in a black notebook, now in the new Bureau of Program and Management.

on over the tax debacle, the lawmakers had to show some legislative action, in order to justify their presence. With this combination of the long session and the increased amount of organized citizen participation, Leader's first legislature enacted more laws than any other session in the history of the state.[108] Each of Leader's advisory committees and commissions had its own *raison d'etre,* but the total effect was to shock Harrisburg with this new burst of citizen activity. The Earle administration is another parallel. After having been out of power some forty years, the Democrats at that time passed more social legislation than ever before in the history of the state.[109]

Pennsylvania had, of course, had advisory committees and commissions before, such as these four notable ones initiated during Governor Fine's administration (1951–1955):

1. The Pennsylvania Tax Study Committee (Buehler Committee).
2. The State Government Survey Committee (Chesterman Committee).
3. The Devers Committee (on penal and correctional affairs).
4. The Pennsylvania Commission on Intergovernmental Relations (described below, page 235).

Each of these operated much as Leader's advisory groups. The Administrative Code specifically provides for advisory committees, commissions, and boards, some of which had been authorized by statute for many years.[110]

---

[108] The governor approved 678 general laws and 150 appropriation bills, 1955 session.

[109] 93 *Pa. Manual,* p. 1025.

[110] *E.g.,* the Veterans' Commission, the State Forest Commission, the Flood Control Commission, the State Welfare Commission, and

What was new under Leader was the large number of such groups, particularly new ones, their location close to the governor under the guidance of a bureau in the Office of Administration, and finally their increased interest in major program and policy questions. Some of Leader's groups, such as the Commission on Governmental Reorganization and the Commission on Constitutional Revision, were established by the legislature with the support of the administration. Others were simply called together by the governor or created by executive order. Both the statutory and nonstatutory groups were serviced by the Bureau of Program Evaluation, which operated as "home base" for most of this activity. A few groups operated directly under the department most concerned, the more customary pattern, which was revived somewhat in the succeeding Lawrence administration.[111]

It was made clear that most of these groups were not created primarily to advise department heads. Most of them were committees to whom the governor could turn for policy advice or support, as well as for program review or initiation. However, the emphasis, whether program review, policy advice, legislative support, or departmental assistance, depended upon the subject matter. For example,

---

the Advisory Health Board, to which Leader added the Advisory Council on Mental Health on December 16, 1955, P.L. 853. *The Administrative Code of 1929* (1957 ed.), as amended (Article IV, Section 448). See also, *Purdon's Pennsylvania Statutes Annotated,* Title 71, 1958 pocket (Ch. 3), #1042.1 to #1564.1.

[111] The Lawrence administration adopted the policy of establishing advisory commissions with terminal dates, in order to prevent them from ranging far beyond their original mandate. Interview with Mr. David R. Baldwin, deputy secretary of administration, October 6, 1960.

the Committee on Fair Employment Practices was called together by the Governor's Office primarily to mobilize support for such a bill, and in this Leader succeeded where previous administrations had failed. In contrast, the professional groups secured by the governor to evaluate the Highway Department (the Automotive Safety Foundation, which reported in 1958), and the consultants on the Sales Tax Bureau, were specialists recruited primarily to review and improve particular agencies or programs. Such paid consultants departed from the usual pattern of volunteer citizen groups.

Most of the advisory committees had in their midst a sprinkling of state officials, representing not only the Governor's Office, but also the state agencies most directly concerned. Thus the problem of separation of the thinking and planning from the actual experience was at least somewhat solved. One result of the advisory committee operation was to help remove the "egghead" charge leveled by critics against the Office of Administration. Policy recommendations which were rather revolutionary in scope could be described as the proposals of citizen groups instead of from governor's "brain trust" alone. Besides, each of these committees had a mandate more specific than the original Governor's Advisory Committee, which undertook to assess the entire state administration. Such a division of labor permitted more thorough treatment than the original Advisory Committee could provide with its limited number of consultants. These advisory committees and commissions (and there appears to have been little clear distinction between the terms, though the statutory ones were usually designated as commissions) became, in effect, an extension of the resources and services provided by the Bureau of Program Evaluation, which had been created to perform a similar function.

Several of Leader's advisory committees were important because they brought the government into new areas of activity and concern. They also focused expert and informed public scrutiny upon many aspects of the state service, in some cases for the first time. Such an operation could help democratize the public service by educating, stimulating and activating citizen participation and concern. Finally, these committees helped to remove the exclusivist implications of a "high level intelligence unit," by providing some representation of the taxpayer, the consumer, and the state administration's varied clientele. In its work with these committees, the Bureau of Program Evaluation was described as not replacing popular processes, but organizing and serving them in a context less encumbered than the legislative processes had become.

5. INTERDEPARTMENTAL AND INTERGOVERNMENTAL MATTERS

Many of the activities described in the preceding pages involved matters of interest to more than one state department. In fact, one of the objectives of the Bureau of Program Evaluation was to provide communication and coordination for related programs within the various departments.

One example was provided when officials observed a surplus of hospital beds in the tuberculosis institutions under the Department of Health and a critical shortage in the mental health institutions under the Department of Welfare. Although welfare officials were active in seeking transfer of such unused capacity (resulting partly from the benefits of new antibiotic drugs), the working out of this problem was greatly facilitated when the Office of Administration, representing the governor, took an interest in the operation. There were many such cases where the active participation of the governor's staff helped to avoid shortages, surpluses or duplication, by establishing better interdepartmental cooperation. Some were matters of a housekeeping character, such as the better allocation of office space by the Bureau of Capital Expenditures. These problems of interdepartmental concern came to the attention of all bureaus within the Office of Administration at their regular staff meeting.[112]

Several interdepartmental matters handled by the Bureau of Program Evaluation have been mentioned earlier: the central film library, the capitol information center, the proposed Commonwealth open house, "Pennsylvania Week," and the milk promotion program. Many departments were also involved in the bureau's work on biennial reports, statistics, state publications, the Reorganization Commission, forestry camps, migrant labor, recreation, insurance, and other surveys already described. Another example was the Bureau of Program Evaluation's follow-up study of the order prescribing a seven and one half-hour day, 8:30 to 5:00, for all departments. Some of the legislative proposals evaluated by the bureau for the governor

---

[112] Meetings were held by Dr. Charlesworth on Thursday afternoons from about 4:30 to 7 p.m. The Office of Administration was so short-handed and the problems were so legion that, in practice, there was considerable overlapping of function. Interview in Philadelphia, August 26, 1960.

and his legislative secretary also involved several departments, as did its work on the new system of personnel complement control.[113] A few of those assignments resembled organization and methods study rather than a survey of program adequacy—a distinction which is sometimes tenuous at best. The bureau also studied the feasibility of merging the laboratories in several of the state departments.[114]

PROGRAM BUDGETING AND CAPITAL BUDGET

One of the major responsibilities of the Bureau of Program Evaluation was to help the Budget Bureau to shift from the old line-item to the program type of budget. This changeover was greatly facilitated by program evaluation's work in the clarification and redefinition of commonwealth programs. Many of the actual program descriptions for the 1957–59 budget were written by the staff of the Bureau of Program Evaluation. The bureau's work resulted in a gradual shift in the format of the governor's budget from 1955–57 to 1957–59 and ultimately 1959–61, at which time close observers felt that the commonwealth had a genuine program budget for the first time. In the period 1955–57, Dr. Ferguson assigned to the bureau the job of working out a program budget. After careful study,

[113] See "Accomplishments of the Bureau . . . ," *op. cit.,* #10, #37, #7.

[114] Mr. Sailer of the bureau explored the possibility of centralizing all state laboratories in the Harrisburg area in a single building. "This laboratory would be located near the capitol city . . . under one professional head . . . financed by all agencies making use of it. . . . This proposal was submitted to the Governor early in 1958." *Ibid.,* item #49.

the Bureau drew up a "dummy" budget, before the forms went out to the departments for their estimates. At the top of each page was the name of the program, under which was included a short paragraph describing the various activities included in that program. For purposes of securing apropriations, it was also necessary to provide a line-item breakdown at that time; so that the legislature could better compare this with previous budgets. In collaboration with the Budget Bureau, appropriation levels were set under three categories—subsidies, general government, and institutions. The actual appropriations were voted, then, by the departments. What was accomplished at this stage was the grouping of all appropriations into three categories, and the creation of the program breakdowns. Ultimately, it was hoped that at least segments of the budget might be refined beyond the program categories to the more precise measures used in a performance budget.[115]

After completion of the 1957–59 budget document, some members of the Bureau of Program Evaluation helped with various preliminary stages of the capital budget. Though the capital budget project was ultimately taken over by other units, the preliminary examination of departmental proposals for capital expenditures can be described as a specialized type of program evaluation. This job of setting priorities and determining relative program emphases had been included in the original mandate of the Bureau of Program Evaluation.[116]

[115] Interview with Dr. Christie, director of Program Evaluation, at the capitol, August 25, 1959. *Cf.* also the 1955, 1957, and 1959 budgets to observe the progression indicated.

[116] That mandate is summarized in 93 *Pa. Manual*, p. 308.

FEDERAL AID

Dr. Ferguson's appointment as director of program evaluation was announced in connection with a study he had recently completed on the question of the impact of federal aid on Pennsylvania. Dr. Ferguson's study can be accurately described as program evaluation, since it involved both the impact and the extent of Pennsylvania's participation in various federal aid programs. Governor Leader pointed to Dr. Ferguson's finding that Pennsylvania ranked forty-seventh among the forty-eight states in the receipt of federal grants per capita.[117] Such a rank among the states is all the more striking when it is recalled that Pennsylvania is one of the more highly industrialized states, which contributes heavily in federal taxes. Taking federal grants as a percentage of income payments, Pennsylvania was also near the bottom, with only Connecticut and New Jersey showing a lower percentage in 1953.[118] Although the total volume of federal grants had been growing rapidly, resulting in "a 68 per cent increase in federal aid to Pennsylvania from 1942 to 1953, Pennsylvania's share decreased

[117] Federal Commission on Intergovernmental Relations, *The Impact of Federal Grants-in-Aid on the Structure and Functions of State and Local Governments.* (Washington, D.C., 1955), pp. 332–348. Dr. Ferguson and Dr. Charles F. LeeDecker were coauthors of Chapter 18 of the above survey, dealing with the impact upon Pennsylvania.

[118] Commission on Intergovernmental Relations, *Report to the President.* Washington, D.C., June, 1955, p. 309. The percentages, as described, are: Pennsylvania, .57 per cent; Connecticut, .53 per cent and New Jersey, .43 per cent. (This volume is also known as the Kestnbaum Report.)

from 7.6 per cent of the total for the United States in 1942 to 4 per cent in 1953." [119]

Governor Leader's major point was that research was needed to discover ways of increasing Pennsylvania's share of federal funds. He gave these two reasons for Pennsylvania's disadvantageous position:

1. The federal government's philosophy is that the so-called "wealthy states" should receive less aid than "poorer states," although the former pay a much larger share of taxes.

2. This State in recent years has been lax in appropriating matching funds for federal aid.[120]

The situation seemed to require thorough explanation and evaluation. Failure to do so might open any governor to serious political criticism, should such facts be uncovered as a "surprise" by an opposition party. One reason for Pennsylvania's poor showing in the receipt of federal funds is the fact that several conservative Republican governors were generally opposed to federal aid, though they accepted "grants for popular programs" that were readily available.[121] In the 1930's and 1940's, however, "the im-

[119] Ferguson and LeeDecker, *op. cit.*, pp. 332, 333. In 1953, federal grants to Pennsylvania were "the equivalent of 3.6% of federal income and employment tax collections. . . ."

[120] In 1953, Pennsylvania received $102,549,000 in federal funds, which represented 12.8 per cent of the general expenditures. *Press Release* #264, July 14, 1955. According to Appendix Table 5 of the main Kestnbaum Report, this state grant amounted to $10.04 per capita, as opposed to the national average grant of $17.19 per capita in 1953.

[121] Ferguson and LeeDecker, *op. cit.*, p. 340, 341. "Governor Arthur James, a Republican . . . registered numerous complaints. In 1939 he urged Congress to put control of the W.P.A. 'back into the States' and remove it 'completely from political domination.' In

perative need for federal assistance" (Governor Pinchot's words) had been utilized by the more liberal Governors Pinchot, Earle, and Duff, as an argument for securing greater authorizations from the General Assembly. Of these three governors, only Earle belonged to the Democratic party. Thus, the issue of federal aid was not entirely a partisan one, though some partisan differences could be observed.

As Ferguson and LeeDecker pointed out, some persons objected to federal aid because the number of patronage positions in aided programs was seriously limited.[122] Others objected to federal controls *per se* on the grounds of general "home rule sentiment." Inertia, rather than direct opposition, was another factor. As Leader noted, Pennsylvania had lost considerable aid simply because the legislature had been lax in appropriating matching funds.

The larger question of the proper federal–state relation-

1941 he complained that the federal government was taking much more money out of the State than it was returning for aided programs. He also charged that the Commonwealth was being penalized for having standards which the Governor considered to be higher for aid to the blind and aged than those required by the federal government. In 1942 Governor James was engaged in serious controversy with the federal government because funds were withheld for administration of unemployment compensation until the State modified its civil service law to assure permanent employes the right of appeal before being discharged.

"Governor Edward Martin . . . was involved in a controversy . . . over standards for some of the aided programs. More recently, Governor John S. Fine . . . advocated abandonment of the federal grant-in-aid system because more funds were taken out of Pennsylvania than were returned. He also made a strong plea for the federal government to repeal its tax on gasoline and leave highway building entirely to the states."

[122] *Ibid.*, p. 346.

ship had received some serious attention in the previous administration. Simultaneously with the study by Ferguson and LeeDecker, a Pennsylvania Commission on Intergovernmental Relations was exploring this very question. Appointed by Governor Fine in January, 1954, this twenty-five-member Commission was headed by Dr. Alfred G. Buehler, a leading authority on public finance on the faculty of the University of Pennsylvania. This commission's first report on September 3, 1954, pointed out that Pennsylvania's state and local taxes were low in comparison with the rest of the nation. Paradoxically, the implication was that the rejection of federal aid was partly responsible for that presumably advantageous tax position.[123]

The Final Report of the Buehler Commission on Intergovernmental Relations further elaborated the case against federal aid.[124] However, this commission was interested

[123] ". . . per capita state and local taxes in Pennsylvania in 1953 amounted to $110.88 as compared with $129.65 for the United States average." Pennsylvania Commission on Intergovernmental Relations, first report, *Federal Grant-in-Aid Programs in Pennsylvania, 1941–1953* (1954, mimeographed), p. 14.

Without questioning these figures, one can challenge two aspects of the above implication: first, that low taxes are always good, and second, that the rejection of federal funds is one way, or at least the best way to keep taxes low. The Commission's assumption on the second point overlooks the fact that the largest portion of federal taxes goes for military and "defense" expenditures for which matching funds are not required.

[124] "1. Our state is economically . . . able, except in cases of extreme emergency . . . to finance the programs which are now being furnished with . . . federal aid . . ." p. XIV of the Final Report.

"3. Federal aid is logically justified only in those cases where it is needed to initiate a necessary new public service to raise standards . . ." p. XIV.

"5. . . . appropriate weight should also be given to . . . ineffi-

in suppressing all governmental expenditure, and in "federal withdrawal from those tax fields which state and local governments could effectively utilize . . . to obtain increased revenues." Thus it was no wonder that Pennsylvania's share of federal money had lagged if the attitude of this commission reflected faithfully the viewpoint of its official sponsors.[125] The Buehler Commission on Intergovernmental Relations was not entirely out of touch with public opinion. Ferguson and LeeDecker reported encountering, at times, a similar viewpoint:

> . . . federal assistance means surrender of local control, added red tape, extravagant expenditures and loss of moral fiber because people think they get something for nothing, and a breakdown of the historic division of powers in the American federal system.[126]

The conflict between the attitude of the Leader administration, which wished to increase Pennsylvania's share of federal aid, and the viewpoint just described was sharp

---

ciency entailed in further extending federal responsibilities, the dangers to human liberties . . ." p. XV.

And later, *"If federal aid is to be continued, a number of reforms should be introduced to overcome abuses . . ."* p. XV (underscored in the original).

[125] Although at various places in its final report, the Pennsylvania Commission stated that "Pennsylvania would share more equitably in federal aid if the allocation formulas were revised," the commission's attitude is revealed by this quotation from page 37:

"The question is pertinent, why should Pennsylvania press for federal aid?"

[126] Ferguson and LeeDecker, *op. cit.*, p. 345. These sentiments were attributed to a former governor, the secretary of one of the state departments, and the mayor of a third-class city in Pennsylvania.

enough to make any administration wary of forging ahead without careful study. To unravel the many threads of this controversy and to provide a factual basis for the policy decisions involved, Leader turned to the Bureau of Program Evaluation.

The Bureau of Program Evaluation made a survey of all state programs which might qualify for federal funds, in cooperation with the departments involved. Aid currently received was then shown in parallel columns with the projected or possible increase if proper action were taken. Though such a process might result in expanding programs out of proportion to the actual need, the survey at least supplied the figures required to see the total picture, and hence to make such decisions on a rational basis. According to a staff report,

> Partly in consequence of this study, federal aid was increased from $188 million in the 1953–55 biennium to about $208 million in 1955–57 and an estimated $435 million during the current [1957–59] biennium.[127]

Such a project had great significance not only for the state government itself, but also for the citizens at large who might look forward to added services, and additional funds for the state as well. Moreover, the study was more than a mathematical calculation. The bureau went beyond the mere estimate of possible increases and investigated the steps or methods required for increasing Pennsylvania's share of federal aid. Forecasts were made beyond the immediate future. Thus Governor Leader referred in his second budget message to the federal funds, which, accord-

[127] "Accomplishments of the Bureau . . . ," *op. cit.*, item #3.

ing to present trends, might be "available for Pennsylvania's use in the next ten years." [128]

In other words, as a result of these efforts the Leader
administration more than doubled the amount of federal
aid received in Pensylvania. Though such an increase of
dollar grants is deceptive in the face of continuing inflation, the accomplishment was still sufficient, at least in
terms of Leader's philosophy, to justify the existence of
the bureau, although that agency was not alone responsible for the increase. But the study of federal grants was
one of the more important research projects of the Bureau of Program Evaluation and the fact that the grants
to Pennsylvania increased can be documented from other
sources.[129]

[128] On page six of the printed message, Leader referred to an
estimated $100,000,000 of federal money for redevelopment projects
in Pennsylvania in the next decade.

[129] The Tax Foundation of New York, Inc., shows the following
increase in federal aid payments to Pennsylvania state *and local*
governments, in selected *fiscal years:*

1954: $133,400,000,   1956: $156,500,000,   1957: $170,600,000
Source: *Facts and Figures on Governmental Finance,* 10th ed., 1958-
59, Table #68, p. 93. Though these figures are based upon *United
States Treasury Department* data, they are not directly comparable
to the staff report quoted on the preceding page, because local as
well as state grants are included, and these are annual, rather than
biennial figures.

The 1958–59 *Book of the States* also shows an increase for Pennsylvania, but has a larger beginning figure for 1955. Here there is a
problem of dealing with a similar definition of "Federal aid." See
Tables 1, 2, and 3, pp. 236–238.

See also *Statistical Abstract of the United States,* 1959, p. 414, the
Pennsylvania Statistical Abstract, published by the Department of
Internal Affairs, 2nd ed., 1959, Table 86, pp. 84, 85, and in the
Leader Papers, "Balance Sheet and Related Financial Statements,"

The story of this increase of federal aid to Pennsylvania would be deficient if it were not pointed out that direct cash grants constitute only a part of the total federal aid. There is also a large operation at Harrisburg and elsewhere involving the distribution of federal surplus foods and other goods to needy persons and institutions. The Leader administration was equally concerned with retaining and, in many cases, increasing this type of direct "commodity" aid. Governor Leader issued over a dozen press releases on various aspects of the federal surplus problem. Less than ten days after he took office, on January 27, 1955, Leader publicized his letter dealing with the surplus food distribution in Westmorland and Allegheny Counties (*Press Release* #16). On May 5, Leader testified in Washington, D.C. on behalf of federal assistance for the Delaware River area (*Press Release* #179). Other problems arose which prompted the governor to lobby for a large tract of federal timberland within the state, which he secured (*Press Releases* #214, #215, and June 2, 1955). He also sought increased federal support for the National Guard (#249, June 24, 1955), for public housing (#250, June 27, 1955), and for civil defense. In addition to surplus food, the Leader administration received an increasing amount of federal surplus property.[130] By 1959, the

---

prepared by the Bureau of Accounts, Office of Administration, and submitted to Governor Leader by Dr. Ferguson July 15, 1957.

Further data on federal aid to Pennsylvania (the state) in fiscal year 1957 can be found in *Compendium of Government Finance,* United States Bureau of the Census, Vol. III, No. 5, subtitle, "1957 Census of Governments."

[130] *Press Release* #906, January 22, 1957, summarizes the quantity of surplus property received by the commonwealth in 1956.

State Department of Property and Supplies had an enormous operation receiving and handling surplus property.[131] Thus the Leader administration's increased interest and attention to federal aid resulted in a significant expansion in Pennsylvania's share, both of money and of goods. Program evaluation played a part in this operation, but by no means the only part.

WHITE HOUSE CONFERENCE ON CHILDREN AND YOUTH

It has been said that one reason states get federal money more readily for highways than for schools is that children do not vote, whereas members of truck and automobile associations do. However, in recent years the problems of youth have become too persistent to be overlooked by government at any level. While the child population in the United States increased only twenty-five per cent since 1948, it has been reported that juvenile delinquency increased 150 per cent. The amount of illegitimacy has also skyrocketed in recent years. Philadelphia's illegitimacy rate is reported to have increased 121 per cent since 1940, while its population increased only thirteen per cent.[132]

Widespread concern over conditions of this kind triggered energetic action at the end of Leader's term on the problems of children and youth. These efforts were stimulated and directed in preparation for the White House Conference on Children and Youth, which took place shortly after Leader's term in March, 1960. This event

[131] Based upon an interview at that department December 3, 1959.

[132] *Proceedings of Planning Conference,* Governor's Coordinating Committee for the 1960 White House Conference on Children and Youth, Harrisburg, July 13, 1959, pp. 4, 5. (Introductory speech by Robert C. Taber, chairman of the Governor's Committee.)

was billed as the golden anniversary of the first such conference announced on Christmas Day, 1908, by President Theodore Roosevelt upon the urgent request of Theodore Dreiser and James West. Later conferences were held in 1919, 1940, and 1950 under Presidents Wilson, Hoover, Franklin Roosevelt, and Harry S. Truman. Elaborate preparations were undertaken to make the 1960 conference the most important of them all.[133] The spade work for this conference involved an organizational job at the federal, state, county, and local levels. Thus children and youth became an important new program in the area of intergovernmental relations.

To serve as liaison with President Eisenhower's advisory committee, and to organize the program in Pennsylvania, Governor Leader appointed a Governor's Committee on Children and Youth in the spring of 1956.[134] Such a state committee had actually been operating on a continuing basis since 1949, when it was originally appointed by Governor Duff. The old committee was reconstituted by Governors Fine and Leader and ultimately by Governor Lawrence.[135] Pennsylvania was one of twenty-five states which had such a continuing committee during the past ten years.[136] Governor Leader's new committee took action in September, 1958, and called together the heads of the Departments of Health, Justice, Labor and Industry, Pub-

[133] Charge to the committee by Governor Lawrence, *Ibid.*, p. 8.
[134] *Press Release* #626, May 11, 1956. See also #850, December 11, 1956.
[135] *Preparing Today's Youth for Living in Tomorrow's World*, Proceedings of the Conference of State-wide and Regional Organizations, Sponsored by the Governor's Committee . . . , Harrisburg, January 9, 1959, p. 1.
[136] *Proceedings of the Planning Conference*, July 13, 1959, p. 3.

lic Instruction, and Public Welfare. These department heads were asked to provide facts for the formulation of ten-year goals, and also to suggest the names of organizations who might participate in this task. This was the first time that these regular state departments were involved in such an effort at the outset. Here was another kind of program evaluation, pointed more towards the future than the past—really an effort at program planning, on an inter-departmental as well as an intergovernmental level. In September, 1958, the Governor's Committee set up a state-wide conference, entitled "A Call to Youth and Parents," which was attended by 100 youths and their parents.[137] Workshops combining both generations were conducted at this day-long conference on such questions as student morale, post-high school opportunities, and job availability. Ten of these young people were then appointed to serve as representatives to the governor's overall committee.

On January 9, 1959, another conference was held by the Governor's Committee on Children and Youth, this time including representatives of over sixty state-wide organizations, mostly drawn from the educational, sociological, medical, religious, and child welfare fields. About 180 persons attended this Harrisburg conference at which Mrs. Katherine B. Oettinger, chief of the United States Children's Bureau, was the keynote speaker. An elaborate regional and county organization was then set up in all sixty-seven counties, each of which was grouped into one of ten areas. Ultimately, the organizational structure, from the Governor's Committee, down, included Professional Advisory Committees, Consultants on Special Service

[137] *Press Release* #A868, September 19, 1958.

Areas, county coordinators, and a Council of State Organizations.[138]

This elaborate organization enlisted the services of nearly 250 persons in Pennsylvania.[139] Only 136, or slightly over half of these, were scheduled to attend the White House Conference in 1960. Though Governor Lawrence and Mrs. Ruth Grigg Horting, secretary of the new State Department of Public Welfare, became honorary chairman and co-chairman of the expanded Governor's Committee, Mrs. Lorna Sylvester, in the same department, carried forward the actual work as executive secretary of this committee. Numerous guides, conference proceedings, and other materials were published by this committee describing its work in considerable detail. It can be argued that organizational work of this kind has considerable political potential for any state administration, since it provides an organizational tie between several state departments and their normal clientele or supporting private organizations. Although it may be an overstatement to assert that "everybody loves children," nevertheless the validity of undertaking serious planning for the improvement of the rising generation can hardly be challenged. In any case reports indicate that this effort evoked a widespread public response of a generally positive nature.

[138] *A Guide for County Committees,* prepared by the Governor's Coordinating Committee, 1960 White House Conference on Children and Youth, Harrisburg, June 1959, p. 6.

[139] Governor Leader's committee of forty-six, including ten youths, was expanded to eighty-seven by Governor Lawrence. Then representatives of eighty-eight state-wide organizations, plus sixty-seven county coordinators, departmental advisors, and others were added. According to Robert Taber, chairman of the Governor's Committee, Pennsylvania was, in July 1959, somewhat ahead of other states which had just begun organizing. *Proceedings of Planning Conference,* p. 3.

When this committee was in its initial stages, it relied, as did other governor's committees, upon the Bureau of Program Evaluation for staff assistance and for official support. When that bureau came gradually to be merged with the Bureau of Management Methods in the early days of the Lawrence administration, the home base of the Committee on Children and Youth shifted over to the Department of Public Welfare, where Mrs. Sylvester, its able executive secretary, was located. Further research is needed to judge whether this committee with its many branches did an effective job of pulling together and evaluating Pennsylvania's total program for children and youth. The records indicate that the committee did at least collect and enlist the services of responsible personnel, qualified to carry out such an evaluation. The reports do not reveal whether the circumstances of their recruitment and deliberation were such as was needed to produce results of a high quality. However, the ambitious organizational job that was done here, originally under the aegis of the Bureau of Program Evaluation, is an example of the Bureau's mandate in the area of interdepartmental, and in this case, also intergovernmental matters.[140]

[140] In fact, three of the official duties of the Bureau are illustrated by the foregoing example:

"#2. To encourage sound program planning in the agencies.

"#3. To lead and coordinate the efforts of agency staffs in the development of program plans, or in the conduct of studies of programs involving two or more departments or agencies.

"#5. To provide staff services for *ad hoc* committees established by the Governor."

Source: "The Role of the Office of Administration," Section on the Bureau of Program Evaluation, Governor's Office, August, 1958. (Mimeographed.)

We have now described the activities of the Bureau of Program Evaluation in five areas: departmental reporting, governmental reorganization, substantive program appraisals, investigation of proposals, and interdepartmental or intergovernmental matters. No attempt was made here to provide inclusive coverage of all activities of the bureau, but several examples have been given of the type of problems handled by the Bureau of Program Evaluation in each area. In many, if not most cases, the exploration of the substantive problem or proposal was not completed by the bureau itself, but was done with the help of outside consultants, specialists, committees or advisors. Such a procedure does not negate the significance of having a staff service or facility within the Governor's Office charged with the responsibility for pulling together such specialized, technical, or mature vision. The validity of such a staff arrangement and its contribution both to the Office of the Governor and to the theory and practice of public administration will be reexamined in the concluding chapter.

CHAPTER VI

CONCLUSIONS

George M. Leader stands in rather sharp contrast to the typical Pennsylvania governor. Elected at thirty-six, he was sixteen years younger than his average predecessor. Leader also brought to the executive chair a different background. Although he was active in politics from an early age, his immediate background was primarily that of a successful farmer, freshman legislator, and county chairman. He slipped into the running unexpectedly in February, 1954, when the leading prospective candidate for the democratic gubernatorial nomination, Philadelphia's Richardson Dilworth, decided not to run. Thus Leader had not been carefully groomed for the post by powerful officials in his party. Nor was his nomination so much the result of elaborate commitments made to rival factions.

Elected in November, 1954, with a comfortable majority of 279,000, over three times that of his predecessor or his successor, Leader's accession represented a political upset at Harrisburg. He was the first Democrat sent to the State House in twenty years, and the third governor from that party in nearly a century. By 1955, Pennsylvania had shifted from a one-party system at the state level to something much closer to a genuine two-party system in both the legislative and executive branches. Leader also helped to spearhead a new liberal movement within his own party. Thus his administration represented an important break in Pennsylvania's political history, as well as an occasion for far-reaching administrative reform. Despite his great political interest and appeal, Governor Leader was much more concerned about "purely administrative" matters than most of his predecessors. He tried to make many of his decisions on what he regarded as an "objective" basis. For this purpose Leader surrounded himself with a group of staff assistants and advisors noted for their technical competence in particular areas. One such group of experts served as consultants to the Governor's Advisory Committee even before his inauguration. Leader continued to rely upon such a "brain trust," composed largely of university professors under the leadership of political scientists who served in various capacities throughout his administration.

Leader also had his purely "political" advisors, some of whom felt their wishes were too often pushed into the background for other, less partisan considerations. One result was that various segments of the Democratic party gave the governor only superficial or lukewarm support towards the end of his term. The details of internal party politics are largely outside the scope of this study, except as they affect either the achievement or the permanence of Leader's administrative reforms. Most of the data examined and the conclusions which follow deal with Leader's contribution to the governorship, particularly on the administrative side.

LEADER'S MAJOR ACHIEVEMENTS
IN ADMINISTRATIVE REFORM

Some of Pennsylvania's important administrative problems arise from constitutional provisions, which are not easily changed. For example, Leader could not succeed himself because of the Pennsylvania Constitution, which prohibits successive terms. The governor's power is also limited by the elective status of four other administrative officials, as well as by various outmoded departmental structures, which have accumulated over the years. Leader tackled many of these reorganizational problems by means of a statutory Reorganization Commission and a Commission on Constitutional Revision, which reported in 1957 and 1959, respectively. Although Leader's second legislature refused to enact many of the recommendations of these commissions, many changes were accomplished by executive order and by other means. For example, Leader brought the State Planning Board into the Governor's Office under the Reorganization Act of 1955, and the Constitutional Commission's recommendation of annual legislative sessions took effect by amendment, following a popular referendum in the fall of 1959.

The basic engine of administrative reform was the Office of Administration, which Leader created within the Governor's Office. Other structures within the executive office were slightly expanded, but operated much as they had before. The expansion of the Governor's Office was important, however, because Leader was the first recent Pennsylvania governor to be equipped with the managerial tools needed to do an effective job as chief administrator.[1] The basic plan for the reorganized Governor's Office had originally been prepared for Leader's predecessor, Governor Fine, by the Pennsylvania Economy League. Leader's only important addition to that plan was the Bureau of Program Evaluation, which has been given special consideration in this study.

Leader's new Office of Administration introduced a number of important administrative reforms, most of which served to strengthen the governor's leadership and control of the administration. One of the most important was the development of a program type budget, which presents each agency's plans and activities better than the old line-item type of budget. It is now claimed that Pennsylvania has one of the most modern budget systems in the United States.[2] The basic format and many of the program descriptions for this budget were the work of the Bureau of Program Evaluation in cooperation with the Bureau of the Budget, which units were in Leader's time physically adjacent within the Office of Administration. Fiscal planning and control were further improved by developing more adequate budget units within many of

[1] According to records of the Bureau of Personnel, Office of Administration, the personnel assigned to the Governor's Office increased from sixty-three in January, 1955, to 121 in April and June, 1957, followed by a subsequent drop to about eighty-three at the end of Leader's term. However, in the later months additional clerical staff for the Governor's Office was carried on departmental payrolls. Governor Leader himself said that the total personnel working in his office rose from about seventy-eight to ninety-eight during his term. Interview at Dover, Pennsylvania, August 14, 1960.

[2] *Final Message* of Governor Leader, January 6, 1959, p. 19. (Supplement by Secretary of Administration Ferguson.)

the departments. Improved budgeting meant that the governor now had a more integrated, balanced and consistent program to promote and administer. A modern system of periodical allotments was also put into effect. The governor achieved firmer control over the departmental operations by reducing the number of agency controllers from thirty-one to eighteen (some covering more than one agency), mechanizing their operations, and placing them directly under the supervision of the secretary of administration rather than primarily under the department head. Toward the end of Leader's term, the Office of Administration developed the Commonwealth's first capital budget, which was finally released, although in somewhat tentative form, early in the succeeding Lawrence administration.

Governor Leader's keen interest in administrative improvement also found expression in a new Bureau of Management Methods, which spearheaded the training and assignment of some fifty management analysts in the various state departments.[3] Payroll reform, forms control, management surveys, organizational studies, and a records management program were among the accomplishments of this central staff unit. The use of electronic data processing and computing was also standardized and greatly expanded with the installation of a new Univac machine at the capitol. After two or three years of experimentation and use this equipment's full potentialities were not yet realized by the end of Leader's term. The governor's eagerness to explore such new ventures as electronic computing

[3] In 1957, Dr. Alderfer reported that "about 65 management analysts are serving in 23 agencies." 9 *GRA Reporter* (Governmental Research Assoc.), 3rd Quarter, 1957.

infused a new spirit into the state government, at least at the upper levels. Persons in state government declare that Leader mounted an administrative revolution of such scope that after him the government at Harrisburg will never be the same again.

Equally significant was the accounting reform initiated by Leader's new Bureau of Accounts. The former method of single-entry cash accounting had made it impossible for the governor to know the true state of fiscal affairs at any one time. A new accrual type of accounting was installed in 1956 in the form of a new double entry system, formalized in a new *Manual of Accounting Procedures,* prepared for the governor by the Public Administration Service of Chicago. Leader claimed that Pennsylvania would now have its first effective system for financial management in about twenty years. Other fiscal reforms initiated by the Office of Administration and its numerous advisory or constituent units included improvements in central purchasing, as for example, in surplus property, hospital drugs and institutional food services.[4] A new automobile fleet purchase plan resulted in substantial economies, as did a private trunk-line telephone circuit from Harrisburg to Philadelphia and Pittsburgh. Even greater savings resulted from such measures as placing automobile insurance and employee fidelity bonds on a fleet or "blanket" rather than an individual basis. Leader's other insurance reforms, such as the reduction of commissions, and the shift from the advance to the "earned" basis,

[4] Described by Dr. Robert A. Christie at an Institutional Food Services Conference, State College, Pennsylvania, January 27, 1959. (Unpublished, six-page typewritten address secured from the Office of Administration.)

were worked out by a group of experts attached to the Governor's Advisory Committee, and resulted in better insurance coverage at a fraction of the former cost. Here, as in other patronage matters, Leader's administrative reform encountered the opposition of political groups, whose largess was correspondingly restricted. Such experiences constitute an interesting vignette of the larger problem of the relationship between politics and administration. In this case, at least, administrative reform was achieved at the cost of some political disaffection. Here, also, political considerations imposed some limitation upon full-scale administrative reform.

The keenest conflict of political and administrative objectives took place in the area of personnel. Observers differ as to how much Governor Leader accomplished here, some claiming that he tried to go too far in one big jump, and others complaining that he did not go far enough. All agree that state government personnel had so long been neglected that energetic action was required at Harrisburg to correct inequities as well as to revamp the whole employment system. There were problems of recruitment, salary, training, supervision, promotion, merit coverage, and morale. All these and many related matters received the tireless attention not only of the governor, but also of his new Bureau of Personnel within the Office of Administration. A new and more "scientific" classification and compensation system was developed by Public Administration Service and installed throughout the state service— the first such reform in many years. Other changes were made raising salaries and standards, not only for the merit positions, but also for many of the patronage positions, which continued to be in the majority. A system of cenralized personnel complement control was instituted, which became the subject of controversy in some departments. All these changes served to strengthen the governor's hand by providing additional and more professional controls over state personnel.

The key issue in the personnel field was Leader's action in expanding the merit system coverage by nearly 10,000 positions. When it proved impossible to get such protection for professional and technical employees by legislative action, Leader extended the system by Executive Board action. This step was certainly more than a "middle-of-the-road" position. Governor Leader now feels that he was not given the credit he deserves for establishing such a substantial "beachhead" upon the territory of the old patronage system, since he risked his whole political future for the cause of good government.[5] Neither the press nor the public generated much enthusiasm for these personnel reforms.[6]

Some observers felt that Leader tried to change too much all at once, and for that reason many of his reforms would not endure. But Leader himself felt that the administrative situation in Harrisburg was "so bad" that many things had to be tackled simultaneously. The major changes just described in budgeting, accounting, reorganization, and personnel, have been continued by the succeeding Lawrence administration, though some changes of emphasis can be observed. Leader presents, then, the picture of a young governor with tremendous drive for administrative reform, extending actually into many more areas than those just

[5] Interview with Governor Leader, August 14, 1960.
[6] The Harrisburg and York press, by exception, generally supported Leader's personnel reforms in the latter part of his term.

mentioned. These changes produced a certain amount of shock within the bureaucracy, where many operations were jolted abruptly into the twentieth century.

These long overdue changes proceeded along lines that have been fairly well charted elsewhere in government and in the general literature on public administration.[7] The major themes were administrative reorganization, consolidation, enlargement of central staff, fiscal, budgetary, personnel, and procedural reform. In many aspects such managerial improvement was nonpartisan. It might well have been sparked by a "modern chief executive" recruited by either party. Similar reforms, though perhaps less bold in conception, had been advocated by such groups as the Chesterman Committee, which was appointed under Republican auspices. The stillbirth of that committee's recommendations resulted partly from vested interests and inertia within the bureaucracy, but also from peculiar intraparty circumstances. Leader came in fresh with a new party and was able to do things which would have been more difficult for the *ancien régime*. He had a new team with fewer commitments to the old order.

[7] Lipson summarized the aim of the reorganization movement as the recognition of the governor's responsibility for directing all the administrative activities of the state. See his *American Governor From Figurehead to Leader* (1939), p. 66. F. M. Marx further elaborated these ideas in his description of the Bureau of the Budget, which he regards the fore-runner of the Executive Office of the President. "The Bureau of the Budget: Its Evolution and Present Role, I." 39 *American Political Science Review* (September, 1945), pp. 653–684. See also, Executive Office of the President, Bureau of the Budget, *Excerpts from Staff Orientation Manual*, April, 1958, 65 pp., plus the Bureau's five-page mimeographed sheet, "Functions and Organization," November 1, 1958.

The significance of Leader's innovation, the Bureau of Program Evaluation, can be measured in terms of what it contributed to the Office of Governor. How much did program evaluation strengthen the governor's leadership and control of the state administration? Governor Leader himself said that the bureau was most helpful to him. It did valuable research for him on many important program and policy questions. There were so many of these that he could have used a much larger staff than he had available. Basically, the Bureau of Program Evaluation brought to the Governor's Office the services of a trained and mature political scientist with his staff. The value of such an advisor rests not only on what he does but also on what he knows. The old type of governor who was chiefly a figurehead with largely ceremonial functions had less need for persons with such training and perspective. The positive leadership now demanded of the governor in a state such as Pennsylvania cannot be adequately supplied by merely popular, amiable and well-meaning amateurs, as many governors and their advisors were. Even those few governors like Leader, who have special interest or training in public administration, cannot give much personal attention to many of the substantive questions requiring top decision. As the American state in the mid-twentieth century assumes so many additional services, problems of balance, priority, and perspective become all the more pressing.

This analysis is clarified by making a distinction between

the governor's external and internal roles. Some studies of the Bureau of Program Evaluation contributed to his external leadership of policy questions. However, more of its activity was directed towards his internal role, as chief administrator and leader of his own administration. Yet, major shifts of administrative direction, as in building schools or in mental health, required external leadership as well. These were not just "administrative questions." They soon became public or political questions as well. Thus program evaluation can never be completely detached from public debate if it deals with significant areas. Still, the program analysts can make a contribution, if the issue is not "too hot to handle."

As Bennett M. Rich recently noted, "The governor's role as the representative of the whole people is a many-sided one with various groups and interests vying for his attention or loyalty." [8] In this situation a governor needs the judgment and factual support of experts who are part of his own team, to sift and help to balance the advice of special pleaders, who come from many directions. A strong governor is, in part, one who can make up his own mind and not be too easily buffeted by the prevailing winds, some of which bring ill-considered counsel of doubtful value. Even advisory committees with eminent members and a representative base have their limitations because they are always outsiders looking in. Leader found this to be true of some of his advisors on state finance during his gubernatorial campaign. They were eminent authorities but not fully informed, since they were not on the inside.

In its work on departmental reports and the governor's

[8] Rich, Bennett M. *State Constitutions: The Governor.* National Municipal League (New York, 1960), p. 18.

budget, the Bureau of Program Evaluation was doubtless seen from below as more of a control than a leadership or advisory operation. Such services were of great value to the governor, although they were not always appreciated by those over whom the new controls were exercised. Some agencies, for example, resented the new budget allotment system and the practice of having all departmental controllers report directly to the secretary of administration. Others objected that the Governor's Office talked about decentralizing, while it was, in fact, centralizing all the time. However, most of this resentment of central staff was directed primarily towards other units within the Office of Administration. Thus the Bureau of Program Evaluation suffered a kind of guilt by association. There were, however, some of the bureau's operations which involved controls, as already noted. On other occasions, review of program resulted in action which altered the equilibrium represented by the status quo. In such circumstances, the program evaluation personnel felt some of the unpopularity which accompanies any administrative change, whether under the heading of leadership or control. Although it was part of the mandate of the bureau to help prune activities which were obsolete, excessive, or duplicating, more often their studies resulted in recommendations for expansion. Thus the bureau's emphasis was generally of a positive, rather than of a negative character—as, for example, in such areas as industrial development, children and youth, higher education, mental health, and recreation. In all these cases program evaluation enhanced the governor's leadership role by providing a more factual, authoritative, and where advisory committees were attached, a more representative basis for his major program emphases. In many of these areas, the Bureau of Program Evaluation was itself a minor actor in an operation which extended political ripples in all directions. As a point of contact between the public and the governor's official family, its position was strategic and sometimes important, as well.

A further qualification should be added to this discussion. In so far as the permanent bureaucrats mentally associated program analysts with the "egghead" epithet, the latters' contribution to the governor's leadership was correspondingly reduced. At certain periods and in certain agencies this reaction was serious enough that the bureau's contribution was minimized. In such agencies the impact of the entire Office of Administration was more a product of its controls then of its leadership. Yet other agencies, particularly the newer ones with younger and more energetic leadership, were most appreciative of the Office of Administration with its staff services, of which program evaluation was one somewhat less visible than the others.

On the positive side, program evaluation often served as a catalyst to action. Certain programs had been neglected partly because little interest had been indicated from the governor on down. When the Bureau of Program Evaluation undertook to investigate an obscure program, such was a tremendous spur to action. Even in large operations, when it was known that the Governor's Office had taken a special interest in the matter, progress could be noted. The same program analysts would have far less influence if they did not operate out of the Governor's Office. Here is an example of how a staff unit may have an unexpected effect upon line operations. In these cases the Bureau of Program Evaluation became not just the eyes and ears of the governor, but an extension of his arm as well. The bureau strengthened the governor here not only by supplying staff information and advice, but also by stimulating action—partly as a by-product of its own research contacts and studies.

A final question remains. Was Pennsylvania's experience with program evaluation a successful one? If the bureau failed, or failed to achieve what it was created for, questions could be raised as to how sound an idea it was. Theory unrelated to experience can be rather barren. The evidence presented in Chapter V is not a record of failure. A great many important problems were tackled by this fledgling bureau and on many of them its work was a valuable contribution. This can be said of its assistance with departmental reporting, the program budget and governmental reorganization, including the merger of two large state departments. Many of the areas the bureau studied, such as federal aid, higher education, insurance, and migrant labor, resulted in progress and much greater attention to these areas by subsequent groups and by the succeeding administration. Limitations of budget and staff prevented the Bureau of Program Evaluation from ever completing, or really undertaking, a systematic evaluation of all commonwealth programs. This would probably have been impossible even with a larger staff within the span of a single administration.

The bureau's work took place in the midst of a vast administrative revolution in Harrisburg, which will doubtless be more significant in the long run than the 1954 political upset itself. Though the bureau contributed to the Office of Administration and to the overhauling and revitalization of all central procedures which that office achieved, the Bureau also suffered from the somewhat hectic atmosphere of change into which it was born. Problems resulted from instituting so many changes in such a short time. Had the bureau been introduced in calmer times, or had the legitimacy of its umbrella agency, the Office of Administration, been better accepted, program evaluation would doubtless have had a more solid record of achievement under its own name. As it was, the director of program evaluation became one of the top "trouble shooters" for the governor and for the secretary of administration. This was sometimes a matter of genuine program evaluation, but at other times the bureau's director was but another hand recruited to help solve some thorny administrative problem. It was difficult for the bureau to keep itself sufficiently free from immediate managerial problems to pursue the course for which it was created. On some occasions when the bureau did undertake to explore a substantive program area, it uncovered such a morass of faulty and inefficient procedures that it had to help strengthen these out before it could really examine the question of program content. That such problems were uncovered and dealt with does not indicate, however, the failure of the bureau, as these were often areas which were otherwise neglected. The record here points, rather, to the difficulty of maintaining the distinction, at least under those conditions, between managerial and program or policy questions. Here also is illustrated the difficulty of keeping an advisory staff to the governor up-to-date and well informed, without its getting enmeshed in managerial operations.

The Bureau of Program Evaluation was ultimately merged with the former Bureau of Management Methods to form the new Bureau of Program and Management, about a year after the end of the Leader administration, in February, 1960. A similar fate overtook Leader's Bureau of Capital Expenditures, whose work was merged with that of the budget bureau early in the Lawrence administration. These changes were the result of a number of factors, most of which are beyond the scope of this chapter. The Lawrence administration did retain the basic pattern of central services established by the Office of Administration and many of the same staff. There was a feeling that perhaps some of the functions of the Governor's Office had been over-structured under Governor Leader. At the least it became the task of the Lawrence administration to consolidate some of the policy initiative and administrative reforms undertaken by Leader, and this was undertaken with some reduction of emphasis upon new program and policy questions. Thus there was less need for a program and policy research staff. There were also circumstances involving personalities and the operational methods of the Office of Administration which contributed to the decision to merge the Bureaus of Program Evaluation and Management Methods. Until 1962, the merged bureau was so busy dealing with problems connected with the full utilization of the Univac electronic data processing equipment that there was rather little opportunity to undertake program research on its own account. Early in 1962, the Bureau of Program and Management revived its program planning and evaluation, designating a section by that name.

In any case, Governor Leader made a significant contribution to the governorship of Pennsylvania. His philosophy of government was more liberal and progressive than that of his recent predecessors, a fact which was reflected in his legislative program. More social and economic legislation was passed under Leader than at any time since 1937. Leader's achievements in administrative reform were even more striking, and were given special attention in this study. His administrative reforms can be summarized under two major headings—state personnel and central staff services. During Leader's term tremendous strides were taken to attract to the state service better qualified and more highly trained personnel. These employees infused new life and competence into the state service. The number of technical and professional personnel under the merit system was almost doubled by executive action. Leader brought new people and new structures into the Governor's Office, and with them came a different administrative atmosphere at Harrisburg. Program evaluation was but one of these innovations which was less well known. Since these reforms were largely internal ones, Leader's public image omitted many of the chief contributions which he made. There is little drama and political appeal in administrative reform.

But Leader was also program minded. He dug into all aspects of state government, searching for ideas and opportunities to improve state services. Though he had a keen intellectual interest in the problems of government and society, Leader was a doer, not merely a theorizer. He was a pragmatic idealist, always interested in results. The experiment with program evaluation was particularly well adapted for a governor with such a bent for exploration and action. Sometimes Leader pressed too vigorously for ideas which were not yet politically feasible—as in the case of his classified income tax, and his plan for community colleges. He acted too much like an ardent New Dealer in a state which had long been conservative and Republican. In his determination to stand by his pledge to abolish the sales tax, Leader held out too long and embittered legislative–executive relations. This long struggle hung like a cloud over Leader's public image throughout his term. Leader also suffered from a hostile press, in Philadelphia on the pardon question and in Pittsburgh on the question of his tax program. Had fiscal realities not forced him to seek such increased funds, Leader's program leadership might have been better known and accepted. Yet Leader's program was by no means stalemated. His administration was one of rapid change, great energy, and accomplishment in such substantive areas as mental health, highways, parks, industrial development, and schools. A number of persons close to the state government have said that Leader is the best recent governor Pennsylvania has had.

APPENDIXES

PENNSYLVANIA GOVERNORS SINCE CONSTITUTION OF 1874—I.

	John F. Hartranft (1873–79), 2 terms	Henry M. Hoyt (1879–82)	Robert E. Pattison (1883–87, '91–95) 2 terms
1. Age at inauguration:	43, 46.	49.	33, 41.
2. County and section of residence:	Montgomery (near Philadelphia).	Luzerne (upstate).	Philadelphia.
3. Party:	Republican.	Republican.	Democrat.
4. Size of majority:	35,587 (1872). 12,030 (1875).	22,253.	40,202 (1882). 16,553 (1890).
5. Per cent of total vote for governor:	52.6%, 49.9%.	44.9%.	47.8%, 50.0%.
6. Education:	Union College (1853, civil engineering).	Williams College (1849).	High school valedictorian.
7. Previous occupation:	Lawyer (since 1859).	Lawyer (1853) and teacher. Appointed county judge (1867).	Lawyer (1872).
8. Military and/or political experience:	Civil War—Major General. Deputy sheriff; auditor general (2 terms).	Civil War—Brigadier General. Internal revenue collector, 2 cos.; chairman, Rep. State Committee (1875).	Philadelphia city controller (2 terms).
9. Relation to Republican "machine:"	Nominated by Cameron machine, as was predecessor, Gov. Geary; both governors very popular, however.	Bolted the Cameron-Quay machine, which contributed to its defeat in 1882.	Attacked Cameron machine vigorously.

267

PENNSYLVANIA GOVERNORS SINCE CONSTITUTION OF 1874—II.

	James A. Beaver (1887–91)	Daniel H. Hastings (1895–99)	William A. Stone (1899–1903)
Age at Inauguration:	50.	46.	53.
County and section of residence:	Centre (upstate).	Centre (upstate).	Allegheny (Pittsburgh).
Party:	Republican	Republican	Republican
Size of majority:	42,651.	241,397.	117,906.
Per cent of total vote for governor:	43.4%.	60.3%.	49.0%.
Education:	Jefferson College (1856, forestry).	? (Was a teacher).	Mansfield State Normal School.
Previous occupation:	Lawyer	Editor, lawyer (1875–88), then coal interests.	Lawyer (1870).
Military and/or political experience:	Civil War—Brigadier General (lost one leg).	Adjutant gen. under Gov. Beaver. (Popular for his handling of Johnstown flood relief operations).	District attorney (Western district of Pennsylvania); congressman, 4 terms (1891–).
Relation to Republican "machine:"	Bolted the Quay machine in Rep. primary, 1890. Thus, Pattison, Dem., re-elected in the fall.	As gov. led revolt vs. Quay, 1895. Almost unseated him.	Dominated by Quay.

268

PENNSYLVANIA GOVERNORS SINCE CONSTITUTION OF 1874—III.

	S. W. Pennypacker (1903–07)	Edwin S. Stuart (1907–11)	John K. Tener (1911–15)
Age at Inauguration:	60.	54.	48.
County and section of residence:	Philadelphia.	Philadelphia.	Washington (Southwest of Pittsburgh).
Party:	Republican	Republican	Republican
Size of majority:	143,350.	48,364.	33,487.
Per cent of total vote for governor:	54.2%.	50.4%.	41.6%.
Education:	Univ. of Pa. law dept.	Philadelphia schools.	Public Schools.
Previous occupation:	Lawyer, county judge, scholar.	Leary's Book Store.	Professional baseball, and bank president.
Military and/or political experience:	Pa. Historical Assoc. and Univ. of Pa. (writer on Pa. history).	Mayor of Philadelphia.	Congressman (1909–11).
Relation to Republican "machine:"	Gov. attacked by anti-Quay press. Some disputes with machine over appointments.	Party on defensive, due to graft disclosures (gov. not implicated).	Tener nominated by the Penrose group. Both parties split and insurgents ran an independent candidate. Tener won 3-way race.

PENNSYLVANIA GOVERNORS SINCE CONSTITUTION OF 1874—IV.

	M. G. Brumbaugh (1915–19)	William C. Sproul (1919–23)	Gifford Pinchot (1923–27, '31–35) 2 terms
Age at inauguration:	53.	49.	58, 66.
County and section of residence:	Philadelphia.	Delaware (near Philadelphia).	Pike County (upstate).
Party:	Republican	Republican	Republican
Size of majority:	135,325.	247,222.	250,071 (1922). 58,670 (1930).
Per cent of total vote for governor:	53.0%.	61.1%.	56.9%, 49.0%.
Education:	Juniata College, University of Pa.	Swarthmore College (1891).	Yale University (1889), and forestry study in Europe.
Previous occupation:	Superintendent of Phila. schools, college president.	Newspaperman and business (mining, banking and transportation).	Chief, U.S. Forest Service under Th. Roosevelt (began 1898).
Military and/or political experience:	Superintendent of Phila. schools.	State senate, 1896 for 22 years, until he became governor.	Besides the above, served on Pa. State Constitutional Revision Commission (1920).
Relation to Republican "machine:"	Brumbaugh's nomination forced upon Penrose by the Vare organization of Philadelphia.	Penrose died 1921, led to split in the Rep. party. Sproul a presidential "hopeful."	Pinchot represented the reform or progressive wing of the party. Opposed the former Penrose forces. He was supported by Mr. Grundy.

PENNSYLVANIA GOVERNORS SINCE CONSTITUTION OF 1874—V.

	John S. Fisher (1927–31)	George H. Earle (1935–39)	Arthur H. James (1939–43)
Age at inauguration:	60.	45.	56.
County and section of residence:	Indiana (upstate).	Montgomery (near Philadelphia).	Luzerne (upstate).
Party:	Republican	Democrat	Republican
Size of majority:	737,543.	66,329.	279,148.
Per cent of total vote for governor:	73.3%.	50.1%.	53.0%.
Education:	Indiana State Normal School (1886).	Harvard University.	Dickinson College (law, 1904).
Previous Occupation:	Lawyer (previously teacher, 7 years).	Business, also diplomacy, army, and navy.	Lawyer and judge (Superior Court).
Military and/or political experience:	State Senate, 1901, 2 terms. Chairman, Capitol Investigating Committee. Banking commissioner (1919).	Ex-minister to Austria; with Pershing in Mexico; Navy Cross W.W. I. Supported FDR, 1932.	District attorney Luzerne Co., 2 terms; lt. gov.; Superior Court judge, elected 1932.
Relation to party organization:	Completely subservient to the party organization, though he carried forward Pinchot's administrative reforms. Despite party split among Vare, Pinchot and Mellon–Grundy factions, Republicans reached peak per cent in 1926.	1937 marks peak of Dem. control in Pa. since Civil War. Democrats sent Guffey to U.S. Senate 1935 and held at least 1 senator till 1949. Serious party splits: J. L. Lewis from the gov., also Atty. Gen. Mergiotti and Phila. Mayor Wilson.	Gov. James was the most conservative of the recent Republican governors. A Luzerne judge, like Governor Fine, James ran the State on a patronage basis though he claimed to be fighting "bureaucracy" and waste. Had his own party "machine."

271

PENNSYLVANIA GOVERNORS SINCE CONSTITUTION OF 1874—VI.

	Edward Martin (1943–47)	James H. Duff (1947–51)	John S. Fine (1951–55)
Age at inauguration:	64.	64.	58.
County and section of residence:	Washington (near Pittsburgh).	Allegheny (Pittsburgh).	Luzerne (upstate).
Party:	Republican	Republican	Republican
Size of majority:	217,634.	557,515.	85,746.
Per cent of total vote for governor:	54.0%.	58.5%.	50.7%.
Education:	Wayne College (1901; bar, 1905).	Princeton, 1904, Univ. of Pa. and U. of Pitt. Law, 1907.	Dickinson Law School, 1914 (Dublin Univ).
Previous occupation:	Military, politics, banking, oil and transportation.	Lawyer, plus oil and real estate.	Lawyer, judge.
Military and/or political experience:	Rep. state chairman, 1928–34. Military career in Philippines, Mexico. DSC from W.W. I. Adjutant gen., Pa. 1939–43 (exc. 1941–42); auditor gen. 1925–29; state treasurer, 1929–33; U.S. Senate (1946).	Attorney Gen. under Martin. Counsel to Pa. Oil and Gas Mfg. Assoc. 1942. Rep. nat'l. conventions 1936, 1940. No military experience. "Bull Moose," later backed James, Martin.	W.W. I veteran, overseas. Appointed country judge by Pinchot (1927) at age of 33, county chairman, age 25. Appointed to Superior Court by Duff.
Relation to party organization:	Closely connected with the party bosses since the days of Penrose. Elected partly on his military record. Helped consolidate party, then dominated by PRR, Grundy and Pew (railroad, business and oil).	Duff represented insurgent western branch of Rep. party, somewhat more progressive than eastern Grundy–PMA brch. Duff also personally blunt, somewhat resented by regular party organization. Elected U.S. senator after term as governor.	Fine, an up-state political chairman for some thirty years, had supported the Pinchot and then Duff factions of the party. Lost control of his own party in the Rep. controlled state legislature.

272

PENNSYLVANIA GOVERNORS SINCE CONSTITUTION OF 1874—VII.

	George M. Leader (1955–59)	David L. Lawrence (1959–63)
Age at inauguration:	37.	68.
County and section of residence:	York (upstate).	Allegheny (Pittsburgh).
Party:	Democrat	Democrat
Size of majority:	279,196.	76,083.
Per cent of total vote for governor:	53.6%.	50.8%.
Education:	Gettysburg College and Univ. of Pa. (teacher training).	Parochial schools.
Previous occupation:	Chicken farmer. Military experience.	Politics, insurance.
Military and/or political experience:	Justice of the peace and county chairman; state Senate, 1950–54; ran for state treasurer, 1952.	Over 50 years of political life. Mayor of Pittsburgh, 4 terms, 1945–59. When elected gov., was leader of state Dem. party. Secretary of commonwealth under Earle; state Dem. chairman since 1935.
Relation to party organization:	Received largest Dem. vote in recent times, especially rural sections. Was a compromise candidate between the Phila. and Pittsburg branches of the Dem. party. Represented the liberal and reform branch, along with Dilworth and Clark in Phila., but tried to cooperate with the Lawrence–Green organizations as well. Defeated for senator in 1958, due to party split.	In 1962 election Dilworth was defeated as Dem. candidate to succeed Lawrence as governor, by William E. Scranton, Republican. In 1963 Gov. Lawrence joined Pres. Kennedy's staff in Washington as chairman of the President's Committee on Equal Opportunity in Housing.

273

APPENDIX B

ORGANIZATION OF THE GOVERNOR'S OFFICE, 1960

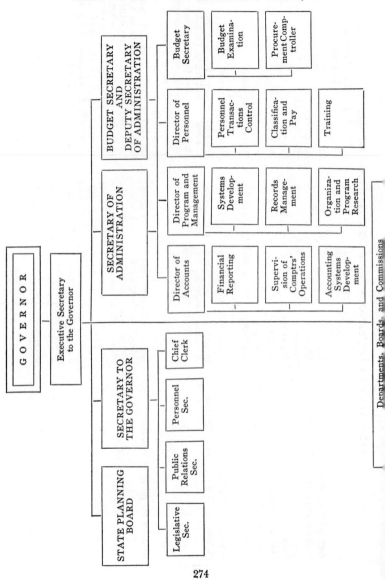

BIBLIOGRAPHY

I. PRIMARY SOURCES

A. Interviews

Governor Leader, several interviews between August 14, 1960, and March 7, 1961. Dover, York, and Philadelphia.

Mr. Henry B. Leader, governor's legislative secretary, 1955–59. Philadelphia, November 12, 1959; Dover, August 14, 1960; York, September 13, 20, 1960; January 10, 1961.

Mr. David V. Randall, secretary to the governor, 1955–58. Philadelphia, September 18, 1959; February 8, 1960; July 12, 1960; August 10, 1960.

Dr. Stephen B. Sweeney, chairman of the Governor's Advisory Committee. Philadelphia, March 24, 1959, August 29, 1960; Harrisburg, August 25, 1959; Washington, D.C., September 10, 1959.

Dr. James C. Charlesworth, Leader's first secretary of Administration. Philadelphia, September 8, 1959, June 27, August 12 and 26, 1960.

Dr. John H. Ferguson, successor to Dr. Charlesworth as secretary of Administration and budget secretary, 1956–59. Also, second director of Program Evaluation, 1955–56. State College, Pennsylvania, March 25, 1959; December 12, 1959; Harrisburg, August 25, 1959; Washington, D.C., September 10, 1959; Philadelphia, November 3, 1960.

Dr. William C. Seyler, first director of Program Evaluation, 1955. Harrisburg, April 8, 1960, January 10, 1961.

Dr. Harold F. Alderfer, successor to Dr. Ferguson as director of Program Evaluation, 1956. Philadelphia, October 1, 1959; Harrisburg, December 3, 1959.

Dr. Robert A. Christie, successor to Dr. Alderfer in the above position. Harrisburg, August 25, 1959; Philadelphia, October 16, 1959.

Dr. Gayle P. Lawrence, Leader's first director of the Bureau of Personnel, Office of Administration. Philadelphia, June 30, 1960.

Mr. Russell D. Johnson, successor to Dr. Lawrence in the above position. Harrisburg, December 3 and 4, 1959, March 7, 1961.

Mr. Donald K. Probert, assistant director, Bureau of Management Methods, Office of Administration. Harrisburg, August 25, December 4, 1959, March 7, 1961.

Mr. Hubert Simpson, Bureau of Accounts, Office of Administration. Harrisburg, December 4, 1959.

Mr. David Baldwin, budget secretary and deputy secretary of Administration under Governor Lawrence. Philadelphia, October 6, 1960.

Mr. Robert Middleton, Bureau of Program Evaluation. Harrisburg, August 25, 1959, December 3 and 4, 1959, April 8, 1960, *inter alia*.

Mr. David DeLong, Bureau of Program Evaluation. Harrisburg, December 3, 1959, April 8, 1960.

Mr. Harry Griffiths, Department of Forests and Waters. Philadelphia, May 19, 1960.

Mr. Guy Davis, director, Joint State Government Commission. Harrisburg, October 4, 1960.

Mr. Charles Cella, Government Consulting Service, Fels Institute, Consultant on Department of Welfare. Philadelphia, March 2, 1960, February 29, 1960.

Dr. Edward F. Janosik, Political Science Department, University of Pennsylvania. Philadelphia, December 22, 1959, May 22, 1960, June 7, 1960.

Hon. Gerald A. Gleeson, Leader's first secretary of Revenue. Philadelphia, October 16, 1960.

Mr. Harry Shapiro, Leader's secretary of Welfare. Philadelphia, October 13, 1959.

Mr. Lewis M. Stevens, Leader's second secretary of Highways. Philadelphia, August 12, 1960.

Mr. John P. Robin, Leader's first secretary of Commerce and chairman, State Planning Board. Philadelphia, December 5, 1960.

Mr. John Baer, capitol correspondent, *The Harrisburg Patriot*. Harrisburg, December 4, 1959.

Mr. John Calpin, editorial department, *The Evening Bulletin*. Philadelphia, June 23, 1960.

Mr. James Higgins, editorial department, *The Gazette and Daily*. York, September 20, 1960.

Mr. J. W. Gitt, owner and publisher of the above paper. Hanover, November 29, 1960.

Mr. J. Dean Polen, chairman of the House Democratic Caucus, 1955–56. Harrisburg, October 4, 1960.

Mr. Hiram G. Andrews, speaker, House of Representatives. Harrisburg, October 4, 1960.

Mr. Charles Weiner, Democratic leader in the Senate. Philadelphia, telephone interview, c. June 30, 1960. Also, a brief conversation in Harrisburg.

Mr. William J. Lederer, formerly of Department of Revenue. Philadelphia telephone interview, c. June 30, 1960.

Mr. Ed Toohey, Labor's League for Political Education. Philadelphia telephone interview, June 30, 1960.

Mr. H. C. Erickson, Department of Property and Supplies, and Cumberland County Democratic party chairman. Harrisburg, December 4, 1959.

Mr. LeRoy Greene, Post Office Department. Philadelphia telephone interviews, December 5, 1960, February 24, 1961.

Plus several other persons who prefer to remain anonymous.

B. State Government Documents

Leader Papers. The Pennsylvania Historical Collection, The Pennsylvania State University Library, University Park, Pennsylvania. Including particularly the press releases, speeches and messages to the General Assembly, executive directives, and files under Ferguson, Office of Administration, and related subjects.

Final Message of George M. Leader to the General Assembly. Harrisburg, January 6, 1959, 116 pp. with Supplement.

Final Messages of Governors Earle, James, Martin, Duff, and Fine. Harrisburg, January, 1939, 1943, 1947, 1951, 1955.

The Legislative Journal, 1955, 1957 Sessions. Harrisburg, 12 vol. in 1955.

Statements by the Democratic State Committee. Harrisburg, 1955–59, in the Leader Papers.

Report of the Citizens' Committee on the Finances of Pennsylvania to Hon. Gifford Pinchot. 1922.

Pinchot, Gifford. *The Extra Session: A Report to the People.* Harrisburg, 1926.

Legislative Reference Bureau. Bulletin #36, revised, *The Administrative Code of 1929,* as amended, including 1957. Harrisburg, 1957.

Department of Property and Supplies, Commonwealth of Pennsylvania. *The Pennsylvania Manual.* Vol. 92 (1955–56), Vol. 93 (1957–58). Harrisburg.

Commonwealth of Pennsylvania. *Report of the Commission on Economy and Efficiency.* Harrisburg, 1915.

Commonwealth of Pennsylvania. *Report of the Commission on Constitutional Amendment and Revision to the General Assembly.* Harrisburg, 1920.

———. *The State Government Survey Committee Report* (Francis J. Chesterman, chairman). Harrisburg, February 11, 1953.

————. *The Tax Problem,* Report of the Tax Study Committee (Alfred G. Buehler, chairman). May 29, 1953. Also, same title, Harrisburg, January, 1955.

————. *Report of the Pennsylvania Commission on Intergovernmental Relations* (Alfred G. Buehler, chairman). Harrisburg, January, 1955.

General Report of the Joint State Government Commission to the General Assembly of the Commonwealth of Pennsylvania. Harrisburg, January 1953, 1955, 1957, 1959.

Commission on Governmental Reorganization, Commonwealth of Pennsylvania (Anthony J. Drexel Biddle, Jr., chairman). *Recommendations Made to the General Assembly.* Harrisburg, March 11, 1957.

Joint Legislative Committee on Finance. *Report on the Organization and Administration of the Government of Pennsylvania* (Phillip Sterling, chairman). Harrisburg, 1934, 687 pp.

Joint State Government Commission. *Report on the Organization and Administration of Pennsylvania's State Government* (Ellwood J. Turner, chairman). Harrisburg, January, 1941, 3215 pp.

Report of the Commission on Constitutional Revision (Robert E. Woodside, chairman). Harrisburg, March 9, 1959.

17th, 18th, 19th *Biennial Budget of the Commonwealth of Pennsylvania.* Harrisburg, April, 1955, February, 1957, March, 1959. (Governors Leader and Lawrence.)

Pennsylvania Constitution of 1874.

Debates of the Convention to Amend the Constitution of Pennsylvania. Harrisburg, 1873.

Report of the Committee on Style, to the Commission on Constitutional Amendment and Revision. Harrisburg, October 25, 1920.

Pennsylvania Archives, Series IV, Papers of the Governors, 12 Vols., Harrisburg, 1902. (Dr. George Edward Reed, editor, under W. W. Griest, secretary of the Commonwealth.)

History of House Bills and Resolutions. Harrisburg, 1953, 1955, 1957, 1959.

History of Senate Bills and Resolutions. Harrisburg, 1953, 1955, 1957, 1959.

Wilkinson, Norman B., Pennsylvania Historical and Museum Commission. *Bibliography of Pennsylvania History,* by S. K. Stevens and Donald H. Kent, eds. Harrisburg, 1957.

Department of Internal Affairs, Commonwealth of Pennsylvania. *Pennsylvania Statistical Abstract.* Harrisburg, 1958, 1959, 1960.

Fertig, John H. *Scope of the Legislative Power of the General Assembly.* Harrisburg, 1931. (Legislative Reference Service.)

Pennsylvania Governor's Office, Office of Administration. *Report of Activities.* Harrisburg, August 15, 1956, 6 pp.; Same title, April, 1958, 9 pp.

Pennsylvania Governor's Office. *The Role of the Office of Administration.* August, 1958, 8 pp. (Mimeographed.)

Staff Report, Bureau of Program Evaluation, Office of Administration. "Accomplishments of the Bureau of Program Evaluation: 1955–1958." (Typewritten copy, unsigned, undated. 13 pp. written by Robert Middleton, Harrisburg, 1959.)

Report of the Governor's Committee on Higher Education. Harrisburg, 1959.

Commonwealth of Pennsylvania. *Report of the Governor's Committee on the Merger of the Department of Welfare and Public Assistance.* Harrisburg, February 9, 1959. (Also, Interim Report of the same committee.)

Bureau of Personnel, Office of Administration. *Biennial Training Report, 1956–1958.* Harrisburg, 1959, 5 pp. (Mimeographed.)

Bureau of Personnel, Office of Administration. *Report on the Personnel Council, October 1956–January, 1959.* Harrisburg, 1959, 2 pp. (Mimeographed.)

Commonwealth of Pennsylvania. *Manual of Accounting and Related Financial Procedures,* Prepared by the Public Administration Service, issued by Governor Leader, August 1, 1956. Harrisburg, 1959, as amended.

Governor's Office, Commonwealth of Pennsylvania. *Five Fiscal Facts About Pennsylvania.* Harrisburg, September 28, 1959, 41 pp.

Budget Bureau, Governor's Office of Administration, Commonwealth of Pennsylvania. *Digest of Federal Aid Programs in Pennsylvania.* Harrisburg, November, 1960.

Pennsylvania Economy League. *A Suggested Plan for the Organization of the Governor's Office, Commonwealth of Pennsylvania.* (Submitted to Governor-elect George M. Leader, December 9, 1954.) Harrisburg, third printing, January 17, 1958, 11 pp. (Type-offset.)

Pennsylvania Economy League. *Recommendations Concerning the Future Organization and Functions of the Office of Administration.* (Prepared for Secretary John H. Ferguson by the State Division, Pennsylvania Economy League.) Harrisburg, June 18, 1958.

Pennsylvania, Governor's Advisory Committee. "Consultants' Reports." Harrisburg and Philadelphia: unpublished, typewritten reports, January, 1955. One copy on file at the Fels Institute, University of Pennsylvania.

Department of Internal Affairs. *Directory of State Publications.* Harrisburg. (Periodical.)

Internal Affairs. Monthly Bulletin, Department of Internal Affairs. In 29th volume in 1959.

Commission on Governmental Reorganization. *Consultants' Reports.* Harrisburg, 1956, 1957. (Mimeographed; Dr. Stephen B. Sweeney, Principal Consultant.)

Michigan Joint Legislative Committee on Reorganization of State Government. *General Management of Michigan State Government.* Report No. 30; Lansing, Michigan, November, 1951.

New Jersey Budget Bureau. *State Government Management Improvement Programs.* Budget Bureau, Department of the Treasury, Trenton, July 31, 1958, 36 pp.

C. United States Government Documents

Commission on Intergovernmental Relations. *The Impact of Federal Grants-in-Aid on the Structure and Functions of State and Local Government.* Washington, D.C., 1955.

Statistical Abstract of the United States, 1959.

U.S. Bureau of the Census. *Compendium of Governmet Finance,* III, No. 5, 1957 Census of Governments. Washington, D.C., G.P.O.

Committee for the White House Conference on Education. *Report to the President.* Washington, D.C., 1956.

D. Pennsylvania Court Cases

Hartranft's Appeal. 85 *Pa.* 433 (1877).

Commonwealth v. *Barnett,* 199 *Pa.* 161 (1901).

Kelly v. *Kalodner.* 320 *Pa.* 180 (1935).

In re: Investigation by Dauphin County Grand Jury, June, 1938, 322 *Pa.* 289.

McSorley v. *Pennsylvania Turnpike Commission,* 300 *Pa.* 81 (1957).

H. K. Butcher et al v. *J. S. Rice,* Dauphin County Court, (1958).

II. SECONDARY SOURCES

A. Books

1. General

The American Assembly. *The Forty-Eight States: Their Tasks as Policy Makers and Administrators.* New York: Graduate School of Business, Columbia University, 1955.

American Society for Public Administration. *Strengthening Management for Democratic Goverment.* Digest of A.S.P.A. National Conference in New York City, March 23–26, 1958; Chicago: American Society for Public Administration, 1959, 159 pp.

Bone, Hugh A. *American Politics and the Party System,* 2nd ed. New York: McGraw-Hill, 1955.

Bowen, Don L. and Pealy, R. H. *Administrative Leadership in Government: Selected Papers.* Ann Arbor: University of Michigan, 1959.

Bryce, James. *The American Commonwealth.* New York: Macmillan and Company, 1895.

Buck, A. E. *The Reorganization of State Governments in the United States.* New York: Columbia University Press, 1938.

Charlesworth, James C. *Governmental Administration.* New York: Harper & Brothers, 1951.

Corwin, Edward S. *The President: Office and Powers,* 4th ed. New York: New York University Press, 1957.

Council of State Governments. *The American Governors: The Backgrounds, Occupations and Governmental Experience of the Present Governors.* Chicago: Council of State Governments, 1959. (Mimeographed.)

————. *The Book of the States,* XII, 1958–59; XIII, 1960–61, Chicago: The Council of State Governments, 1958, 1960.

————. *Organization of State Departments of Administration and/or Finance.* Chicago: Council of State Governments, November, 1958.

————. *Reorganizing State Government.* Chicago: 1950.

————. *A State Department of Administration.* Chicago: Council of State Governments, 1957.

————. *State Government, Annotated Bibliography.* Chicago: Council of State Governments, September, 1959.

Current Biography, XVII, New York: H. W. Wilson Company, 1956.

Emmerich, Herbert. *Essays on Federal Reorganization.* University of Alabama Press, 1950.

Encyclopaedia of the Social Sciences, XI, New York: The Macmillan Co., 1937.

Fenno, Richard F., Jr. *The President's Cabinet.* Cambridge: Harvard University Press, 1959.

Ferguson, John H. and McHenry, Dean E. *The American System of Government,* 5th ed. New York: McGraw-Hill, 1959, 780 pp.

Gosnell, Harold F. *Machine Politics: Chicago Model.* Chicago: University of Chicago Press, 1937.

Graves, W. Brooke. *American State Government,* 4th ed. Boston: D.C. Heath and Company, 1953.

Herring, E. Pendleton. *Presidential Leadership.* New York: Rinehart and Company, 1940.

Index Digest of State Constitutions, 2nd ed. New York: Legislative Drafting Fund, Columbia University, 1959.

Key, Vincent O. *American State Politics: An Introduction.* New York: Alfred A. Knopf, 1956.

Lancaster, Lane W. and Breckenridge, A. C. *Readings in American State Government.* New York: Rinehart and Company, 1950, 347 pp.

Lipson, Leslie. *The American Governor from Figurehead to Leader.* Chicago: University of Chicago Press, 1939.

Lubell, Samuel. *The Future of American Politics,* 2nd ed. rev. Garden City, New York: Doubleday Anchor Books, 1956, 297 pp.

McKean, David Dayton. *The Boss, The Hague Machine in Action.* Boston: Houghton Mifflin Company; and Cambridge, The Riverside Press, 1940.

March, James G. and Simon, Herbert A. *Organizations.* New York: John Wiley and Sons, 1958, 262 pp.

Marx, Fritz Morstein. *The President and His Staff Services.* Chicago: Public Administration Service, publication #98, 1947.

The Model State Constitution. The State Constitutional Studies Project, Series I, No. 1. New York: The National Municipal League, 1948.

Neustadt, Richard E. *Presidential Power: The Politics of Leadership.* New York: John Wiley and Sons, 1960.

Phillips, Jewell Cass. *State and Local Government in America.* New York: American Book Company, 1954.

Ranney, Austin and Kendall, Willmore. *Democracy and the American Party System.* New York: Harcourt, Brace and Company, 1956, 550 pp.

Ransone, Coleman B. *The Office of Governor in the South.* University of Alabama Press, 1951, 256 pp.

————. *The Office of Governor in the United States.* University of Alabama Press, 1956, 417 pp.

Rich, Bennett M. *State Constitutions: The Governor.* State Constitutional Studies Project, Series II, No. 3. New York: The National Municipal League, 1960.

Sarasohn, Stephen B. and Vera H. *Political Party Pattern in Michigan.* Detroit: Wayne State University Press, 1957.

Scace, Homer E. *The Organization of the Executive Office of the Governor.* New York: Institute of Public Administration, 1950.

Schlesinger, Joseph A. *How They Became Governor. A Study of Comparative State Politics, 1870–1950,* Governmental Research Bureau, Michigan State University, East Lansing, 1957, 102 pp.

Steffens, Lincoln. *The Autobiography of Lincoln Steffens.* New York: Harcourt, Brace and Company, 1931.

Swarthout, John M. and Bartley, Ernest R. *Principles and Problems of State and Local Government.* New York: Oxford University Press, 1958.

Sweeney, Stephen B., ed. *Education for Administrative Careers in Government Service.* Philadelphia: University of Pennsylvania Press, 1958, 366 pp.

Stein, Harold, ed. *Public Administration and Policy Develop-*

ment: A Case Book. The Inter-University Case Program; New York: Harcourt, Brace and Company, 1952, 860 pp.

Waldo, Dwight. *The Administrative State: A Study of the Political Theory of American Public Administration.*

Wasserman, Paul and Silander, Fred S. *Decision Making, An Annotated Bibliography.* Ithaca, New York: Graduate School of Business and Public Administration, Cornell University, 1958, 111 pp.

————. *Measurement and Evaluation of Organizational Performance: An Annotated Bibliography.* Ithaca, New York: Graduate School of Business and Public Administration, Cornell University, 1959, 110 pp.

Who's Who in America. Current Biographical Reference Service. Chicago: Marquis Who's Who, Publishers, May, 1955. Also, Vol. XXX, 1958–59.

Who's Who in United States Politics and American Political Almanac. New York: The Macmillan Company, 1952 edition.

Young, John D. *Taking Over a New Executive Post.* Brussels: International Institute of Administrative Science (United Nations), 1952, 26 pp.

Zeller, Belle, ed. *American State Legislatures.* Report of the Committee on American Legislatures, American Political Science Association. New York: Crowell Publishing Company, 1954.

Zink, Harold. *City Bosses in the United States.* Durham: Duke University Press, 1930.

2. Pennsylvania Politics and Government

Alderfer, Harold F. and Luhrs, Fannette H. *Gubernatorial Elections in Pennsylvania, 1922–1942.* Pennsylvania Municipal Publication Series, University Park. Institute of Local Government, The Pennsylvania State University, 1946, 64 pp.

————, Harold F. and Young, Louise M. *Know Pennsylvania: Your State and Local Government, A Handbook of Basic Information*. Harrisburg: The Telegraph Press, 1946, 180 pp.

————, H. F. and McGeary, M. Nelson. *Pennsylvania Government: 1950. The Shape of Things Today and the Shape of Things to Come*. State College: Institute of Local Government, Pennsylvania State College [1950].

————, Harold F. and Luhrs, Fannette H. *Registration in Pennsylvania Elections, 1926–1946*. University Park: Institute of Local Government, The Pennsylvania State University, 1948, 68 pp.

Allen, Robert S., ed. *Our Fair City*. New York: The Vanguard Press, 1947. (Chapter 3, O'Neil, Thomas P., "Philadelphia: Where Patience is a Vice," pp. 59–76.)

————. *Our Sovereign State*. New York: The Vanguard Press, 1949. (Chapter 4, Lowe, Herman A., "Pennsylvania: Bossed Cornucopia," pp. 96–131.)

Armor, William C. *Lives of the Governors of Pennsylvania. With the Incidental History of the State from 1609–1872*. Philadelphia: J. K. Simon, 1872, 528 pp.

Baltzell, E. Digby. *Philadelphia Gentleman: The Making of a National Upper Class*. Glencoe, Illinois: The Free Press, 1958, 440 pp.

Bowden, Robert Douglas. *Boies Penrose, Symbol of an Era*. New York: Greenberg, 1937, 274 pp.

Branning, Rosalind L. *Annotated Bibliography on Pennsylvania State Government*. Pittsburgh: University of Pittsburgh (Dept. of Political Science), 1959.

Cooke, Edward F. and Janosik, G. Edward. *Guide to Pennsylvania Politics*. New York: Henry Holt, 1957, 120 pp.

Crumlish, Joseph D. *A City Finds Itself: The Philadelphia Home Rule Charter Movement*. Detroit: Wayne State University Press, 1959, 105 pp.

Deatrick, Elinor S. *The Pennsylvania Citizen*. New Brunswick, New Jersey: Rutgers University Press, 1958, 374 pp.

Dunaway, Wayland Fuller. *A History of Pennsylvania*. 2nd ed. Englewood Cliffs, New Jersey: Prentice-Hall, 1948.

Franklin, Benjamin. *An Historical Review of Pennsylvania from its Origin*. Originally published in London, 1759. Philadelphia: E. Olmsted and W. Power, 1812.

Gosnell, Harold F. *Grass Roots Politics: National Voting Behavior of Typical States*. Washington, D.C.: American Council on Public Affairs, 1942, 195 pp.

Greene, Le Roy. *Shelter for His Excellency, The Story of Pennsylvania's Executive Mansion and the One Hundred Governors of the Commonwealth*. Harrisburg: Stackpole Books, 1951.

Institute of Local and State Government, University of Pennsylvania. *Bibliography on Pennsylvania Local and State Government*. Philadelphia, 1941.

————. *Manual of Pennsylvania Local and State Government*, rev. ed. Philadelphia: Fels Institute of Local and State Government, University of Pennsylvania, 1958. (Mimeographed.)

————. *Proposed Reorganization of the Executive Branch of the State of Pennsylvania*. Philadelphia: Fels Institute of Local and State Government, University of Pennsylvania, 1949, 31 pp. with charts. (Mimeographed.)

Kurtzman, David H. *Methods of Controlling Votes in Philadelphia*. Philadelphia: University of Pennsylvania, 1935.

McClure, A. K. *Old Time Notes of Pennsylvania*. Philadelphia: John C. Winston Company, 1905. 2 Vol.

McGeary, M. Nelson. *Gifford Pinchot, Forester Politician*. Princeton: Princeton University Press, 1960.

Martin, Edward. *Always Be On Time*. Autobiography, Harrisburg: The Telegraph Press, 1959, limited edition.

Pennypacker, Samuel. *Autogiography of a Pennsylvanian.* Philadelphia: J. C. Winston Co., 1918.

――――. *Desecration and Profanation of the Pennsylvania State Capitol.* Philadelphia: William J. Campbell, [1911], 104 pp.

Purdon's Pennsylvania Statutes Annotated.

Reichley, James. *The Art of Government, Reform and Organization Politics in Philadelphia.* A Report to the Fund for the Republic. New York: The Fund for the Republic, 1959.

Salter, J. T. *Boss Rule, Portraits in City Politics.* New York: McGraw-Hill, 1935.

Scott, Samuel Bryan. *State Government in Pennsylvania: A Manual of Practical Citizenship.* Philadelphia: Harper Press, 1917, 272 pp.

Sigafoos, Robert A. *Guide to Public Affairs Research in Pennsylvania.* University Park: The Pennsylvania State University, March, 1959, 97 pp.

Stackpole, E. J. *Behind the Scenes with a Newspaper Man: Fifty Years in the Life of an Editor.* Philadelphia and London: J. B. Lippincott Co., 1927, 320 pp.

Stevens, Sylvester K. *Pennsylvania, The Keystone State.* New York: American Historical Company, 1956. (Historical volume and documentary volume.)

Tanger, Jacob, Alderfer, H. F., and McGeary, M. Nelson. *Pennsylvania Government, State and Local,* rev. ed. State College: Penns Valley Publishers, Inc., 1950, 442 pp.

Vare, William S. *My Forty Years in Politics.* Philadelphia: Roland Swain Co., 1933, 225 pp.

Wanamaker, John. *The Speeches of Hon. John Wanamaker on Quayism and Boss Domination in Pennsylvania Politics.* Philadelphia: Business Men's Republican League. (Undated, c. 1898.)

Wood, Ralph, ed. *The Pennsylvania Germans.* Princeton, New Jersey: Princeton University Press, 1942.

B. Articles

1. General

Berdahl, Clarence A. "Party Membership in the United States II." 36 *American Political Science Review* (1942), p. 241. Also Part I, p. 19.

Bosworth, Karl A. "The Politics of Management Improvement in the States." 47 *American Political Science Review* (March, 1953), pp. 84–99.

———. "Law Making in State Governments," *The Forty Eight States: Their Tasks as Policy Makers and Administrators.* American Assembly (December, 1955), pp. 85–110.

Graves, W. Brooke. "Criteria for Evaluating the Effectiveness of State Government," 32 *American Political Science Review* (1938), pp. 508–514.

———. "Some New Approaches to State Administrative Reorganization." 9 *Western Political Quarterly* (September, 1956), p. 743.

Gurwell, John K. "The Governors of the States." 14 *State Government* (1941), p. 157.

Highsaw, Robert B. "The Southern Governor—Challenge to the Strong Executive Theme." 19 *Public Administration Review* (1959), pp. 8–11.

Jewell, Malcolm E. "Party Voting in American State Legislatures." 49 *American Political Science Review* 3 (September, 1955), pp. 773–791.

Kaufman, Herbert. "Emerging Conflicts in the Doctrines of Public Administration." 50 *American Political Science Review* 4 (December, 1956), pp. 1057–1073.

Key, V. O. "The Lack of a Budgetary Theory." 34 *American Political Science Review* (1940), p. 1138.

McKean, Dayton D. "The Politics of the States." *The Forty-*

Eight States: Their Tasks as Policy Makers and Administrators, American Assembly (December, 1955), pp. 65–84.

Marx, Fritz Morstein. "The Bureau of the Budget: Its Evolution and Present Role—I." 39 *American Political Science Review* (September, 1945), pp. 653–684.

Perkins, John A. "American Governors—1930–1940," 29 *National Municipal Review* (March, 1940), p. 178.

Ranney, Austin and Kendall, Willmoore. "The American Party Systems," 48 *American Political Science Review* (June, 1954), pp. 477–485.

Sayre, Wallace S. Review of six books on the functions of the chief executive, 16 *Public Administration Review* (Autumn, 1956), pp. 307–312.

Scace, Homer E. "The Governor Needs Staff," 40 *National Municipal Review* (October, 1951), p. 464.

Solomon, Samuel R. "United States Governors 1940–1950," 41 *National Municipal Review* (1952), pp. 190–197.

———. "Governors, 1950–1960," 49 *National Civic Review* 8 (September, 1960), pp. 410–416.

Tompkins, D. C. *Organization and Reorganization in State Government, 1958–59: A Bibliography.* Bureau of Public Administration, University of California (Berkeley, 1959).

2. Pennsylvania Politics and Government

Alderfer, Harold F. "Pennsylvania's Office of Administration." 9 *G.R.A.* (Governmental Research Assoc.), *Reporter* 3 (third quarter, 1957).

Barth, Harry A. "Proposed Reorganization in Pennsylvania." 12 *National Municipal Review* (June, 1923), p. 330.

Bronner, Edwin B. "The New Deal Comes to Pennsylvania: The Gubernatorial Election of 1934." *Pennsylvania History* (January, 1960).

Charlesworth, James C. "Pennsylvania's High Level Seminars

in Administration," 29 *State Government* 4 (April, 1956), p. 67.

England, R. W., Jr. "Pardon, Commutation and their Improvement." 39 *The Prison Journal,* Pennsylvania Prison Society (Philadelphia, April, 1959), p. 30.

Fox, Leonard P. "Pennsylvania Reorganizes: Pinchot Code Now Effective." 12 *National Municipal Review* 9 (September, 1923), pp. 526–528.

Hawkins, Frank. "Lawrence of Pittsburgh: Boss of the Mellon Patch." 213 *Harper's* 1275 (August, 1956), pp. 55–61.

Higgins, James. "Election Preview—The Picture in Pennsylvania." 178 *Nation* 13 (March 27, 1954), inside the cover.

———. "Pennsylvania." (One of a series: "An Eight State Analysis."), 179 *Nation* (November 13, 1954), pp. 416–417.

———. "Pennsylvania's Leader," editorial, 180 *Nation* (February 19, 1955), p. 151.

———. "Two Obstructive Votes in the Keystone State." 181 *Nation* 19 (November 5, 1955), p. 372.

Howe, Leslie D. "Pennsylvania Governor's Office Revamped." 44 *National Municipal Review* (July, 1955), p. 366.

Keefe, William J. "Parties, Partisanship and Public Policy in the Pennsylvania Legislature." 48 *American Political Science Review* (June 1954), pp. 450–464.

King, Clyde L. "Fiscal and Administrative Reorganization in Pennsylvania." 17 *American Political Science Review* (November, 1923), pp. 597–608.

Kraft, Joseph. "Pennsylvania's New Breed of Politicians." 217 *Harper's* (October, 1958), pp. 46–50.

Kurtzman, David H. "Ramifications of a Central Administrative Management Unit." Unpublished address to the Philadelphia regional chapter of The American Society for Public Administration, Fels Institute, University of Pennsylvania, January 12, 1960. (Tape-recorded.)

Leader, George M. Address on Civil Rights, 300 *Annals of the*

American Academy of Political and Social Sciences (July, 1955), pp. 1–3.

————. Commencement Address, University of Pennsylvania, February 9, 1957, issued as *Press Release* #934, February 9, 1957.

————. "Recent Developments in Pennsylvania State Administration." Address to the Pennsylvania Political Science and Public Administration Association, Harrisburg, April 12, 1957, issued as *Press Release* #A–71 3 pp.

Leader, George M. "Taxes, Governmental Efficiencies and Urbanization." 15 *Township Commissioner* 1 (Winter, 1956) pp. 2–5.

Macdonald, Austin F. "The Governor and the Public Service Commission of Pennsylvania." 15 *National Municipal Review* (March, 1926), pp. 184–188.

McGeary, M. Nelson. "The Governor's Veto in Pennsylvania." 41 *American Political Science Review* (October, 1947), p. 941.

Margiotti, Charles. "Why We Must Revise the Pennsylvania Constitution." 181 *Annals of the American Academy of Political and Social Sciences* (September, 1935), pp. 19–26.

Nurich, Gilbert. "Much Ado About Something: The Story of Administrative Chaos in Pennsylvania." 45 *Dickinson Law Review* (1941), p. 85.

Paxton, Edward T. "Feuds and Politics in Pennsylvania." 10 *National Municipal Review* 1 (July, 1921), pp. 366–368.

————. "Gifford Pinchot's First Legislature." 12 *National Municipal Review* (October 1, 1923), pp. 567–571.

Sorauf, Frank J. "State Patronage in a Rural County." 50 *American Political Science Review* (December, 1956), pp. 1046–1056.

————. "The Relationship Between State and Presidential Nominating Politics." Unpublished paper presented at the Pennsylvania Political Science and Public Administration Association, Harrisburg, April 9, 1960. (Typewritten.)

Wolfgang, Marvin E. "Analysis of Selected Aspects of the Board of Pardons." 39 *The Prison Journal* 1 (Pennsylvania Prison Society, Philadelphia, April, 1959), p. 9.

C. Academic Dissertations and Related Sources

1. General

Barth, Harry Aldin. *Financial Control in the States with Emphasis on Control by the Governor.* Ph.D. dissertation; Philadelphia: University of Pennsylvania, 1923, 87 p. (Privately printed.)

Bell, James Robert. *The Executive Office of the California Governor Under Earl Warren, 1943–1953.* Ph.D. dissertation, University of California: 1955, Berkeley, California. (Unpublished.)

Blue, Leonard A. *The Relation of the Governor to the Organization of Executive Power in the States.* Ph.D. dissertation, University of Pennsylvania, 1902, 47 pp. (Privately printed.)

Bollens, John C. *Administrative Reorganization in the States Since 1939.* Sacramento, California: California Bureau of Public Administration, Legislative Problems Report No. 6, 1947.

Crennan, Charles Holloway. *A Survey of State Executive Organization and a Plan of Reorganization.* Ph.D. dissertation, University of Pennsylvania, 1961, 87 pp. (Privately printed.)

Nispel, Benjamin. *The Office of Lieutenant Governor in the United States.* Ph.D. dissertation, University of Pennsylvania, 1957. (Unpublished.)

Rosen, Leopold. *Major Trends in State Reorganizations with Special Reference to the Period 1945–1954.* M.G.A. thesis, Fels Institute, University of Pennsylvania, 1955, 86 pp.

Schlesinger, Joseph A. *Methods of Ascendancy to the Office of Governor in the United States.* Ph.D. dissertation, Yale University, 1957.

2. *Pennsylvania Politics and Government*

Bell, William J. *A Study of Personnel Practices in a State Administration Under a Merit System* (The Pennsylvania Bureau of Employment Security). Ph.D. dissertation, Indiana University: Bloomington, Indiana, 1957, 269 pp. (Unpublished.)

Burns, Edward McNall. *The Office of Governor in Pennsylvania.* M.A. thesis, University of Pittsburgh, 1927, 216 pp. (Unpublished.)

Davy, Thomas J. *The Public Service Institute in Pennsylvania.* Ph.D. dissertation, University of Pennsylvania, 1957.

Hellerich, Mahlon Howard. *The Pennsylvania Constitution of 1873.* Ph.D. dissertation, University of Pennsylvania, 1956, 513 pp. (Unpublished.)

Hogarty, Richard A. *The Department of Administration as a Current Development in American State Government Reorganization.* M.G.A. thesis, Fels Institute, University of Pennsylvania, 1959, 71 pp. plus charts. (Unpublished.)

Kehl, James A. *Ill Feeling in the Era of Good Feeling: Western Pennsylvania Political Battles—1815–1825.* Ph.D. dissertation, University of Pittsburgh Press, Pittsburgh, 1956.

Keller, Richard C. *Pennsylvania's Little New Deal.* Ph.D. dissertation, Columbia University, 1960.

Reynolds, Harry Wesley, Jr. *Gubernatorial Coordination of Administrative Boards and Commissions in Pennsylvania.* Ph.D. dissertation, University of Pennsylvania, 1954, 354 pp. (Unpublished.)

Salter, J. T. *The Non-Partisan Ballot in Certain Pennsylvania Cities.* Ph.D. thesis, University of Pennsylvania, Philadelphia, 1928. (Privately printed.)

Wike, Jesse R. II. *The Pennsylvania Manufacturers' Association: A Study of a Political Interest Group in the Governmental Process.* Ph.D. thesis, University of Pennsylvania, 1955.

D. Newspapers and Periodicals

Bulletin Almanac and Yearbook, 1954–1960, Philadelphia, Pennsylvania.

Citizens Business, published by the Pennsylvania Economy League and the Bureau of Municipal Research, Philadelphia, 1959, 1960.

Civic Affairs, published by the Committee of Seventy, Philadelphia, especially 1959, 1960.

The Evening Bulletin, Philadelphia, especially November 3, 1954, January 18, 1955, ff.

Harper's Magazine, 1956, 1958.

The Harrisburg Evening News, 1954–1959.

McClure's Magazine, July, 1903.

Nation Magazine, especially 1954, 1955.

New Republic, especially October 20, 1958, November 3, 1958.

News from the Civil Club of Allegheny County, especially January–February, 1959.

Newsweek, especially November 15, 1954 and October 17, 1955.

The New York Times, 1954–1959.

PCA Reports, (Pennsylvania Citizens Association for Health and Welfare), especially April, 1955.

Pennsylvania Road Builder, 1955–1959.

The Philadelphia Inquirer, especially November 3, 1954, Jan. 1, 1955, Magazine Section and July 3, 1955.

The Pittsburgh Post Gazette.

Saturday Evening Post, especially February 23, 1957 and December 5, 1959.

State Government News, Council of State Governments, Chicago, especially February, 1959.

Time, 1954–1959, especially November 15, 1955, January 15, 1955, September 26, 1955.

U.S. News and World Report, especially November 12, 1954.

The York Gazette and Daily, 1955–1959.

INDEX

Accounts, accrual type, 251; Bureau of, 51–57; 65; manual of, 54, 251; recruitment of accountants, 57, 58

Administrative Code of 1929, 28, 32, 45, 52, 225, 226

Administrative reform, Pinchot's, 28; Leader's, *see* Leader administration; Office of Administration

Administrative reorganization, 28–43; *see* reorganization act; Commission on Governmental Reorganization; governmental reorganization

Advisory Committees and Commissions, Fine administration, 225; Lawrence administration, 226; Leader administration, 220–228; limitations of, in general, 256; on Public Education, 218; *see also* Governor's Advisory Committee

Agriculture, Department of, 67, 92; and migrant labor, 202; secretary of, 92 (Henning); stimulating sale of milk, 190

Albers, H. Michael, 70, 80

Alderfer, Harold F., 6, 28, 29, 33, 34, 62, 68, 80; and program evaluation, 134, 146, 149; director of program evaluation, 135; and the merger, 178; on number of management analysts, 250

Allen, Robert S., 9

Anderson, Paul R., 215

Appointment, power of, 91; *see* patronage, personnel, civil service

Army Corps of Engineers, 205

Atterbury, Gen. William Wallace, 9

Athletic Commission, state, reorganized, 175

Attorney general, and Pardon Board, 123, 130; Governor Leader's, 89; opinions, 82, 111, 173

Automotive fleet purchase plan, 60, 251

Automotive Safety Foundation, 227

Bailey, Stephen K., 160

Baldwin, David R., 158, 226

Banking Department, 114; examiners, 114; *see also* Myers

Barr, Joseph M., 52, 100, 102

Batt, William, Jr., 97, 103, 202, 211; *see* Labor and Industry

Bell, John C., 125–26

Biddle, A. J. Drexel, 100, 103; and Reorganization Commission, 173

Bigler, Governor William, 22

Board of, Pardons, Finance, Revenue, etc., 82; *see* commissions, independent; Teachers' Colleges, 90; Welfare, 85

Boehm, Charles H., 98, 103; and NDEA, 217; *see also* Public Instruction, Department of

Bok, Curtis, 89

Book of the States, 127, 238

Bowden, Robert D., 9, 17

Bradley, Andrew, 100, 101, 102, 103

Brain trust, and advisory committees, citizen groups, 227; Governor's Advisory Committee, 68, 74;